There's Something in a Name

Louis Berry

Orlando, Florida, USA

ISBN 1448663857

Cover Photograph © Louis Berry, May, 2000

Author Photograph by David Goldman

Printed in the United States of America.

Chapter One

Owen had been running for nearly an hour. The road behind him had to be forgotten. He must focus on what lie ahead and push through the pain. Lactic acid burned his muscles.

An opening in the Mangrove trees ahead offered a place to stop. The waters of the Atlantic Ocean were shallow there and the bottom was sandy so he could remove his shoes and walk without shredding his feet against the coral that surrounded the islands.

Thoughts occupied his mind about how he had come to associate with the malcontented characters he called friends. He never knew if any of them would turn on him, yet was quite certain someone already had. What he was sure of was his knowledge of sunken treasure could easily lead to his demise.

He saw the opening ahead. The gap wasn't obvious, but was marked by a large coral formation. It seemed as though he had been running from something all of his life. His thoughts turned to the mother he knew as Jenny. She raised him from the time he was five years old, when his parents were killed while attempting to rob a bank. The household consisted of her husband Bobby and his younger sister Sylvia. The fact that his parents were crooks was lauded over him and used with great precision, to belittle and emotionally castrate the young man; effectively wresting away any ambition that might have been innately bestowed upon him. What he wasn't told was that Bobby was the cop who shot both of his parents during the robbery.

One bit of advice given to him by his mother stayed with Owen throughout his adult life. She pulled him aside on his thirteenth birthday and told him, in an unusually caring tone, 'Son, if you are ever in an un-comfortable situation, just remove yourself from it.' He never knew whether her intent was to keep him away from drugs or from turning to a life of crime, but he was sure it was the reason he continually found himself running.

He struggled up an incline as he recalled his seventeenth birthday. A girl he fancied was at their house for dinner. The length to which his father exerted himself for Owen on his birthday consisted of well-charred burgers and crispy hot dogs. Jenny took the trouble to make a cake and allowed him to have com-pany.

Bobby drank one can of beer after another and tossed the empties into the back yard as he grilled. The man and alcohol were a volatile concoction Owen avoided by staying inside. He lay on his side on the sofa as he watched television. Tranquil behavior was meant to avoid drawing anyone's ire. His girlfriend Sara had gone to the bathroom. While he stared into space with his mind on nothing in particular, a gentle hand came from behind him and began to gently caress his arm. She squeezed his muscular bicep and then moved to his chest. With her fingertips, she traced the valley created by his overly developed pectorals. Owen thought about Sara and how he desired to make love to her that night. She was beautiful and shapely, with long blonde hair. Oh, how he wanted to hold her in his arms. It made him feel good to be sought after.

He rolled over to face her and make his desires known. Instead, he saw Sylvia standing over him, grin-ning. The look on her face conveyed ambiguity. Owen was not sure if she actually wanted to sleep with him, or if her actions were meant to freak him out. Without a word he stood, walked out of the house and into the back yard. A drunken Bobby became preferred company.

Owen approached the opening in the trees. The sun had yet to breach the morning sky. Sweat formed on the top of his head and dripped into his face. Salty perspiration stung his eyes and his shirt tail was the only thing he had to wipe away the excess moisture. It was half past six in the morning on the eastern side of Barracuda Key. Owen made his way through the trees then stopped short of the water and removed his shoes and socks before proceeding. Twenty yards from shore was a large piece of driftwood that protruded from the ocean floor. It was from a large, stout tree; like nothing that could be found on the island. He had come there on many occasions. When he reached it he sat, placing his shoes and socks on the log next to him.

I'm still pretty young. I have time to change my life for the better, right?, he thought to himself as he stared out over the ocean. Lack of self-esteem triggered questions that crept into his psyche on a regular basis. It was the only way he knew to forget his past, but he never convinced himself. Doubt caught up to him as it always had and yanked Owen down. The stakes were higher. He knew that he was being followed and feared for his life. Maybe it was a combination of Jenny's advice and the beatings he received at the hand of her husband, but his instinct had always been to run. *Maybe it's time for me to stand and fight for something?*

Owen felt safe sitting on the log, hidden by the thick Mangroves. Solitude had always been good to him. The sun rose above the horizon and the sky lightened from black to deep blue. Minutes passed and it changed to a beautiful Carolina shade. His sweat soaked shirt sent a chill over his body as the wind blew. He removed it so that he could bask in the warmth of the sun. He peered beneath the surface of the water and watched as he swirled his feet, stirring the soft sand on the bottom. Each time he stopped, the silt settled. Several minnows darted aimlessly back-and-forth. His thoughts raced just as quickly. He traced the timeline of his life as he sat with nowhere to go. There was something about not being responsible for, or to, anyone that appealed to him. Somewhere deep within him he knew that was not how he wished to live out his life. What was the alternative? The abuse he suffered at the hands of the only family he had known had a great deal to do with his inability to commit to anyone or anything. That not only included relationships with lovers, but friends. He was a loner and appreciated being one; most of the time.

Owen spied a seashell that lay near his feet. He reached into the water, retrieved it, and threw it as far as he could from his seated position. When it impacted the surface ripples spread in the calm morning ocean.

Only one woman made him wonder what would have happened if they had stayed together. Her name was Julia. She was the most beautiful person he had ever met. It was the way she carried herself, with confidence that made him respect her. He saw in her the qualities he longed to possess. The relationship didn't last, and as always, Owen took responsibility for its failure. That did not prevent him from remembering the day they met with fondness. It was on a trip he made to Florence, Italy. The memory was three years old, but

stimulated his mind as vividly as if he were there enjoying the sights and sounds of the vibrant, ancient city.
Owen searched for the final resting place of a great-
uncle he had never known. What they did share was
their name.

Brilliant cognitive images took him to the courtyard of the Uffizi Museum. Several street vendors
spread blankets onto the ground. Their wares ranged
from wood carved animals to designer handbags. Owen
sat on the top of four steps watching; not altogether interested in what happened below. His mind was filled
with visions of the art he had seen in the gallery. Works
by the masters; Michelangelo, Leonardo Da Vinci and
Bottacelli had only been two dimensional and not altogether real to him until his visit. For the first time in his
life he understood genius could only be appreciated
when it was beheld by someone open to the experience.

A flurry of activity below scattered the images
in his mind and his attention focused on something other than his tour through the museum. Every street
vendor picked up their blankets by the corners and
slung them, filled and bulging with their merchandise,
over their shoulders. Moving from his left were two
Italian Policia walking and rhythmically swinging their
batons. Each wore a smug and cocky grin. Owen
watched as they walked exaggeratingly slowly, from
one end of the courtyard to the other. When they passed
each purveyor, blankets and merchandise were placed
back onto the ground and hurriedly spread behind the
officers. For each peddler it became business as usual
mere paces behind the police. It was so cadenced it exuded the air of choreography. Owen laughed under his
breath as he stood and picked up his backpack. He

walked behind the officers toward a piazza adjacent to the museum. There was a little café where he could get a cold beer to offer some relief from the warm spring day.

When he reached his destination he was delighted to see several available tables. He approached the host and asked to be seated, trying his best to speak Italian without an accent, "*Posso avere una tavola per uno, per favore.*"

The maitre D' removed a single menu from a pocket on the side of his stand and without a word showed Owen to a table. It was the middle of the afternoon and the café had cleared of its lunchtime patrons. He dropped his backpack in an empty seat and sat down. The waiter approached quickly and eagerly. Fearing the server would begin to speak in his native language, he asked for a beer before being challenged to decipher an unfamiliar greeting. "*Una birra, per favore.*"

The waiter detected the accent he tried so hard to conceal. "Peroni okay?"

"*Si, grazie,*" Owen said, graciously.

The waiter brought the beer out quickly and he drank and watched the people in the square. After several moments of examining the different faces and manner of dress, he made a game of picking out the tourists and those who were local. He listened intently to the conversations going on around him. After a couple of hours and a few large glasses of beer, Owen felt confident in his ability to discern those who were speaking Italian, but not well enough to be native to the wonderful city.

The sun set over the piazza and Owen had a glow about him that was the result of ingesting several '*birra grandi*.' He wiped the sweaty film from his forehead and realized he needed something to eat before alcohol consumed his every faculty. A good brisk walk would do him well.

"*L'assegno, per favore*," Owen asked as he signed the palm of his left hand with the imaginary pen he held in his right. It did not matter that he knew the waiter spoke English.

"Right away," the waiter replied.

Paying in Lira and the substantial amount of currency it represented caused him to worry about leaving too much. He shook away his fear and picked up his backpack and walked out of the café. When he reached the entrance, he looked toward each corner of the piazza. They all appeared the same. In addition to the exits at each corner, there was a large archway in the middle of one side of the square. Five choices were available and he was certain he could get back to his hotel via the portico. He slung his backpack over his shoulder as he began to walk.

Just as Owen turned the corner and walked through the massive opening, a group of young Italian girls approached laughing and having a good time on a Friday night. There were five of them and he hesitated, shifting left and then right, trying to avoid a collision. One young lady walked backwards in front of the others as she spoke loudly. She was being very demonstrative, using her arms and hands to place emphasis where it was needed. Displaying a single consciousness, the others saw Owen and began to direct their companion under the guise of helping her. Instead, they guided her into his path. He countered each of her moves, but the collective was deft at the game. With a final wave of a hand, one young lady completed the decisive action that brought the tourist and her friend together. Just before they collided, another of the girls, in a moment of conscience, yelled, *"Vigilanza favori."*

The young girl turned just in time to meet Owen face-to-face as they ran into one another. He dropped his backpack. She fell backward, away from him. His momentum and stature propelled her to the ground. He felt horribly as he stood witnessing the incident. She was stunned, and her friends fell silent. They rushed to her aid. With their help she stood and flipped her coal-black hair that had fallen into her face over the back of her head with her left hand. It took him a few moments to regain his composure.

"Mi Scusi ... I'm sorry. I'm sorry. How the hell do you apologize in Italian?" Owen became frustrated with his inability to properly communicate his regret. The girls looked suspiciously at him. Nervously he searched for the words, but it only made matters worse. He stared at the cobblestone street, unable to face the young lady he feared he may have hurt. Owen took a deep breath, looked up at the group of girls who stared at him condescendingly. He searched for a glimmer of forgiveness on just one face. Finally, he looked at the young lady who stood in front of the group with her arms folded across her chest. When he took the time to appreciate her for the first time, he was captivated. The others quickly faded into the background. His nervousness was obvious to her, so she smiled to let him know everything was okay.

Her dress was white with small purple and pink flowers intricately stitched into its fabric. It perfectly complimented her dark skin. Owen noticed how the frock conformed to her hourglass shaped body. The hem hung to mid-thigh, revealing very long legs. With his eyes he followed the outline of her skirt. "Oh my god! You're absolutely gorgeous!" Owen was stunned to confession by her beauty. He continued to stare. Her eyes were the shape and color of fresh almonds. They were bright and possessed a smile all their own. Her skin was smooth, brown and flawless. Every detail of her body was sculpted and magnificent. "She is the most amazing woman I've ever seen and I can't even communicate with her." He became frustrated at the prospect of not being able to tell her how he felt. Fear that he would never see her again lowered his linguistic skills to that of a caveman. He placed his hand on his chest, "Owen."

Her friends watched and copied his gesture. "Owen," they repeated, mockingly, in unison.

"Okay smart guy, what now?" Suddenly, his attempt seemed hopeless. He bent over, picked up his backpack and smiled graciously in an effort to bid *arrivederci*.

The young woman placed her hand on his shoulder as he began to walk away, then placed the other on her chest and deliberately said, "Julia."

"Well Julia … the most beautiful woman I've ever seen, and possible love of my life … I have no way to tell you how sorry I am that I ran into you." The language barrier and his despair fueled his boldness; "Who am I kidding? I wish I could run into you every day for the rest of my life." She stared at him blankly.

Owen continued, "Your beauty is burned into my memory. You'll be the first thing I think of every morning for the rest of my life and the last thing each night. I will dream of holding you close to me. *You* belong in the Uffizzi." Owen shook his head. "Why did I not spend more time learning Italian? This is useless."

"No it isn't," she said.

Her friends walked away engulfed in laughter and mocking Owen in English, "Love of my life! The *Uffizzi!*" Julia did not move.

Suddenly, a loud thunderous clap shook him from his daydream. One of his shoes flew from the log and landed ten feet away with a splash. He fell into the water using the tree for cover. After a few seconds he lifted his head and peered toward the highway. A car sped away. Its rear tires threw up oyster shells and dust as it struggled to gain traction. Keeping his head low, he moved toward his shoe. When he retrieved it from the water he saw that a bullet had pierced the circle on the back that once contained the likeness of a puma. His heart pounded in his chest. Someone obviously knew he had information that could lead to great wealth.

Chapter Two

The house sat atop the only bluff in the area and provided a view over the roof-tops of homes that dotted the landscape. Owen stopped at the front door and removed his shoes by prying them off with the opposite foot as he leaned against the door-frame. He picked up the one that had been shot by sticking his finger through the bullet hole, then shook his head in disbelief. His shirt was slung over his shoulder, and he held it in place as he leaned over and neatly placed both shoes next to the doorway before walking to a spigot and turning on the water. After rinsing his feet of the sand that had dried on them he walked into the house and closed the door behind him.

From the foyer he looked through the living room and the wall of glass that enclosed the back portion of the house. The day had become cloudless and the sun's rays reflected off the canal, brightening its interior.

His legs ached from the morning's activity. Pain radiated through his thighs with each step on the ceramic tile floor as he walked toward the rear of the house. When he reached the massive sliding-glass doors, he grabbed the handle of one and shifted his weight to aid in opening it. Owen walked onto the pool deck and closed the door behind him. The bones in his tender feet shifted and sank into the gaps between the pavers adding to his discomfort. Nevertheless, he continued toward the edge of the pool. He stopped and posed at the shallow end, slung his arms behind him and then forward as he performed a picturesque shallow dive. Once his body entered the water he glided motionless toward the deep end. When he approached the wall he held his arms out to stop his momentum. After his head breached the water he gasped for air then grabbed the edge and pulled himself up until his forearms rested on the deck. The sun provided instant warmth against his back while he thought about the events of the morning. He had no idea who took a shot at him, but the possibilities were many.

Suddenly the urge came over him to check on something stored in his guest house. He placed his palms flat on the edge of the pool and effortlessly lifted his body out of the water. Once he had both hands and feet firmly on the ground he stood straight, walked across the patio and into the outer quarters.

The interior was covered in wood paneling. Owen shook his head as he realized this was the only room in the house he had not taken the time to redecorate. Several brass portals hung on the walls as did a Jolly Roger, completing its nautical theme. He walked over and opened a drawer in the small kitchenette and removed a screwdriver before moving toward an air conditioner intake.

Kneeling down, he began to unscrew the bolts along the corners of the slotted metal plate. Once they had all been removed he did the same to the cover, placing it on the floor next to him. He reached in and grabbed a black leather carrying case that lay on the bottom of the vent. It was too heavy for him to lift at that angle, so he slid it out and onto the floor. It took a great deal of strength to lift the bag as he stood. His arms flexed to their maximum as he carried it across the room and laid it on the coffee table before sitting on the edge of the couch. After unzipping it he pulled apart the sides revealing its contents. Owen ran his hands across the bumpy contours of the hundreds of coins contained in the case. It was filled with Spanish Pieces of Eight. He chuckled as he recalled that until 1857 the Spanish coins had been the preferred legal currency in the United States. *They're obviously my preferred currency*, he thought smugly to himself.

Over a half million dollars was in the case that lay before him, and there had been many multiples of that stored in his guest house over the years. It was the method by which he had come to possess the coins that at one time made him uncomfortable. Guilt had been successfully rationalized away years earlier. The mere fact that Owen was in possession of such artifacts made him a criminal amongst the collective intellect of the State of Florida; no matter the means employed to procure the items. He had never been one to subscribe to any set of rules. They were seen as a way to control and manipulate. For someone who never experienced economic freedom, he gravitated to everything that afforded him that sense. Money perched him upon the greatest emotional pedestal he had known. Its source and the physical price he paid to obtain it were brushed aside as easily as his past.

Chapter Three

Later that morning Owen stood in front of the wall of glass at the rear of his house. His gaze fell beyond the pool and onto the vessel that hung from a winch in the boat house. Pure mathematics dictated that each time he went out on it the chances of something dire happening increased. It was a dangerous game he played. No matter how civil humans think they are, when millions of dollars are at stake, the kindest person could easily be transformed into a vicious marauder. He never thought of himself as a pirate. Instead, he rationalized away responsibility by eliminating the victims from his crime. The shipwreck he plundered sank over three hundred years earlier. Identifying heirs would be next to impossible. He smiled as he drank from a coffee mug that he held near his chest; emptying it.

Guilt was pushed into his subconscious, yet again. The void was filled by memories of how he came to live on the small island. An ad for a ship's mate caught his attention as he surfed the internet. Bone Key Salvage advertised the position. He chuckled at the irony of how he had gotten his start like many of the pirates of the sixteenth and seventeenth centuries, working to recover valuables from wrecked ships.

His work ethic made Owen a great deck-hand. He set about doing his job as quickly as possible and without a lot of talk. Captain Tull never felt compelled to exact discipline upon him. Life on the seas did not afford many opportunities for friendship, or to build trust in individuals. There was an intangible about him; something that went far beyond hard work, which caused the captain to immediately trust his charge.

His mentor was a man of considerable age when they met. Many years in the sun had worn his appearance to a craggy and gaunt shell of the man he once was. He was thin and shriveled with deep lines that cut into the dark skin on his face. A cigarette was perpetually clamped between his lips. Never once did he recall the man using his hands to hold it; only to insert it, or remove the butt and flip it over the side of the boat. His hands were either gripped firmly on the wheel of the boat, or occupied doing some task that required immediate attention. During the many times Tully cussed out the crew, never once did the butt fall from his mouth as it bobbed violently, reflecting the captain's rage.

Owen's mood became melancholy as he thought about how the captain was the one man in his life who had taken the time to teach him. His knowledge may have been limited to the sea, but he did everything he could to impart every bit of it into his young protégée. It may have been his advanced age and the realization he spent his entire life at sea that caused the captain to nurture what he viewed as the final relationship of his life. Their friendship was fresh and devoid of any history that may have caused the harboring of contempt. In the captain's eyes Owen could not get away with anything the other members of the crew couldn't. However, he was a little more tolerant of his young mate's screwups, especially when he first entered the captain's employ. Owen proved to the other members of the crew that he could hold his own and then some. He had their respect. They had his.

The most valuable lesson the captain taught him was how to read nautical maps, and to understand the affect the ocean's current had on the sandy bottom;

shifting tons of silt along with whatever salvageable booty lay there. That knowledge helped when he began researching the old Spanish Galleons that were ship-wrecked along the Florida coast. He was able to de-termine the position of one. In 1622 an unlucky vessel was decimated by an unforeseen hurricane, and Owen was able to anticipate its position within a mile. For months he took his twenty-three foot Boston Whaler out daily until he had zeroed in on its exact location. By the time he found the ship, Tully had passed away. Owen ached to share his good fortune with the man who meant so much to him and who had given him the skills to reap such a bountiful harvest.

The bullet that barely missed him caused him to question the wisdom of opening that Pandora's treasure chest. He stared out at his brand new thirty-six foot Sea-Ray as the dichotomy of money became clear. The currency offered the much needed liquidity for him to carry on an existence filled with excess. As a store of wealth it became worthless to a man who never felt worthy of it. No long term aspect of his life had ever been valued. But he didn't know how he would live without the one thing that brought him security; his for-tune.

Owen took his empty mug into the kitchen. He wore a bathrobe; hair still wet and mussed from a shower meant to wash away the stench of his morning activity. He opened the refrigerator and removed the or-ange juice container. Just as he carried it to the counter, the phone rang. He looked at the glass and wondered if he had time to pour the juice before the caller hung up.

He decided not to, and placed the carton on the counter. He walked to the phone and picked up the receiver. "Hello."

"Owen Taylor?" the voice on the other end asked.

"You got him," he said, smugly.

"My name is Pedro Melendez. I am a Special Agent with the Federal Bureau of Investigation office in Miami. I am outside your gate. Can you buzz me in?"

Owen walked back to the counter where he left the orange juice container. He picked it up and calmly poured a full glass of juice. "Have you got some kind of search warrant?"

"Oh no. This is not that kind of visit. You know the FBI. If it were, we'd just burn your house down."

Owen did not laugh at the agent's feeble attempt at humor. "That should be my line." He furrowed his brow, realizing most FBI agents were straight-laced and devoid of a sense of humor, especially the self-deprecating variety. He walked to the front door where a small television screen was mounted to the wall, and turned on the monitor. The video feed was from his neighborhood's front gate. There he saw a man and no one else in the car. "Can you show me your identification, Agent Melendez?"

"Certainly. Where is the camera?"

"Just hold it up in front of the key pad. I'll be able to see it."

The man removed the identification from his coat pocket and held it up. Owen looked closely at the screen. Although he was no expert in forged documents, the ID looked legitimate. "Okay. I'll buzz you in." He looked at his phone and pushed a combination of buttons to open the gate, then dropped it into the left pocket of his robe. From the small table positioned against the wall beneath the closed circuit monitor he removed a .38 caliber handgun and put it into his right robe pocket.

After a few minutes the doorbell rang. Owen waited coolly before looking through the peephole. He saw the same man he had seen at the gate. There were no signs of anyone else lurking about, so he unlocked the door and slowly opened it before placing both hands in his pockets and gripping the gun firmly. He backed away from the door as it opened. The man he knew as Agent Melendez cautiously walked inside, looked to the left and then to the right. Owen took the man's identification that had been offered in his left hand and examined it very closely, never allowing the agent out of his peripheral vision. When he was done, he handed the document back to the man. "So, what's all this about?"

"Can I sit down?" The man pointed toward a sofa across the room.

Owen paused. "Okay." He extended a welcoming, yet cautious hand.

His guest led the way and he followed with both hands in his pockets. The man sat down on the sofa and Owen sat on a love seat. He leaned forward in an aggressive manner. Between the two was a glass top coffee table. They stared in silence at each another until the agent spoke. "This is a nice home you have."

"It's not a part of the Parade of Homes tour," Owen replied, glibly. "You didn't come here to compliment me on my house."

"You're right. I'm here because I need ... the bureau needs a favor from you."

"What's that?"

"Are you familiar with a man named Owen Franklin who lives in Florence?" the agent asked.

"Florence, Alabama?" Owen's attitude spoke volumes about his lack of desire to cooperate.

Agent Melendez smiled and replied calmly. "Italy."

"Come on! You're an intelligent man. You can come up with a better excuse for your visit than that." Owen replied sarcastically as he leaned back.

"We have reason to believe that Mr. Franklin has been trafficking in stolen merchandise."

"What kind of merchandise?"

"Historical artifacts," Melendez explained.

Owen paused. "I guess you know that three years ago I took a trip to Florence?"

"I do."

"I can assure you the only purpose of my trip was to find the final resting place of my uncle." He paused again. "My great uncle is dead and has been since World War II."

The agent did not respond immediately. He considered his confession carefully. "The F.B.I. has a dossier on you."

Owen sat silently, contemplating the agent's admission. "What does it say?"

There was no response. The men sat staring at each other, neither blinking nor showing any sign of weakness. After carefully choosing his words the G-man broke the silence. "Let me ask you this. How do you support yourself here? A man of thirty-five living in a multi-million dollar house with no visible means of support tends to raise a few eyebrows. I know that you have one and a half million dollars in cash sprinkled in small banks from Key West to Jacksonville. I know that your stock portfolio is valued, at the close of trading yesterday, at three and three quarter million dollars; give or take a few thousand. I know there is no mortgage on this house. You don't even have a car payment on that nice BMW 650i convertible parked outside. If you refuse my offer, I will dedicate every waking hour of my life tracking down exactly where all your money came from. I don't care how petty you may think it is, I will push for the stiffest penalty I can get."

Just as the agent finished his threat, the phone in Owen's pocket rang. When he removed it the man looked at his robe and saw the bulge in the other pocket. "Hello." He listened. "Hey Lilith … Islamorada?! Why way up there? … Sure. Come by here about five thirty." Owen pushed the off button on the phone and placed it back into his pocket. Agent Melendez smiled. Owen did not volunteer any information.

"Who's Lilith?"

"A friend."

"Girlfriend?"

"Not in the least. Just a local I hang out with," he replied.

"Well, since you have refused my offer I'll be leaving now. If you have a change of heart and want to tell us what you know about Owen Franklin, here is my card." The agent handed him a business card.

"I'm not promising anything," he replied as he took the card. Melendez stood and walked to the front door. Owen followed. Before his guest had a chance to turn the doorknob and open the door, Owen said, "You know, my father told me when I was ten years old,

'Son, life's tough. Don't sit around bitching about it. You either get into the game, or sit on the sidelines.' That was the single best piece of advice I've ever gotten. I got into the game, and I play it well."

"I don't understand," The agent confessed.

"There is nothing illegal about how I made my money. I am simply very good at acquiring it," he explained.

"One day you'll have to explain its source; to me, or to someone who would rather kill you than risk losing it." The man walked through the door and onto the patio.

"I just have one more question."

Melendez turned around. "What's that?"

"Why did you bring my uncle Owen into this?"

He thought carefully before answering. "If I told you that your great uncle was alive and living outside Florence … Italy, would you help me, help him?"

"Is he really in trouble?"

"Let's just say that if you offered your help, I'm sure he would welcome it."

Owen did not reply as the two parted ways; closing the door only after the agent had descended the steps and driven away. If what the man said was true he found himself in the unfamiliar position of being able to help someone. Value was an attribute he was only able to apply to possessions. It never occurred to him he could be of benefit to someone beyond the superficial underpinnings that defined all of his relationships.

Chapter Four

The deep water port in Key West was discovered in the early nineteenth century by men who took on the mundane task of salvaging wrecked ships, eventually turning it into an art-form. From causing the wrecks by extinguishing the lighthouse's lantern, to cleaning up afterward, these men knew how to maximize the return on their investment. The port from which they operated was a tourist attraction where people gathered nightly to celebrate the end of their day and the beginning of debauchery filled nights. Mallory Square played host to the festive atmosphere each evening. It started with the celebration of the sunset marked by a booming canon at the exact moment the sun dipped behind the horizon. Street performers entertained in a carnival-like atmosphere, vying for the attention of tourists and the change in their pockets with which they were willing to part. Lillith cancelled their date because two of her employees had called out sick.

Owen walked alone through the crowd stopping to watch a little bit of each act. A young man wearing a green and gold blouse juggled various items. At one point during his show he held aloft a sledgehammer, a basketball and a camcorder, unwittingly donated by a passing visitor. Mimes, singers, and a lady playing tunes by running her moistened finger-tip around the rim of crystal goblets filled with varying amounts of water all attracted Owen's attention at some point during the night.

Suddenly, an elaborate stage production caught his eye. It was set up on the southern side of the promenade. At first, all he saw were three large squares outlined in bright white lights. When he approached he could see over the crowd was actually nine squares; three by three. A mock performance of The Hollywood Squares was being staged. Owen became intrigued. He watched the inter-play between characters. Two contestants appeared to have been plucked from the audience, based on their poorly timed responses. Questions along with quick witted answers were heavily scripted. Uproarious laughter filled the night.

In the center square was a Paul Lynde look-a-like. To his left was a man dressed as Cher during her eighties period with very full hair and a dress made of mesh. Three patches of black leather covered the parts any gentile lady would want concealed. He watched for several minutes as the contestants and audience bantered back-and-forth. When he grew tired of the show, he decided to buy a beer from one of the many vendors who offered refreshing libations.

For hours he wandered aimlessly; making what amounted to several laps around the square, viewing the different street performances. A couple of entertainers smiled and nodded at him as he passed for the third and fourth time. He knew they recognized him and that their congeniality was fueled by the hope of securing a tip. Several times he dug into his pocket and removed a bill and dropped it into whatever receptacle they made available for donations.

When the night grew late and morning became a consideration, a drunken Owen Taylor strolled along the waterfront. The only people left were guests of the various hotels along the wharf; making their way back to their rooms after a night of revelry. A film of alcohol ladened sweat covered his body. His eyes were bloodshot and scratchy. Focusing clearly on anything was

nearly impossible. It appeared to him that his Rolex
Submariner read '1:15.' The impaired wisdom of walking around at such a late hour with an expensive watch
prominently displayed became apparent. Nonchalantly
he removed the chronograph and dropped it into his
front pocket. The last shuttle left at midnight. Catching
a cab was his only alternative. Owen wanted to forget
that the F.B.I. was a part of his life.

Living out his days in a quiet and unassuming
manner was no longer an option. *Bobby was right. I am
just a fucking dumb-ass,* he thought to himself. *Maybe I
shouldn't go home tonight. I could walk to Higgs Beach
from here and hang out with the homeless people. I
could probably get away with that for a couple of
weeks before they found me.* He felt more helpless than
when he lived with Jenny and Bobby. Self destructive
urges raged within him. Alcohol would do, but all of the
vendors had closed for the evening.

His emotions were raw and inevitably exposed
all that was wrong with his life. His cousin Bill had
worked his way through pharmacological school. He
was eight years older than Owen and fancied Sara. On a
trip to Islamorada, Sara and Bill slipped a drug into
Owen's breakfast to provide the opportunity for them to
carry on a day-long tryst. It knocked him out for nearly
twelve hours. At first he attributed his exhaustion to all
the partying they had been doing. When he and Sara
broke up during a heated argument, she employed her
confession as an emotional dagger. Loneliness became
his preferred companion.

His walk became a stagger as he attempted to
make it across the square toward Duval Street and a
waiting cab. He felt himself exaggerating his steps in an

attempt to appear sober and laughed out loud at his own ineptitude.

"What the fuck are you laughing at?" a voice asked, from the darkness.

He tried to focus on where it came from, but could not see anyone.

"Shut-up, Jack," a female voice answered, from the shadows.

Moving toward the voices he was able to see several shadowy figures sitting on a wall that was about two feet high. Cautiously he walked closer. They sat at a point where two walls came together at a ninety degree angle. He recognized them as the street performers he watched earlier. The prospect of their association he found intoxicating. Slowly he sauntered closer. The pungent smell of marijuana stopped him in his tracks. It had been several years since he had smoked pot. He quit because he felt it exacerbated his depression. Getting high became an enticing alternative. "I was laughing at myself," Owen said, as he attempted to focus on each face. Identifying the person who spewed hatred seemed prudent. When no one responded, he asked, "Do you mind if I sit with you?"

The continued silence cut into his psyche. He knew his intentions were honorable, but they did not. What could he say to convey that? Before he had the chance, a voice spoke. "Where's your watch?"

Owen looked at his naked left wrist and rubbed it with his right hand. "I don't wear one."

"Bullshit! I saw you with a Rolex Submariner on earlier this evening." The man who spoke was older than the others. He wore a white Hoss style cowboy hat that was filthy from years of wear. Long, stringy, gray hair hung past his shoulders. His face was round and red, and he spoke with a southern accent.

"I … took it off," Owen admitted.

"Can't be wearing that watch around a bunch of undesirables like us, huh?"

"That's not it. I took it off an hour ago."

"Sure you did."

Just as Owen felt like he needed to dismiss himself the young lady said, "Dutch, give the guy a break." Then she looked at him. "Go ahead and have a seat, sweetie."

Euphemisms delivered in a condescending tone had always irritated him, but he made an exception and hurriedly found a seat amongst his new friends. There were two others sitting on the same wall with him and four along the adjacent one. He looked at the only girl in the group and smiled hoping to convey his thanks. She returned the gesture, but it was tinged with skepticism. She was pretty and must have dealt with men hitting on her a lot. The girl's appearance was clean and unsullied, unlike anything one would expect from a person who makes their living nightly in a public park. He watched as she placed a joint to her lips and inhaled. The embers cast an orange glow on her smooth, thin neck. Just behind her ear was a tattoo of three stars. Each one was a little larger than the one before and they curved along the gentle bend of her ear-lobe. There was no other way to describe her than refreshing. She seemed quite out of place with the riffraff.

He watched her pass the joint to the gentleman sitting next to her; who quickly inhaled, holding his breath as he passed it along to the next person. The inebriant was handed around the corner and made its way toward Owen. He worried whether or not he should partake. It didn't seem as though he was too popular.

"Here dude," the guy next to him said without exhaling as he pivoted on his butt to hand over the cigarette.

Without a word, he put it to his lips and inhaled as deeply as he could. His pre-middle age body was in such good shape he was able to take a lot of the drug into his lungs, maybe too much. It began to burn and he coughed. The others laughed at his blunder. Embarrassed, he quickly handed it back to the young man. This continued until it was merely ash held at the end of a roach-clip.

"Hey friend, where are you from?" The fresh-faced girl asked.

"I live here," Owen replied.

"Cool," was her only response.

"I'm sorry I was such an asshole earlier," Dutch apologized. "And it ain't just the pot talkin'."

"That's alright."

Without acknowledging his acceptance, Dutch continued. "It's just that these goddamned tourists come down here with all their money and they think they are better than us. Don't ever become a street performer, friend. You'll end up nothing more than a jester."

"My name is Owen, *friend*."

Dutch smiled.

The young man next to him turned and held out his hand. "My name is Jack." The two shook hands. "It is frustrating. I've got an Ivy League education and this is what it has gotten me."

With conspicuous admiration, Owen replied to them all, "But don't you all enjoy a freedom that no one else can say they have?" He saw all of their shoulders shaking in silent laughter.

"That was the dream," replied a black man whose shorts were made from a Jamaican flag. "By the way, my name is Winston."

At that moment everyone else said their name in unison. Owen focused on the young girl. Her name was Saffron. He had never known anyone with that name. It was as unusual and distinct as he found her. He turned to Dutch. "Tell me, how did you remember me out of all of the people that were here tonight?"

He smiled. "Son, when you've been at this for as long as I have you develop the ability to carry on your show while scoping out the crowd. You look for signs of wealth, like Rolex watches, in order to focus on those folks so that you can take home a bigger haul."

"Do you remember whether or not I placed anything in your bucket?"

"I don't use a bucket. That's Jack. I use a treasure chest, and yes, you placed a ten dollar bill in it." Owen smiled. He was impressed by the man's ability to recall their brief meeting in such detail.

"Just because I'm not an educated man, doesn't mean I'm not an intelligent man," he proclaimed.

"I'm well aware of that fact," Owen responded.

"What is it that you do for a living?" Saffron asked.

He hesitated briefly. "I'm a salvage operator."

"Oh, a pirate!" she said.

He laughed nervously without saying a word. The last thing he wanted was to get into a discussion about how he made his money.

Brief silence allowed their altered minds to entertain whatever metaphysical thoughts happened to present themselves, until a man walked up to them. He was heavily intoxicated and staggered, unable to maintain his balance while trying to close the distance between himself and group. "How ya'll doin'?"

No one answered.

"My name is Tom Harper. I'm down here with the Interfaith University Search For Christ," he proclaimed, arrogantly.

Dutch immediately pointed to a spot down by the water. "I saw him walking across the bay to Sunset Key a little earlier." That elicited a chuckle from everyone except Tom. It was obvious he was trying to wrap his Gin soaked brain around the joke.

"Where are you from, Tom?" Owen asked.

"Atlanta," he boasted.

"Have you got a wife?"

"And two kids," the drunk man added as he held up the same number of fingers.

Owen shook his head. "Does she know you drink so heavily?"

"Oooh, no. We could never tell the little lady about that," he wagged his finger back and forth, as he spoke in a condescending tone.

Jack exploded. "What the fuck do you want?"

Tom was offended by the language, but it did not deter him from making his move. "I was wondering if I could buy this pretty little girl here a drink," he said, as he pointed toward Saffron.

Owen looked at Dutch immediately. His face became beet-red. "That's it friend. You need to leave and the first thing you need to do when you get home is to ask your wife's forgiveness. And then you need to do the same with your God."

Understanding it was time to leave Tom disappeared as quickly as he had shown up.

"That asshole would probably be my boss if I still lived there," Dutch pointed aimlessly in the direction of an existence that had become surreal to him.

Owen chuckled. "I guess that's why we are all here."

"Why's that?" Saffron pressed.

"Because I'd wager that none of us have ever had a relationship that we've found to be satisfying. If it's not heartache, it's betrayal. And if it's not that then it's hypocrisy, just like our friend Tom. Every one of us had the same visceral reaction to him."

"So what are you trying to say?" Jack asked.

"What I'm trying to say is that I think all of us are looking for that one ... *just one* relationship that is oblivious to all outside forces. There won't be a woman or a man who could come between us and our uber-lover. Trust won't be questioned. Blind faith won't be necessary because the love will be palpable." Owen paused. "We are all searching for perfection and it pisses every single one of us off that we haven't found it."

Contemplative silence fell over the crowd until an unnamed young man spoke. "Dude, I want to get high with you again!"

Owen surprised himself with how his altered mind articulated his feelings about what he desired from a relationship. His brush with death provided an entirely new outlook on life. He was caught between a shipwreck he no longer felt safe to visit, a fed who wanted the treasure for himself while lying about his great uncle, and someone who took a shot at him. People he counted as friends might have been moved to orchestrate any of these situations. It was up to him to figure out who; or as he had always done, run away.

Chapter Five

Owen slid from one side of his bed to the other. The sheets were cooler there. His head was heavy and he had no desire to leave the security of his duvet. Staring at the ceiling he was unsure of whether he could go back to sleep, but wanted desperately to do just that. The bones in his neck creaked as he rolled his head over on his pillow and looked at the alarm clock. It read, '9:11.' He returned his gaze to the ceiling.

The people he met the night before consumed his thoughts. To a person he could find no reason to doubt their genuine disposition. It was a quality he never looked for, but one he craved with so much uncertainty surrounding his future. Dizziness, exacerbated by the remnants of the mind altering substances consumed the night before, caused him to feel as though his body were floating above his mattress. The pungent taste of marijuana lingered in the back of his throat. Circumstances of his life guaranteed a future he wasn't sure he could change. It was laid out for him like a long stretch of highway that disappeared into a barren desert.

Owen picked up the remote control from his bedside table, pointed it at the ceiling fan and pushed the button that increased its speed. The cool breeze was meant to overtake the nausea he felt. Instead, he sat up quickly, ready to spring from his bed in order to make it to the bathroom in case the need to vomit overtook him.

Moments later the feeling subsided just before the phone rang. He looked at the receiver, reached over and removed it from its cradle. It was his friend. "Hey, Lilith."

She spoke excitedly. "Turn on the T.V."

"Why? What's up?" Owen asked, as he reached for the television remote.

"We've been attacked."

"Who has?"

"The United States."

Owen turned on the local news station and watched in awe as he saw one of the towers of the World Trade Center burning near its top. "*What happened*?"

"A plane flew into it."

Owen thought for a moment. "Could it have been an accident?"

"No way. How could a plane not see that building?" Her tone got more excited. "If there was ever a pilot that knew he was about to crash, how many would purposefully steer it toward a building?"

"I'm sure there was at least one," Owen said, sarcastically.

Before she had a chance to respond, they watched in horror as another plane came into view of the camera. When it hit the second tower they knew for sure it was a coordinated attack, but had no idea what to do or say.

"Owen, are you there?" Lilith's voice startled him.

"Yeah, I'm here. I was just wondering how many people are stuck on the upper floors."

"This is horrible!"

"It's like watching Pearl Harbor happen in real-time." Owen's tone was dazed.

Lilith did not respond, and the two did not exchange a word for several moments. The horror they witnessed was unlike anything either had ever experienced. Violent images destroyed the efficacy of words.

"Do you think I should open the bar early?"

Owen did not immediately offer his suggestion. He shook his head in disbelief at the surreal vision before him. "I'm sure from a business perspective that might be the right thing to do, but I won't be there until later. I have some things I need to do." Recovering from his hangover took priority. "I've got to go." He hung up the phone without waiting for a response from his friend.

The more he watched constant replays of the second plane hitting the tower, the angrier he became. Sickness in the pit of his stomach was exacerbated by the prior night's debauchery. Memories of the worst times in his life made their way from the deepest recesses of his mind. He never had any control over the circumstances surrounding those times. The fact that there had never been any resolution prevented closure on an unhappy childhood. Minor infractions were met with severe corporal punishment. Maturation and the challenges of adult life helped him to understand that the anger Bobby directed toward him was most likely the result of something the man could not control. If Owen knew the tragic circumstances surrounding his parents' deaths had taken more of a toll on Bobby than he ever experienced, life may have made more sense to him. Without that knowledge he was left to find his own way out of the misery it caused. He recalled how the man would hold him up by the wrist so that his feet no longer touched the floor, and lash a belt across his buttocks repeatedly. Exhaustion was the only thing that stopped the beatings. It did not help that Jenny allowed her husband to dole out punishment. Owen realized it was her way of redirecting the man's anger so she wouldn't have to deal with it. She taunted him by saying, 'wait until Bobby gets home.' Fear caused him much stress as a boy and manifested itself in a perpetual anger he passed along whenever the opportunity presented itself.

The last time the man laid a hand on him was when he was in high school. He was at Sara's house one night past his curfew. It happened to be the same night clocks were turned back. Owen was met by Bobby in the dark hallway of his home. Their argument spilled into his room. When the man yelled at him that it was five o'clock in the morning, he replied, 'it's actually only four o'clock.' Bobby drew back his fist and struck him across the face; knocking him backward onto his bed. He lay there unconscious until nine twenty-three that morning. There had never been any discussion of the incident; never an apology, and never any closure. For the longest time Owen felt like he deserved to be hit for his smart-ass remark.

Julia provided a ray of sunshine that lit his dark psyche. He knew there was no way he could make her happy. She was sophisticated, and he was not. No matter their differences he always remembered their time together fondly. He wasn't sure how to characterize the pleasant feelings he had for a woman with whom he had no future, but he enjoyed thinking of her.

One afternoon was spent at the Piazza de Michelangelo. It sat high atop a hill on the southern bank of the Arno River in the city of Florence. The setting sun appeared to be dropping just over the horizon and into the river. Its rays made the surface of the water shimmer like gold leaf. The experience was vibrant, as were the feelings of the lovers who came to enjoy un-bridled passion. From the moment they met he knew he would be willing to do anything for her. He smelled her perfume as he remembered the two of them sitting on a bench overlooking the river. She laid her head on his shoulder and he nestled his jaw against her crown. Owen slid his hand down her flank and over her hip. It was a gentle touch. Everything about their time together thrived within each of his senses.

Suddenly he shook away the dichotomous nature of the two emotions. For the first time he noticed a distinct cognitive patter. Whenever he became angry, ultimately, recollections of Julia brought him comfort.

Chapter Six

The *Bone Key Pirates Local #69* was at the edge of the tourist corridor. For the most part, it was a place for the locals to hang out after work, but an occasional tourist stumbled in for a drink. It was rare that Lillith left her business for someone else to oversee. Skepticism was in her nature and she had not found the person she knew would hold her interests above their own.

The normally raucous atmosphere was tempered by the events of the morning. Patrons stared at various televisions that hung from the ceiling around the room. Owen sat at a table with three other regulars. Whenever they were there, they were together. Lilith was behind the bar making sure her customers were satisfied.

To Owen's left was a man he estimated to be in his mid-forties. No one knew his real name, because he insisted on being called Ivy. The nickname was based on the fact, or so he told everyone, that he attended one of the more prestigious universities in the United States. No one knew what he did for a living, but he was always dressed impeccably. His shorts and shirts were always starched to a razor-sharp crease. A perpetually tilted head, with his chin buried in his chest, forced him to look down his nose at people. He spoke without moving his jaw freely, and projected his voice from deep within his throat. Owen had never been able to figure out how this person came to associate with the beer-swilling, riffraff they all considered themselves, but his company was usually pleasant. Whenever he got overly pompous the group quickly turned on him like a pack of rabid dogs and gnawed at his ego until he skulked away. He always returned displaying a more pleasant disposition.

Asa Tift had been coming to the bar far longer than any of the four. He introduced Owen to the group. The two met on the salvage boat, and both had great respect for Captain Tull. They kept his memory alive often through discussions about the things they missed the most about their mentor. Asa was the elder member of the group and usually kept quiet, forgoing active participation in most conversations. However, everyone knew that when he felt led to voice an opinion, he had a passion for what he was saying. He was the only one they didn't try to talk over. His beard was long, scraggly and gray. It had yellowed around his mouth from decades of smoking. *Cappy*, as Asa referred to Captain Tull, had given him his first cigarette when he was sixteen years old. He always donned a khaki fishing cap. It had tuxedo-tails that hung from the back meant to protect his neck from the sun.

Susan Swearingen was the final member of the crew. However, she was never the last, nor the least in anything she did. *Stump* was her nickname and the only name to which she answered. It was a moniker she carried with pride and distinction. Most people would have collapsed under its pressure. She was short of stature, but her large, bright smile that beamed from her eyes lifted everyone who had the pleasure to behold it. That was the only silent manifestation of her personality. Her ability to inject heightened enthusiasm into anyone with whom she spoke gave her an airborne narcotic quality. It took a day filled with tragedy to keep Stump silent. She sat staring at the screen across the room, her lips pursed, shaking her head in disbelief.

Owen removed his stare from the T.V. set and looked toward Lilith. On the other side of the bar sat

Agent Melendez. He maintained the same position as every other patron; head leaned back as he watched the constant coverage of the destruction in New York, Washington, and Pennsylvania. His weight rested on his forearms that lay across the edge of the bar. He held a mug of beer with the four fingers of his right hand inserted through its handle. Gently his thumb caressed the condensation on the outside of the glass. Owen did not know what to do. Should he look at him until they made eye contact? If he approached him, it would let the agent know he was not intimidated by him. He decided to face his demons.

Owen stood holding his beer, and not one of his mates noticed. He walked to the nearest end of the bar, turned the corner and made his way toward the agent. On the other side, as he rounded its edge, an extraordinarily beautiful young woman caught his eye. He could not help but stare as he walked toward his adversary. She had jet-black hair and her eyes were dark brown and bright. They sparkled and attracted Owen like a moth to a flame. An orange tank-top complimented her dark skin as well as her shapely body. Khaki green shorts came to mid thigh. Her legs were lean, long, smooth, and craved to be touched.

Owen turned his head as he came within a few steps of the bar-stool the agent occupied. The man had already noticed him.

"You shouldn't stare at women like that. It'll get you in trouble." Agent Melendez extended his hand.

Owen refused it in an effort to intimidate. "Aren't I in enough trouble?"

The agent smiled. "When I get through with you, you will get exactly what you deserve."

His imagination took flight. The man never accused him of anything, but seemed to know an awful lot about his life. He pointed toward the television above the bar. "Shouldn't you be out chasing terrorists?"

"That's not my department," the agent said, conveniently.

"So you're strictly assigned to money launderers … or whatever it is that you are accusing me of doing, right?"

The agent smiled, shrugged his shoulders coyly, and took a sip from his beer.

Lilith walked over to the two men. She had a bar rag in her hand and wiped the counter in front of them. "Can I get you another beer, Luca?"

"*Si, per favore.*"

Owen looked at the man and wondered if he were under-cover. The thought was quickly brushed aside, and given his purpose for confronting the man had been accomplished, making a play for the young lady at the end of the bar was what he desired, so he bid farewell to the man. "Have a good day, Agent Luca." He wanted the man to know he was bold enough to call him out in public. "If you'll excuse me I am going to introduce myself to this beautiful woman over here. The one *you* think I need to stay away from."

The man lifted his glass in bidding adieu.

Owen walked the length of the bar and valiantly sat in the seat next to the object of his desire. He had never been shy about approaching a strange woman, and with the great beauty she possessed, there was no way he would let the opportunity slip away.

"Hi. My name is Owen." He extended his hand in front of her, "I must say, you cast quite an impressive shadow."

She ignored his pass. "My name is Monica." Her response was laden with a Spanish accent.

"Where are you from?" he asked.

"Venezuela."

"Wow! How much longer will you be in town?"

Owen's question confused her. She looked at him curiously and re-translated his question. "No. I live here now. I was born in Venezuela is what I meant."

His heart sank at the realization she was a local. He made it a policy to never get involved with someone who lived in town. They tended to become clingy and breakups were never easy. But there was something that smoldered within him, and he was certain it emanated from her.

"Are you here visiting?" She jolted him from his fantasy.

Promise and optimism filled his psyche. "No. I live here too." When the words escaped his control he wondered whether he should have lied. "How long have you lived in Key West?" he continued, without hesitation.

"We moved here in 1999."

"Do you miss Venezuela?"

"Yes and no." Monica looked at him and realized there was no need to discuss the reasons she and her family moved to the United States. "I miss my country. I don't miss the political environment. *Mi pais es mi orgullo*." She paused before translating. "I am very proud of my country."

"I guess we're both in exile here." Owen did not put a lot of thought into his comment.

"What country did you come from?" she asked.

Owen laughed, sheepishly. "I'm from the U.S. I guess that I don't have the guts to move abroad."

Monica shook her head. "What about your family?"

"I don't have any family left," he said, and then took a large sip from his beer. "I am going to the bathroom. I'll be right back." He employed his urge as a tactic to measure Monica's interest.

After entering the washroom, he stood at the urinal reading a copy of the local newspaper from September 10, 2001. Front page news addressed the growing problem of chickens roaming the streets freely about the island. The unreal happenings of the morning made the mundane seem surreal. The world had changed overnight. It could have easily been a paper from fifty years earlier.

After washing his hands he walked out of the bathroom, around the corner and into the bar. Anxiously he looked for Monica. His heart sank when he saw that she had left. He quickly shook away the disappointment and changed direction toward the table filled with his friends. Wading through the myriad of patrons, he approached and saw that Monica sat in the chair he vacated earlier.

Laughter abounded and everyone appeared happier. The sentiment that life goes on had settled upon the group. Owen grabbed an empty chair from another table and swung it around. He placed it next to Stump and across the table from Monica. He enjoyed looking at her.

"*Ooh … big boy!*" Stump proclaimed, loudly and in a breathy voice as he sat down. "You're gonna sit next to *me*?"

"Yeah. Do you mind?" he asked, stiffly. She was prone to play to the crowd and he embraced his role as the straight-man.

"I ain't never had me no pirate before. I got your booty right here," she proclaimed as she elbowed Owen. "I might have to give you the opportunity to check some of this out." Stump caressed her hands an inch above her overly voluptuous body as she stood and stared directly into his eyes. She turned and bent over, sticking her butt in his face. "See! I got some junk in my trunk." She shook it from side to side. It was hard for him not to be embarrassed. He worried Monica would be offended.

Stump finished her performance and sat down hard in her chair. "Whew! I need a little drinky-drink." She picked up her mug and took a large gulp. Beer poured over her upper lip, down her check and dropped onto her blouse. After setting the mug down she wiped her mouth on the sleeve of her blouse in an exaggerated manner. "*Ah!*" she said, satisfyingly.

The others said nothing. Owen glanced across the table at Monica. Stump saw him and expanded her routine. "Don't you be eyeballin' no other women. You're *my* man!" she said, as she slid her chair closer to him and wrapped his arm in hers. Once again, he looked for Monica's reaction. She still had a smile on her face, so everything appeared copasetic. Stump looked at Monica and asked. "What's your last name sweetie? We never asked when we invited you over."

"Rojas."

Asa looked at the girl. "Are you Mexican?"

"I'm from Venezuela," she responded proudly, and a bit offended.

Asa laughed at himself. "I guess that'll give you an indication of my sophistication. When I was a kid I would watch old westerns, and without fail the banditos that came across the Rio Grande were named *Rojas*."

Everyone laughed at his self-deprecating story, except Ivy. He gave a loud, obnoxious, condescending laugh meant to humiliate. Owen and Stump glared at Ivy, letting him know they were there to make sure their society remained classless.

The waitress approached holding her tray by its edge and slapping it against her leg. "Anybody need anything over here?"

Stump took over. "We'll have another round." She looked at Monica. "Sugar, what are you drinking?"

"Cherry Tom Collins," the guest replied. Her accent was as sweet to the ear as her drink of preference.

Stump turned to the waitress. "Give her one of those and put it on my tab." She plunged her hand inside her shirt and under her bra.

Owen noticed what she was doing and that there was a tube of lipstick nestled in her cleavage. "Aren't you afraid your lipstick is going to melt? After all, you do have quite the ample bosom."

"Ooh, good point," she said, as she quickly grabbed it and slammed it onto the table. She continued searching for her money, and announced, "This is my cash register." She removed a wad of money and slapped it down next to the lipstick. "I gotta pay for Monica's drink somehow." A curious look on Owen's face caught her attention. "What's wrong with you?"

"Nothing. I'm just trying to figure out how your cash register works with only one button!" Everyone laughed.

Drinking continued into the night. The noise level in the bar increased as its usual liveliness returned to the bar. A band came in and set up their instruments on a small stage at one end of the room. Conversation became impossible during each set. With nothing to interrupt their drinking, quite a bit of alcohol was consumed. Emotions that were already raw became personal. Memories oozed from every sweat soaked pore. These stories were better left untold. Some heeded the advice of the voice of reason within their soul. Others could not resist the urge to share. Emotional embers that glowed were sparked by a well timed, yet innocent interrogative. "Asa, have you ever thought about leaving Key West?" Owen knew he was a true Conch, born and raised on the island, and that the answer was, *no*.

Asa swung his head around. His eyes were bloodshot and burned. The chair in which he sat was pushed away from the table and he slouched in it, holding his mug on his thigh. "Once. I felt like I had to get away from a situation," he answered. "My second wife was one of those women who, in her own mind, did nothing wrong, and I could do nothing right. She justified the numerous affairs she had by telling the men she was sleeping with what a horrible lover I was, and how they were the only ones who ever made her feel like a *real* woman. Then when she was with her lady friends she told them how ignorant I was and that I had no prospects to ever make a decent living. The only reason I could think of her doing that was so none of them would want me when she was done with me." He paused. "She was just plain evil, and consumed every bit of me."

Stump could not hold her comment inside. "Damn! You've got to be a man and have some balls. Grow a set would ya'?" Asa didn't flinch. She kept badgering him. "You've got to fight fire with fire. You gotta get down and dirty with 'em if that's how they want to play the game."

Asa slowly shook his head. "Nope, I don't believe in that. The bond between a man and his wife has to be built on trust. No matter what she did or said, she knows to this day that I would never do anything to harm her physically or emotionally."

"*What*? She walked all over you, old man."

"True, but if I had allowed her to drag me into the muck with her, then I would not have been the kind of man my current wife fell in love with." He smiled. "And believe me, having the wife I have now was well worth the pain I went through early in my life."

Stump shook her head. "You're weird, old man."

"You want to know how weird I am?" he asked. "The first woman I had sex with after my divorce was ten times as beautiful as my ex-wife, yet I had a bit of difficulty getting a hard-on because of the guilt I felt over making love to a woman who was not my wife."

Owen smiled. Something inside him identified with Asa. "Asa, how is it that you know that your wife is the one and only woman for you?"

An impish smile grew on the old man's face. He looked around at each person, wondering if he should deflect the question or be completely honest. There was no reason for a man his age to engage in deception. "I knew it the day I asked her what her wildest sexual fantasy was."

"That's it?" Owen asked, a little disappointed.

"No. Every time I make love to my wife I fantasize about her in the exact situation she described for me. I knew that when I could feel happy putting my wife's desires ahead of my own I had the one woman who was truly my soul mate. I'm glad that I sought out the relationship. It wasn't going to just fall into my lap."

Stump stood quickly causing her chair to slide across the floor as her legs straightened. She threw her hands into the air and declared, "That's it! Lord, I've been to the mountain-top and I am now enlightened." She pointed toward Asa. "Sir, you are a better man than I am." She walked across the floor and through the open doors onto Eaton Street. Everyone laughed under their breath, except Monica. Stump was known for making grand entrances and exits, and somehow each one seemed a little different than the last.

"I guess she wasn't man enough to handle that," Asa joked. "Believe me, if you don't think you can handle the answer, don't ask the question. Don't let fear keep you from saying what you truly feel. When you find a partner who accepts you no matter what, you'll know it's right."

Owen and Monica made eye contact and smiled at each other. The energy between them was so strong he was unable to see their relationship for what it was, or what it would become. Such a strong attraction he only felt one other time in his life. Something deep within his soul told him there was more to her than physical beauty. He would willingly take apart every ounce of his flesh to expose the other-worldly force that craved to connect with her.

Chapter Seven

Owen busily readied his boat for a journey to the shipwreck. It occupied a spot on the globe he considered his own. With each successful trip his possessiveness grew. The logical voice in his head continually whispered that this bounty would not last forever, which made each visit more urgent. Agent Melendez was not who he presented himself to be, but Owen couldn't figure out his true motives. He could not rest comfortably until he found out who this man was and what he wanted. His treasure had never been in such peril.

The vessel had been lowered into the water and it swayed gently with the calm morning current. Owen nervously examined each of his neighbor's docks for signs that someone may be readying themselves to follow him. He looked down each of the canals that converged behind his house. Several people carried large duffle bags filled with equipment down to their watercraft. Some held scuba tanks by their valves. The agent was nowhere in sight, but that did little to pacify his paranoia. Once again logic dictated that all of these people lived in the Keys for the purpose of enjoying boating. He would not allow that fact to dilute his overcautious nature.

Although his boat was built for speed, it took him over three hours on a straight path with calm seas. For the first time he felt this could be his last trip. During past visits he had only been able to carry twenty pounds of coins to the surface with each dive. The depth limited him to one dive over a twenty-four hour period due to the nitrogen buildup in his blood. Several would be needed in order to grab as many coins as he would need to live comfortably for the rest of his life at some obscure point on the map. Pushing beyond recommended dive times entered his mind several times. He had to grab as much booty as possible in one dive in order to minimize the danger.

Earlier that morning at a local dive shop he had purchased the largest mesh bag available. Two hundred feet of nylon rope would help bring the coins to the surface. Owen estimated this approach would yield two hundred pounds of coins. It was a lot of weight for one man to lift one hundred feet straight up, with the ocean's current pulling it, but he *had* to do it. Anticipation of a two million dollar yield fell short of his wildest dreams of building a fortune in excess of twenty million dollars before he was forced to abandon it. Owen prepared himself for the possibility of diving at night depending on how long the trip took.

All of the uncertainty that surrounded his life required him to make sure no one followed. His normal route took him through Key West harbor toward the Gulf Stream. A northern route through many of the insignificant islands that dotted the landscape seemed more prudent.

He throttled the boat's motors just enough to engage the propeller. The craft meandered along the Mangrove covered shoreline as he keenly watched every vessel and its occupants. When he maneuvered the boat north of Sugarloaf Key, he turned toward the narrow canal that separated it from Cudjoe Key. His path was meant to expose anyone who followed him. Once he reached the bridge spanning the channel he glanced over his shoulder and then shoved the throttle forward, maxing out the boat's speed.

For over four hours he captained the boat until he reached his destination. A direct path was forgone for a zigzagged one. At each angular point along that course he stopped and scanned the horizon with the aid of binoculars.

Modern Global Positioning Systems allowed him to place his boat in the exact same spot time and again without fail. Once the anchor settled itself on the bottom he adjusted its line on the cleat mounted to the bow. The first order of business was to determine what effect the current had on the treasure. As before every dive Owen found himself hoping he would uncover a jewel encrusted chalice worth millions, eliminating the need to lift thousands of coins to the surface.

When he had his wetsuit, buoyancy control device and mask on securely, Owen stepped off the platform cantilevered from the back of the boat and into the frigid waters of the Atlantic Ocean. He swam as quickly as he could toward the bottom, stopping only to equalize the pressure in his ears. A waterproof flashlight attached to a lanyard dangled from his left wrist, and he held the mesh bag containing the rope in his right hand. Occasionally he stopped and looked toward the surface. The current pushed him off course and he used the bottom of the boat as a guide. It marked the starting point of his search.

When he reached the ocean floor Owen once again looked toward the surface and searched for the bottom of the boat. It was a mere speck that could barely be discerned from the ripples on the surface. He stood on the sandy bottom, centered himself under the marker, and gently dropped the bag and rope at his feet. His main goal was to maintain visibility. A goliath grouper and several nurse sharks swam around a nearby coral reef without noticing him.

Gingerly, Owen brushed aside the sand looking for the reflection of silver coins in the light he shined on the bottom. After several minutes his breaths became quick as they moved through the regulator. He found nothing. Nervously, he looked at the timer on the dive watch he wore on his wrist. The length of dive was seven minutes. Irrational thoughts crept into his mind. *Dive tables were based on total time at depth, not the total time of the dive. Right? I can probably stay on the bottom for twenty-five minutes. It took me five to get down here, so my length of dive is only two minutes.*

No matter how convincing he sounded, he just didn't buy it. Quickly he waved his hand over the bottom. Silt billowed up and engulfed him. He could no longer see what he was doing. Determined not to be defeated, he began plunging his gloved hand deeply into the soft sand. When he could not shove it any deeper he wiggled his fingers vigorously, digging further down. Nothing! He held his watch in front of his mask and pushed the button that illuminated the backlight. The dive was into its twelfth minute. It would take him at least five to make it to the surface. That left only three to continue his search. Owen inhaled deeply and tried to calm himself. He knew that if he had to make another dive, he had to stay on the surface for at least twenty four hours.

Gently, he dug with his hands once again. Suddenly he felt something hard brush against the tip of his finger. It was a familiar feeling. Trying to stay calm he slowly maneuvered his hand deeper. When the texture of the sand against his hand gave-way to the recognizable feeling of a mound of silver coins a smile grew on his face. Ecstasy pushed concern for safety from his mind, and he rationalized staying below another five minutes.

Judiciously he uncovered and placed as many coins as possible into the bag. When there was only a minute left, he cinched it and attached the rope securely. He was so caught up in his joy that he began his ascent without grabbing the free end of the rope. Bubbles burst through the outer valve on his regulator as he laughed at himself for nearly forgetting the one item for which he risked his life. After tying the line to his wrist, he slowly made his way toward the surface.

At the depth of ten feet he exhaled a sigh of relief. His watch automatically calculated the time necessary to stay at that depth. It read '13:00' and began counting down. Disgust over having to hover in the water for so long lingered for only a moment. He knew he had pushed the limit of this dive, and come through it unscathed. Riches that exceeded his wildest dreams soothed his angst.

Thoughts of pulling the heavy bag into the boat filled his mind, until he noticed something moving at the surface. Holding onto the anchor line he swam to take a closer look. When he neared the vessel's hull, he saw the face of a Bahamian pirate leaning over the side, looking into the water. Owen moved quickly under the boat. He let go of the anchor-line so that it would not give him away. After several minutes of treading water to maintain his depth the lactic acid in his arms and legs began to burn. He had not had the opportunity to regulate his buoyancy control device, and there was no way he could give away his position by releasing so much air. Reluctantly, he removed the rope from his wrist and let go. His heart sank as he watched it drift toward the bottom and out of sight. He was stuck. If he descended it would mean certain death. The odds of being able to board the boat and successfully defeat the thief were not good.

Like a hummingbird he frantically waved his arms parallel to the surface, trying desperately to create enough push to keep him from ascending toward danger.

Something shiny caught his eye as it flickered and drifted down through the water. He recognized it as his St. Christopher pendant and gold chain. "Dammit!" The force of his disgust pushed a great deal of air through his regulator. He watched nervously as the bubbles he exhaled floated toward the bottom of the boat. They hit the hull, floated to its edge, and then the surface. He closed his eyes. Childlike hope that the pirates wouldn't see him filled his psyche. Briefly, he considered allowing himself to sink to the bottom to take away the pirate's pleasure of killing him. Just before releasing all of the air in his vest he heard the high pitched whir of a boat propeller. Owen opened his eyes and saw the boat that had been parked at the stern of his cutting through the ocean's surface. As quickly as he resolved to never return, he realized his trip had been for naught. He had to come back, but only after his blood had been cleared of nitrogen.

When the boat was far enough away he surfaced. After peeking over the side to make sure no one had been left behind, he tossed his fins onto the deck. Once onboard he walked directly to the throttle, where he kept his necklace. It was gone. Julia had given it to him and it was the only item from their relationship he had left. His soul ached knowing he would never see it again. Once he had removed his equipment he moved toward the glove compartment and opened it. "*Fuck*! They took my wallet and my Rolex."

It did not take him long to realize a stolen wallet and watch were much better than a lost life. He could not dive again for twenty-four hours, and he had no desire to stay there overnight. They may come back. Owen looked at the ignition switch. The chain that held the keys was attached to the steering wheel, but the keys were gone. There must have been only one pirate; who would certainly come back with friends. He walked to the back of the boat, bent over one of the engine housings and removed it. Duck-taped to its inside was an extra key. He grabbed it and then replaced the housing. After retrieving the anchor he made his way to the helm and inserted the key into the ignition. Quickly he turned it and the engines roared. They weren't allowed to idle long before he engaged their gears and sped toward home.

All he wanted was to make it there safely, lock all of the windows and doors, and foxhole. Solitary existence for a man who spent his entire life alone was not difficult. A second brush with death caused him to realize the emptiness of the house that awaited him. Once again, all of the negatives in his life were overcome by the one bright spot available to him. He craved the effervescence of Monica's energy. Only once before had he ever experienced something so positive. Its power had been inextricably laced into every fiber of his being.

Chapter Eight

Owen paced back-and-forth at the rear of his home. The sky transformed to deep purple and showed signs of a typical late afternoon thunderstorm. Darkness made its way through the expanse of windows and into his soul. Thoughts of the bag containing millions of dollars lying on the bottom of the ocean proved too much for him to easily dismiss. He risked his life gathering it together, and for nothing. Dissatisfaction surrounding the day's events exacerbated his greed. Rationalizations of multiple hauls of that size crept into his mind.

How long should he wait to go back and recover the bag? The pirates were just as far from home as he was. Would they go back to their island or maybe camp out on the ocean in order to make as many raids as they could? Regardless, they were sure to come back to the coordinates that yielded a successful raid, no matter how small. These bandits were smart and knew that boats were anchored in certain spots for a reason.

Depression cloaked his soul as thoughts of failure persisted. The speed at which he paced grew faster as the darkness of the clouds engulfed his house. Gloom soaked through every tissue of his body and resided in the core of his being. Deep-seeded resentment swelled into every nerve. It dawned on him that humans must have struggled with depression whenever they were unable to accomplish the hunting and gathering necessary to feed their families. Someone with whom to commiserate was the only remedy for his despair. Alcohol had always pushed unwanted thoughts from his conscious mind. He walked over to the phone and called Lilith, the person who had always supplied that emotional salve. After four rings it went to voicemail and he hung up without leaving a message. He called all of his friends. No one was available. The only two he did not call were Ivy and Monica. Ivy was not the most enjoyable person to hang out with, and he would not call Monica for fear of appearing needy. His desire to drink and carouse was too great. Acquiescing, he finally called Ivy, who eagerly agreed to meet him later at a bar on Duval Street.

Owen drove downtown alone. Reluctantly, he chose to park in a space behind the *Bone Key Pirate's Local # 69*, but worried Lilith would think he was taking advantage of their relationship. It was a chance he took, because all he cared about was numbing his soul.

After walking through the bar, he emerged onto Eaton Street and moved toward Duval. The mass of people and the noise they created shook Owen from his funk as he turned the corner. He did not worry about finding Ivy because he had no compunction about sitting at a bar by himself, but also had no desire to exist in solitude any longer. Being trapped ten feet below the ocean's surface afforded him plenty of isolation.

Ivy was punctual.

Aimlessly they strolled up and down Duval Street. If the action inside a bar looked appealing, they stopped for a drink. No sense of purpose moved them from bar to bar. Their ultimate goal was inebriation. Few words were spoken between them. Hollow companionship was an obstruction to a permanent bond.

Frozen drink machines lined an entire wall of one bar they chose. All of the colors of the rainbow were represented in the spinning cylinders that kept the drinks mixed. After ordering and receiving two beers the men mingled in the crowd. They squeezed themselves through a sea of nubile bodies as they held their drinks high in the air to avoid spilling a single drop. It did not take long before they grew tired of the scene and left.

Bar after bar offered nothing more than the smell of stale beer and sticky floors. Loud music and raucous crowds provided Owen and Ivy with the perfect excuse to avoid talking to each other. More than once he questioned whether Ivy could have been the shooter. Just as quickly as those thoughts entered his mind he chased them away. Murder was not something he could picture Ivy doing. White collar crime was a more likely pursuit for him.

When Owen felt it was time to go home he wasn't far from Lilith's bar. His alcohol soaked brain had all but forgotten his failure. Numbness took over his mind and body. The desire to pick the ocean floor clean of all the Spanish Pieces of Eight that had been there for centuries welled within him. It was only his life at stake. All he had to do was heavily arm himself each time he dove the wreck.

Just as he was about to suggest leaving, his friend turned and said, with a drunkenly slurred delivery, "Hey man, let's go to the clothing optional bar on top of the Entwhistle Pub."

Owen thought about his friend's suggestion. Of all the times he walked by the pub, and even gone in for a drink, he had never been to the top. Curiosity got the better of him. "You know, that's not a bad idea, my friend."

It was well past midnight and there were considerably fewer people on the street. The two walked at a quick pace, unobstructed, toward their destination. Once inside they followed the signs that were prominently displayed, directing patrons to the roof-top bar. Although each marker was of a different size and color, they all contained a large hand with the index finger pointing toward their destination. As the men approached the door leading to the roof the stairwell narrowed considerably between the third floor landing and the roof. It was obvious the corridor was never meant for any purpose greater than that of a utility access.

When they stepped onto the roof it took several minutes for their eyes to adjust to the dark environment. Lights from the street below glowed along the edges of the building and caused a backlit effect which made everyone appear shadow-like. The experience was ghostly.

Quickly they moved toward the bar. It was small and situated in one corner, and was not large enough for many to gather. Patrons were meant to mingle. Owen and Ivy stood close to it until their eyes adjusted to the dimly lit atmosphere. Vigorously they scanned figures as they came into focus. Several women were in various stages of undress, some topless and others fully nude. Owen remained calm and surveyed the fare. Ivy's reaction was to the contrary. He was giddy and childlike at the sights that lay before him. Owen felt the excitement radiating from his friend, but would not think of killing his buzz by reigning in his enthusiasm.

Ivy nudged Owen's arm with his elbow. "Check out that girl over there," he said pointing toward a woman who was completely naked. Her body was firm, dark and without tan lines.

Patronizingly, he warned his friend. "Do us both a favor and don't point at anyone or *anything* while we're up here, okay?" Ivy dropped his arm to his side and stared at the woman. Owen looked, but with a more discriminating eye.

Ivy attempted to temper a desire burning deep within him. He knew making an advance broke the vow he promised his wife, along with the basic trust between married people. Primal urges took over. "That girl will be mine, tonight," he said, nodding his head in her direction attempting to be discrete.

Owen looked at his friend. He examined his face for some sign of levity. "Are you serious?"

"Never more so," Ivy answered.

Owen shook his head. "First, you should never cheat on your wife. Second, you and that naked guy on that barstool over there," he pointed to a man several stools down from where they stood who wore not a stitch of clothing, "are the only two people here who do not realize that all these women are prostitutes."

Ivy turned his head sharply. "No they're not. They just feel the need to free themselves of the burdens society has placed on them by forcing them to wear clothes."

Owen laughed. "No, my friend, those are prostitutes who are displaying what it is they're selling." Ivy said nothing and he asked a more pointed question. "Why would you consider cheating on your wife?" When he saw the distressed look on Ivy's face he realized that he may have crossed a proverbial line in the sand with his inquiry. "I'm sorry. I should not have asked you that question. It's really none of my business." Owen's acquiescence conveyed sincerity.

"If I live to be a hundred years old I will never figure out how women think."

"So what has she done that confuses you so much?" As the words escaped his control he was surprised, and wondered why he had asked such a ridiculous question. His emotions were raw, as they had been before, but never had he considered the fidelity of relationships to be a cause worth championing.

Ivy was equally stunned. Suspiciously he looked upon his friend as if they had only recently met and there had been a discovery that threw their association's merits into question. "Such drivel from a man so accomplished in the art of casual sex."

"Your praise is appreciated," he answered, emphasizing the sarcasm. "But you have a wife, and I don't."

"Exactly! I've lived with the same woman for fifteen years. The mystery and excitement have long since exited our relationship."

Owen had never been afforded the opportunity to grow tired of a relationship, but understood the need to free one's self from the confines of a bad marriage. Before his friend made the irreparable mistake of an affair he had one more word of caution. "Are you sure that there is no way to salvage your relationship?"

Ivy nodded. "It's over. She knows it, and I know it." He paused. "Why are you so keen on faithfulness all of a sudden?"

"Because I left a woman a few years ago; completely turned my back on her. There's not a day that goes by that I don't think of her and *wish* that she was here with me."

"So, if it's such a lost cause, why do you keep living the way you do?"

"Sorry, man. I was only trying to help. Just do me a favor instead of thinking twice about the viability of your marriage, think twice about how your desires are going to affect it."

Ivy shook his head. "You have no idea what goes on in my marriage."

"You're right. I don't. But what I do know is that when a man and a woman are meant to be together there is something deep within them that connects, and no matter what that bond will never be broken. Only that will lead you out of the tumultuous state you're in and into a peaceful existence with your wife."

An incredulous stare bore into Owen. "What are you, the Dali Lama?" After a moment of silence between the men, Ivy had an epiphany. "You're in love, aren't you? That's it!"

Owen smiled. "Well, there is a woman I would love to get to know better. And we definitely have an energy that draws us together."

"Well fine. I hope the two of you are eternally happy. But you can take your joyous demeanor elsewhere."

"And leave you here to swim amongst the sharks? You'll be eaten alive without my help."

"My I.Q. is one-fifty-two. I think I can handle myself."

"Yeah, but your B.I.Q. is one *seventy-five*. You need the master here with you."

"My what?"

"Blithering Idiot Quotient."

Ivy shook away the insult and walked boldly toward the woman he desired. Owen followed. She saw the two approaching and offered a welcoming smile, and then moved through the crowd of men that hovered around her to greet her newest admirers. The circle that bound this beautiful, nude woman reformed with Ivy and Owen new members if its circumference. She looked deeply into both of their eyes as they exchanged greetings. An intangible quality in a man was what she sought, much to the chagrin of the others. Of all her potential suitors it did not take her long to identify the one most qualified to make the night worth remembering.

Chapter Nine

The door to Owen's house swung open. He and his date stood just outside while engaged in a deep, soulful kiss. She was clothed, unlike the hours spent on the roof-top bar. Her blouse was satin and sheer and only buttoned to the middle of her torso. Owen had driven her home in his BMW with the top down. Her hair had been mussed by the wind. He stroked it with his hands as they kissed. The skirt she wore barely covered her thighs. It was snug and silver snaps secured it and offered a quick exit. One half of her shirt tail hung freely about her waist. Owen reached inside and vigorously caressed her ample bosom.

Tactile pleasure abounded for them both. They walked through the door without losing contact with the flesh that gave them pleasure. Their time was limited and it was all about physical gratification. Once inside Owen lifted his right leg and nudged the edge of the door with his heel with enough force that it gently closed behind them.

Hours were spent talking atop the Entwhistle Pub. His initial impression of her motives proved to be wrong. It was difficult, but he fought the urge to examine every inch of her body as he talked to her. Discussion progressed and he found it easier to focus on the conversation because she was an interesting person, and obviously very intelligent; proved by the Masters degree in Mechanical Engineering she held. Similar views and values were shared by them. He still did not know her name.

Locked in an embrace, the couple made their way to the sofa and fell into its plush leather cushions. Suddenly she placed her hands on his chest and pushed him away. Reluctantly, he leaned back and sat with his butt against his heels. She stood and looked at him. "Where are the controls for your air conditioner?"

Owen thought for a moment. There were three units that cooled his house. He directed her to each control panel and she quickly disappeared. Once upstairs she was gone much longer than it would take to adjust a thermostat. He waited patiently, but could not help feeling like a visitor in his own home. He looked at his watch. It was two o'clock. As he nervously bit his fingernails Owen realized it was seven o'clock in the morning in Florence. He wondered what Julia was doing at that moment. Maybe she was preparing her child for daycare. She and her lover could be lying in bed naked. His mind filled with imagines of sheer white curtains billowing in the morning breeze as the lovers enjoyed a nude embrace.

"Oh, lover," the woman's sultry voice called from the top of the stairs.

Owen turned and saw her standing wearing an old football jersey she found in his closet. It was an early nineteen seventies style shirt that was orange with two white strips at the juncture of the shoulder and the sleeve. The number six was emblazoned on both sides with the last name of 'James' on its back. Thirty years earlier it had belonged to a young punter for the University of Florida named John James. Owen always admired how he could kick a football with a perfect spiral nearly every time. He considered it a sacred garment that had been given to him by John; a gesture the man did not have to make. Owen had never worn it. How could she have the audacity to put it on? Then he saw how nicely it fell over her abundant chest and realized it was his job to remove it as quickly as he could.

He exploded from the sofa and ran over to the stairs, ascending them in a double-time fashion. She ran from the landing and through his bedroom door. After eclipsing the last step he slowly followed her. Once inside he saw that she was sprawled across his bed, still wearing the jersey. They exchanged smiles as he sauntered toward her. The curtains over the sliding glass doors that made up the room's rear wall were open and revealed a full moon. It sparkled across the dark waters of the Gulf of Mexico. She threw her arms over her head signaling him to remove the jersey. He did. A perfectly tanned, stunningly beautiful, naked female lay before him.

For nearly an hour he lay on his side and gently stroked her, barely touching her skin with the tips of his fingers. Showing restraint he avoided contact with her erogenous zones, instead he hoped to stimulate her soul. Owen knew he would never see her again, but something within him wanted her to never forget their time together. Primal urges surged within him, but he quelled them in search of sexual nirvana.

When neither of them could wait any longer she rolled onto her side and pulled him on top of her. They kissed slowly and sensually. Their bodies slid across each other on a film of sweat. He leaned back. "Should I turn the air conditioner down?"

She smiled, sensuously. "No, silly. I turned the heat on so that our sex would be steamy."

An equally impish smile grew on his face as she returned to the slithery embrace. Their passion grew as their bodies became one. Each undulation increased the feverish beasts within. Physical imperfections gave way to a completely ethereal experience. Energy was concentrated and powerful, until it exploded, leaving two exhausted shells of human flesh.

The hue of the sky began to lighten as the sun, not yet above the horizon, began to exercise its influence. Changes were taking place and the eventuality that the evening had to end became apparent. Still breathless, they both lay on their backs and stared at the ceiling. Owen wiped the sweat from his brow and slung it away with a flick of his wrist. She lay with her arms resting on the pillow above her head. Her hair was in disarray and her body glistened. He rolled up on his side and stared at her one last time. The final act of copulation did nothing to diminish his desire. She smiled. "When do you need to be … home?" Owen asked.

"It doesn't matter." She rolled her head over and looked at him. "My husband is on a fishing trip for another couple of days."

The acknowledgement of a mate stung, even though he suspected as much. Fantastic visions rapidly dissipated. His cloak of invincibility was donned once again and suddenly he would not care if she got up and walked out. After several moments of silence the urge to ask a direct question came over him. "If you're married, why do you cheat on your husband?"

She could only bring herself to shrug her shoulders, at first. After a second she defensively declared, "You're not the first and you won't be the last."

Owen was unimpressed. He refused to let the issue rest. "There has to be a reason. You're an intelligent person. Think!"

His prodding touched a nerve. She sat up and faced him, crossing her legs in front of her. "I'm a nihilist. Do you know what that is?" she continued, smugly.

He smiled, wryly. "It means that you don't give a shit."

"Basically." She paused briefly as she gathered her thoughts and continued. Holding her arms out and gesturing toward Owen's house as a representation of all things material. "All of this, doesn't mean shit at the end of the day." She grabbed her breasts. "These fake tits don't mean anything. If I had it my way I would scrap the entire Earth and start over. Society tells me that I can't screw as many men as I want, well screw society. When I have been reduced to mere ashes it won't make any difference who I was married to, or what my job was, or even who I slept with. If this world is without purpose, why not do everything I can to pleasure myself during what little time I have? Money helps to provide that pleasure." She looked for a reaction. When she didn't see one, she pressed even further. "It doesn't matter that I slept with my boss to get a promotion last year."

He interjected. "You strike me as a very intelligent person. Why would you have to sleep with your boss to get a promotion?"

"There are a lot of intelligent people where I work. I'm simply tilting the playing field in my favor." He saw the Devil in her eyes as she continued. "Besides, my boss is so pathetic. He follows me around like a lost puppy sniffing at my heels."

"Is he married?"

"Yeah, but his wife's best days are well behind her. I have the advantage."

Owen could not believe what he was hearing. "I bet you're the type person who sabotages the work of others when presenting it to the C-suite officers?"

"If I have something to gain from it, you're damned right I will."

Suddenly the beauty in front of him became ugly and vile. He opened himself to a spiritual en-counter because of his attraction to Monica. By doing so he became vulnerable like he had not been in years. Yet another disappointment had to be discarded in favor of the hope Julia sparked within him, and whose flames Monica fanned.

Chapter Ten

Something unnatural disturbed Owen's sleep. The sun was high in the sky and his body seemed well aware of that fact. His mind tried to wrest control from that realization, but it only made his slumber more fitful. No end to the night meant he could not begin fresh. Days lost to fanciful excursions made his life a mere blur. Unlike his other encounters there was no kiss or pleasantries in bidding adieu.

His sleep was shallow and void of meaningful rest. He tossed and turned hoping to find a position that would afford him the absolution he desired. Twinges of anger erupted as he punched his pillow, blaming *it* and not his carnal desires for the situation in which he found himself. Every noise the house made was magnified; windows rattled as the wind blew inland off the water; the air conditioner blowing cold air; and, the ice maker as it dumped its load.

Just when those sounds disappeared from his awareness and he drifted away, the phone rang. The first sound brought him back into semi-consciousness. The next one he recognized for what it was, and looked at the alarm clock. It read, '*11:45.*' By the time it rang again he had removed the handset from its base and looked at the caller I.D. It was Monica. He had just enough time to answer before the call was sent to voice-mail.

She wanted to know if they could meet for lunch. He did not have it in him and declined her offer. His suggestion that they meet for dinner and an evening on the square was accepted.

Monica's affect on his psyche calmed him and he was able to fall asleep. He did not awaken until four-thirty that afternoon. Drool soaked the pillow beneath his cheek. The realization that he had been completely unconscious for so long brought a smile to his face. Not a single dream or thought went through his mind during that time.

It did not take long for the excitement surrounding his date to motivate him to get out of bed. Dried sweat and bodily fluids were caked onto his body so badly he could hardly stand to smell himself.

Giddily, he paraded around naked as the shower ran before suddenly running, completely nude, out of his room and down the stairs.

The entertainment center took up an entire wall of his living room. It held the most technologically advanced stereo equipment money could buy. After turning the system on he pushed a combination of buttons on the console that directed the output to his bedroom. When he heard the music emanating from its open door, he ran back upstairs.

Steam fogged the mirror in his bathroom, but Owen was not ready to get in the shower. He walked over to his closet, opened the doors and moved inside. There was an outfit he felt accentuated all of his greatest physical assets, which he removed and laid neatly on his bed before getting into the shower.

Hot water fell over his body and he felt its cleansing affect. He ran his open hands over his body, pressing in order to remove the evanescent film along with traces of the excesses of his life. Once he had scoured away the froth, only then did he use liquid soap and a washcloth.

After stepping out of the shower, he walked to the mirror and wiped away the steam. The towel he dried off with was wrapped around his waist. Moving backward he looked at his reflection, and liked what he saw. Hard work contributed to an abdomen that was thin and muscular. His pectorals, biceps and triceps were equally well defined; flawless as he saw it except for a receding hairline. Bobbing his head to the music, he continued preparing for his date with Monica.

When finished, he walked into the bedroom and plopped his body onto his bed. He stared at the rotating fan. The heat from the shower caused him to sweat, and he did not want to dress while perspiring. Lying perfectly still he willed it to stop. Before he had a chance to accomplish his goal the song Owen considered the greatest dance tune ever recorded blasted through the recessed speakers above his head. He hopped up and danced to the best of his ability. The song was *Here Comes the Hotstepper*. It had a distinctive reggae sound and a benign beat that his Anglo-American rhythmic ability could handle. He swung his hips back and forth to the beat while allowing his head to roll freely atop his shoulders. Finally, he realized he was sweating more profusely and stopped.

He laughed at the realization of the giddiness with which he approached his date. Monica was worthy of the optimism innate in a bright future.

Chapter Eleven

Several world-class restaurants lined both sides of the east end of Duval Street, away from the raucous crowds. Owen and Monica settled on *Jimmy's Bistro* for dinner. She wore an orange sundress replete with a red and yellow flowered print. The colors perfectly complimented her skin's tone. A hair band tightly held a jet-black pony tail, which matched her dress and purse. Owen cherished the effort she made to look nice for him. Self-esteem was the result of her endeavor for beauty. She looked like a woman who knew what she wanted and was in complete control. She had a regal air about her and he found her strength stimulating.

Monica appreciated his appearance equally. The cut of his shirt accentuated the strength in his shoulders and arms and then tapered nicely to his waist. He wore pleated black slacks and Ferragamo Sesto Moccasins. Rarely had he gone out of his way to impress a woman, but Monica was too special to leave their future to chance.

During dinner they talked about the obligatory family history. No embarrassing stories were left untold. The pasts that were discussed were devoid of bad experiences. Everything they talked about was pleasant and meant to reveal a cheerful disposition.

After desert Owen suggested a walk to Mallory Square. She found the proposition desirable. When they walked out of the restaurant he took up a position between her and the street to shield her from any projectiles, verbal or material. It was one of the few lessons Jenny taught him. Something about being a perfect gentleman gave him a sense of purpose. He learned from the way he hastily exited his relationship with Julia and wanted Monica to know he would be there for her.

The conversation during their walk mirrored the one at dinner. It was trivial and benign, yet it was meant to bring the couple emotionally closer. Nothing discussed was of such gravity that either could have been accused of telling their inner-most secrets. However, it was the foundation for building a friendship.

Loud revelers did not bother them, much less make their way into the couple's consciousness as they walked and talked. Mallory square teamed with a mass of humanity that swarmed like ants on a hill that had been disturbed. Neither was interested in watching the performances, so they leisurely strolled and enjoyed the energy the crowd emitted. The sun had long since set and the darkness brought out a wicked boldness among everyone. Men who were with their wives had no reservations about looking over every inch of Monica's wonderfully voluptuous body. The women attempted discretion, but several got an equally satiating look at Owen by following him with their eyes. It was obvious he took great care of his body and they appreciated that as much as he enjoyed the stares.

Owen and Saffron made eye contact as the couple passed her exhibition. She gave him an acknowledging nod of the head. He returned a quick smile that was obviously hidden from Monica's view. Saffron furrowed her brow at the snub. The couple kept walking.

He was not sure what motivated him to ask, "Would you like to go diving with me one day?" It became apparent he was trying to build a bridge toward sharing the only thing he had that held value.

She smiled. "I have no desire to become shark shit!"

He laughed. "Sharks won't bother you while you're diving. Of course, I wouldn't recommend it if you're on your period." Instantly, he feared he had said something too personal.

Without hesitation, Monica replied, "Well then, I guess we won't be going tomorrow."

He chuckled, but wondered whether her statement was true or meant to throw down a *no-sex* gauntlet. Regardless, he knew if he had to wait to make love to Monica, she would be well worth it.

Owen bought two beers at a kiosk. They walked to the water's edge, leaned against the railing and looked out over the channel.

Maybe it was the sense that the evening was coming to an end, but something caused him to become philosophical. "What is it that you fear the most?"

"Hmm," she replied as she turned and faced Key West harbor. "I guess I would have to say that I am afraid that God won't approve of how I am living my life."

Mmm, party girl, he thought. "How is that?"

She hesitated. "I have some personal beliefs that I feel very strongly about that go against the teachings of the church."

"As long as you have conviction in those beliefs, and they don't cause harm to others, I would think God would have an appreciation for that. After all, we were made in his image, both physical and emotional, right?"

She smiled at his supportive words. "What is *your* greatest fear?" His first instinct was to not show weakness, opting for abundant machismo. Too many one night stands had been achieved using that approach. Respect was something he wanted to show Monica, but had no idea how. Conveying truth became a paramount concern. "I'm waiting," she challenged.

"I'm thinking," he responded.

"It takes you that long to think of what scares you the most?"

"Uh, *yeah*."

She shook her head. "Never-mind. Forget that I asked."

"Why? I just need a little time."

"If you need that much time to think about your greatest fear it means that you don't think about it every day. If you are not aware of the feelings you have then it's impossible for you to express the person you are. If you can't do that I have no way of truly getting to know you."

Owen felt sick to his stomach. Without trying he created a barrier between them. Before he had the opportunity to plea for another chance, he heard a voice that seemed to be directed toward him and Monica. "Well, look who we have here."

They both turned to see Ivy standing behind them. He held a cup that once contained beer. Nothing but a foam ring remained in its bottom, but he held it as if it contained something substantial. He wore tan cargo shorts with oversized pockets. A dark blue shirt covered with sailfish was draped over his shoulders and unbuttoned. His overall appearance was slovenly. Ivy could tell they were less than impressed. "I figured if I look like a tourist it will be easier for me to get laid."

Owen had never seen his friend like this. His clothes had always been neatly pressed and he carried himself, albeit obnoxiously at times, with pride. Alcohol consumed nightly had reached deep into his soul and extracted a being that was quickly wresting away his sensibilities. Owen would have rather spent his energy trying to salvage what was quickly becoming a lost first date.

His friend stood, swaying back and forth on unstable legs. Several times he tried to drink from his empty cup. Owen did not know what to say and Monica became uncomfortable. Ivy teetered and watched as people passed. He leered at women and drew more than one angry stare from men who did not appreciate his overt, silent advances toward their dates. Owen watched and realized it would not be long before he and Monica would be drawn into a confrontation in which he had no desire to be involved. "Come on, Monica. Let's start walking back to the car." He held out his hand to take hers, but she refused his gesture of familiarity. They walked away while she looked back at Ivy with sympathy.

"Should we leave him like that?" she asked.

Owen stopped and faced her. He glanced at Ivy and then back. There was not a single reason he should subject them to the contempt for everything his friend seemed so intent on dolling out. Currying favor with his date was an option, but did she have a valid point? If she were not there he would leave. As he debated the pros and cons of being a true friend Owen noticed a commotion. Ivy wagged his finger vigorously in a young, innocent looking girl's face. Owen looked at Monica, rolled his eyes and walked toward his friend.

There's Something in a Name

The girl wore a Vanderbilt University Commodores tank-top. He overheard Ivy say, "If you're so hung up on Harvard then why didn't you go there?" and then answered his own rhetoric. "I'll tell you why, because you couldn't get into Harvard."

Owen forced his way through the crowd that had gathered, put his hand on his friend's shoulder. It was quickly shrugged away. "I'm sorry," Owen apologized to the young lady and her date, a large muscle bound young man who looked like he spent several hours a day in a weight room. Owen grabbed Ivy by the arm and tugged him away from the fracas.

Ivy pleaded his case. "But Owen, she said that she went, 'to the Harvard of the south.' I had to defend the honor of my school." Without responding Owen tugged again and again on Ivy's arm making little progress to remove them from the situation. "I had to defend the honor of my school, right?" Ivy implored.

Owen stopped. With his hand firmly gripping Ivy's arm he turned him around so that they faced each other. "Your arrogance and your desire to associate yourself with something greater than the objects of your disdain are pathetic. It causes everyone around you to dismiss you. And you know what? I'll bet that you're really not a bad guy if you'd ever try to stand on your own two feet and not glom onto Harvard for validation of the man you are ... or want to be." He paused briefly. "I don't even know your real name ... asshole."

Ivy looked at his friend, and then Monica. He snorted his disapproval and staggered away without a word. An evening that held promise quickly turned into one without hope. Desire to be honest with Monica morphed into the anger he learned to use when dealing with situations outside of his control. The absolute nature of both emotions added to his confusion. Not once did he realize the necessities of a successful friendship with Monica were the same required by one with Ivy.

Chapter Twelve

Stump and Asa sat at the table by themselves. Four empty chairs were positioned around it in case any of their group stopped by the bar. It was three o'clock on a Saturday afternoon and the patrons who had come to the *Pirate's Local #69* the night before had ample time to alleviate their hangovers. Several occupied seats at the bar repeating ritualistic behavior.

The day was hot and without a refreshing breeze to offer relief. Most of the faces shined through a thin film of sweat, but no one seemed to mind. It was a simple inconvenience and the price one paid for living in a tropical setting. The high pitched whine of mopeds carrying tourists about the island could be heard outside on the street. Occasionally, the sound of a large truck passing made idle conversation impossible. Nothing more than a finished roof set atop several pedestals gave the bar its form. Collapsible walls allowed occasional breezes to cool the joint. Everyone hoped for constant comfort from them.

The two had been sitting silently for nearly an hour. Neither felt comfortable in the company of the other, so they drank and looked past their counterpart fearing an uncomfortable exchange. Nothing in particular drove their discomfort other than the inability to understand the person who sat across the table.

Asa retrieved his pocket-knife and began to trim his fingernails. Stump's attention was drawn toward him and she shook her head in disgust, then turned away and continued to drink. Her overt disdain for his desire to groom himself was not appreciated. When he finished, instead of folding the blade and returning it to his pocket, he held it firmly by the handle, drew his hand back toward his ear and plunged it into the wooden table in front of him. He let go and it quivered back-and-forth on its tip as Stump investigated the noise that startled her.

"Is that some kind of threat old man?" she asked.

"No threat," he said casually, as he brushed the fingernail shavings from his pants onto the floor.

Before Stump had a chance to respond she spied Ivy walking into the bar. He held his head low and wore a baseball cap. It was pulled down well below his brow. Something was amiss, but she couldn't tell what it was. Her curiosity caused her to forget about her row with Asa, and she watched as Ivy made his way to the table. He pulled a chair by its back and swung his leg over it and plopped down, staring at the floor. Nothing was said; nor did he acknowledge anyone's presence until the waitress came to take his drink order. When he looked up Stump noticed that he had a black eye. "What the hell happened to you?" she asked.

Ivy finished his order and dropped his chin to his chest so he did not have to face either of them. "I got a little drunk last night and somebody decked me. I think it might have been Owen."

Asa sat silent. Stump laughed. "Two things," she started. "First, I've told you a million times that you have got to stop being such a prick, and that one day it would get you in trouble. You're lucky all you have is a black eye. Secondly, I guarantee you that Owen didn't do that to you."

"Well, he was the last person I remember seeing last night."

She smiled. "He doesn't care enough about you to bring himself to the point of hitting you." Looking past him, she said, "You'll have your chance to ask him. Here he comes."

Ivy turned quickly and saw Owen walking toward the table. When he saw the damage done to Ivy's face he laughed. "Nice shiner!"

Ivy's voice shuddered as he asked, "Did you do this to me?"

Owen looked at Asa. "Hey man. What's going on?" he asked as he reached across the table. The two shook hands and then he turned to Stump. "How are you today?" he asked, purposefully ignoring the question.

"Fine," she answered.

Owen sat and turned his chair to face Ivy. "No. I did not hit you last night. I did see you and it must have been just before that happened." He pointed to his eye. "It doesn't surprise me though. I saw you acting like a total asshole, and you deserve what you got, and probably more of the same." When Ivy did not respond he added one last comment. "As a matter of fact, I am surprised I wasn't called to the morgue to identify your body."

Ivy dropped his head. He was embarrassed that he could not remember what happened. "I must have been a total ass." He said from under his ball-cap.

Stump and Owen looked at each other in astonishment. Neither had ever heard him utter a conciliatory word. Maybe a shot in the eye was just what he needed. They could have done that long ago. Then Owen recalled the conversation he and Ivy had on the roof-top bar and began to wonder about his well being. Had things gotten worse at home?

Just as he contemplated his friend's dilemma he felt two feminine, yet strong hands squeeze his deltoid muscles. He looked across the table at Stump with a questioned gaze. She shrugged her shoulders because she did not know this person. Owen allowed the massage to continue. Finally, he could no longer stand the suspense. Without turning he dropped his head back and looked up. The distortion caused by viewing her upside down caused confusion. Once she smiled it became clear that it was Saffron. Her expression was unmistakable and fresh, just like her beauty. Owen looked at his watch. "Shouldn't you be at Mallory Square?"

"I was just leaving," she said as she stepped to the side of his chair. "Lillith makes the best chicken salad. I stopped by to get a sandwich," she held up a paper bag, "for my dinner later on."

Owen politely introduced her to everyone at the table and then asked, "Can you sit down for a minute?"

She hesitated briefly before sitting in the empty seat next to him. "I can only stay a second." Something pressed her. She looked him directly in the eye. "What's up with the snub you gave me last night?"

"What snub?"

"Last night when you were with that lesbian, you barely acknowledged you knew me. You should have stayed until after the show. We could have gotten high again."

He quickly looked at the others fearing their disapproval. When there was no reaction he began his explanation. "I'm sorry, Saffron. I did not mean to snub you, but when I'm on a date I don't like spending a lot of time explaining my relationship with each female friend we happen to meet."

"So, *why* were you on a date with a lesbian?" she insisted.

"I'm not real sure what you're talking about. The woman I was with is not a lesbian."

Saffron cocked her head to the right. "Ah, *yes*, she is. She dated a friend of mine."

Stump, in her usual manner, interjected with an off-the-wall suggestion. "Maybe she's bi?" She looked at Owen. "That's a huge score for you my man!"

He ignored the suggestion. "Are you sure you have the right woman?"

"It's hard to forget someone as beautiful as she is."

Owen nodded. "You've got a point."

Saffron stood quickly. "I've got to get to work and earn a living." She walked away from the table, disappeared through the door and onto the street.

Ivy eagerly spoke up. "You see Owen, things aren't always the way we see them?" He took pleasure in his friend's discomfort.

Owen did not reply. Instead he wondered if there had been an obvious indication, or anything she said that should have given him a clue about her predilection. There was *nothing* he could remember. When he shook away his thoughts he realized the group had gone about doing what they did most of the time; drinking and being obnoxious.

For hours the booze flowed as did the banter among friends. Stump tried unsuccessfully to convince Owen that another trip to the Bahamas was needed for both of their well being. He had no desire to see any

Bahamians until he had his treasure off the ocean floor and stored safely inside the intake in his guest house.

Upon hearing the conversation about boating to Nassau, Asa recalled a story. "Owen's first day on the boat we played a trick on him that we always played on the new deck hands. We told him not to stare at the splashing waves as they shot away from the hull of the boat. Without fail, he sat and stared at them as the boat hopped over the waves. He holds the record for puking the quickest."

Everyone laughed, including Owen. "Alright, in good fun everyone has to share an embarrassing story about themselves." Thoughts of Monica no longer occupied his mind. He settled back into the dynamic of the group he enjoyed.

"More embarrassing than being on a date for an entire evening with a lesbian and not knowing it?" Stump asked.

No one laughed. Everyone looked at Owen. He smiled and said, "Touché." Only then did the others feel laughter was appropriate.

Ivy spoke. "I'll be the first since I am the ass in the group, and you all will get a kick out of this." He looked around the table before continuing. "One night in college I was determined to sneak out after curfew. I got the bright idea to tie bed sheets together and repel from my third story window to the parking lot below. Well, a little less than half way down one of the knots came untied and I fell flat on my back onto the hood of my car. I guess it was poetic justice that it was *my* car that took the brunt of my stupidity." It bothered him when no one laughed heartily. Stump shook her head, Asa sat stoically, and Owen nodded through a chuckle.

Stump was next. "I was at one of the water parks in Miami. I was there with my nieces and nephews; six in all; and my fiancé. We all went on this slide that went straight down. At the top, the guys who worked there told me to take off my glasses; so I did and held them in my hand. These guys pushed me as hard as they could and I flew down that slide. After I plunged into the pool I stood up, but was a little disoriented. My fiancé and the kids were yelling at me, 'Stump! Stumpy!' I waded all the way out of that pool not realizing that my top had come off and my big ole boobs were flapping in the breeze. The rest of the day people at the water park would point me out to their friends and laugh."

The three burst into laughter. They examined her large breasts, imagining what she must have looked like emerging from a wading pool sans bathing suit top. Stump knew what they were doing and egged them on. She grabbed one in each hand and yelled, politely, at the three, "If any of you want to see these, you're gonna have to buy me dinner." They laughed some more.

Owen confessed, "Okay, I've got one more story I want to tell about myself." Everyone turned their focus toward him as he began. "When I was in high school I had a dream of playing college football. My coach convinced me that the best way to market myself was to attend the annual summer football camps that colleges hold for high school kids. I chose to go to the camp at the University of Florida. The dorm we stayed in was a coed dorm that had two wings; one for the men and one for the women. In the center of the wings were bathrooms and showers. I was in the shower one day by myself, and as boys will be boys my camp-mates came in and took my clothes and towel off the bench. When I got out of the shower I realized they were gone, instead of going down to my room I thought they may have hid the clothes in the girl's bathroom. I thought the only camp going on was the football camp, and when I opened the door, there were several girls in there who were attending a cheerleading camp."

"Did they like what they saw?" Stump asked, grinning sensuously.

Owen laughed. "I'm not real sure, but they all had the same astonished look on their faces."

"Were any of them naked?" Ivy asked.

"No."

"Did you get wood?"

Owen shook his head. "Not until that night when one of them invited me to her room."

Jealously, Ivy chirped, "You've got to be kidding me?"

Even though it was true, Owen thought his denial may help Ivy's state of mind, which he knew was sinking fast. "Of course I'm kidding," he replied convincingly. He then turned to Asa and said, "You're the only one who hasn't shared anything embarrassing. Want to give it a shot?"

"Nope."

"Aw, come on, man! You're the one who got this whole thing started by telling an embarrassing story about *me*. The least you could do is give one up on yourself."

Everyone waited, but Asa did not respond. After a few moments the conversation resumed. The subject was not of great importance, but stirred the three into an emotional frenzy helped along by the alcohol they consumed. The sun outside had almost completed its descent over the horizon. The bar turned dark and the inside lights were illuminated. Members of the house band began to set up their instruments for the evening's sets.

Finally, Asa spoke. "I've got a story for you all," he said, as he removed a pack of cigarettes from his shirt pocket; took one from the foil and held it between his lips as he replaced the pack. In one motion he flipped open his silver Zippo lighter, spun the flint-wheel, then held the flame to the tip and inhaled as deeply as he could. The cloud of smoke he expelled hid his face momentarily. When it cleared, he began. "Our ship had pulled into Port-au Prince, Haiti. I was a young snot then, like you when I first met you," he said, as he pointed to Owen. "My shipmates and I had gone into town the first night we were in port. They told me about this witch doctor on the island who no one ever wanted to cross. He was an old guy and his voodoo was said to be very powerful. The first few nights we were in port I hung out with the guys. On the last night, I stayed behind when everyone left for the ship. Then I went to the old man's camp. He allowed me to take part in a voo-doo ceremony." He laughed. "Maybe I should say that I observed it. I had no idea what to do, but I was curious. The old man sensed that I was no danger to them. Later that night, after it was all over, I asked him why he let me stay. He replied, 'When a person perceives a threat, their demeanor is forever affected. More importantly, when someone *knows* that another is accepting of them no matter what, the willingness to share of themselves becomes boundless for both.'" The memory gave Asa reason to smile. "I've never forgotten that bit of advice, and I've tried to live my life by that simple rule."

The other three listened intently. Each one was waiting for a punch line. When Ivy realized that Asa was finished, he asked, "*That's it?*"

"Yep."

"I thought you were going to tell us that the voodoo priest had you running around molesting chickens, or something silly like that."

"I'm sorry to disappoint you," Asa replied. "I just felt that as the senior member of our group I should impart a bit of the wisdom I have acquired over the years. What you do with that knowledge is up to each of you ... and some of you need it, in my opinion." He drank from his beer.

Owen sat silently as he pondered the story his oldest friend told. For the first time he convinced himself he had chosen to live his life in the same manner as Asa. He took comfort in the apparent approval of the man he considered his best friend. "I know what you mean about people," he said smugly.

Asa looked him squarely in the eyes. "Owen, there is a pathway between the two extremes. They are not absolutes. You cannot continue to live your life in a black and white environment."

The criticism stung like a blade that cut to the core of his being. At first there was a chill and then came the ache. He was sure that Asa's comment was directed at Stump and Ivy. "But what about the witch doctor?"

"The witch doctor *knew* that I understood that there was something greater in life and that to get the most from it we must be open and accepting. You, my friend, have not grasped that concept … yet."

Owen did not know how to respond so he sat silently, sulking as he drank from his beer. Before anyone had the opportunity to begin another conversation, Stump stood and grinned heartily. She waved someone toward their table. Owen did not bother to turn and see who it was. The chair Saffron vacated earlier moved as it was pulled by its back and slid it away from the table. Stump sat and Owen saw the grin on her face grow. It conveyed the great pleasure she derived from the situation. Curiosity got the better of him. After calmly taking a sip from his beer, he turned and looked over his shoulder at the person next to him. It was Monica. The pace of his heart intensified as he felt the need to bestow upon her every bit of his anger. He did not appreciate being manipulated.

"Hello everyone," Monica greeted them. Her Spanish accent was still pleasant to the ear.

"*Hey, Monica,*" Ivy's tone was overly friendly.

Asa said nothing, but raised his half-empty beer mug in her direction. Owen and Stump did not reply. Their minds contemplated tactical assaults.

Stump decided to take a friendly approach lulling Monica into a false sense of security before employing emotional daggers meant to demean. "So, you and Owen went on a date last night, I hear." She began with a sugary sweet quality.

"Yes, we did," she responded, pleasantly. She looked at him. "He was the perfect gentleman, too."

Owen gave a half-hearted smile as he glanced over his shoulder at her. He knew that Stump was like a pit-bull. Once she had her jaw tightly clamped onto

Monica's psyche she would not let go. "Yes. He's never been anything less than a perfect gentleman with me, also."

"You don't find a lot of true gentlemen in the world today," Monica added.

"And, you don't find a lot of women who are true to those around them." Stump took a sip of her White Russian.

Monica did not take time to translate her confusion. "*Que?*"

Sarcastically, Stump replied, "*Nada.*"

Monica looked at Asa and Ivy for a glimmer of understanding from their faces. They smiled without saying a word. She then bumped Owen on the arm. "Have I done something to upset your friend?"

He turned and faced her. "I'm not sure what you're talking about. I don't sense any anger from her." It felt good to have an ally. "Maybe she is jealous that we had such a great time together last night. *I know*, maybe she is harboring some deep seeded love for me that she has never talked about, and can't for some strange reason." He turned to her and asked, "Are you secretly in love with me, Stump?"

"I've wanted to have your baby since the day I met you," she replied, breathlessly sarcastic.

He turned back toward Monica and with an equal amount of sarcasm said, "You see, if it weren't for you and your obvious ability to bring truth to every situation, I *never* would have known that."

Monica looked at everyone helplessly. Sarcasm was thick and she had no idea why it was directed at her, until Stump could no longer contain herself.

"Hey Owen, have you ever dated a lesbian?" She knew she could have done a much better job of drawing out the fun they were having at Monica's expense, but the direct approach felt divine.

It did not matter that he perpetuated anger, Owen jumped on top of the emotional saber Stump plunged into Monica's heart and thrust his weight onto it driving it as deeply into her as he could. "Actually, I did. She was a biker chick with a hell of a set of guns on her." He flexed his arms and pointed to his biceps. "It started out we would just hang out together. Then one night we were shooting pool and she picked me up off the floor and threw me onto the table and kissed me. That was the first time I had any indication that she wanted me." He faced Monica. "Of course, I *knew* all along she was a lesbian."

Images became unclear as Monica looked at her friends through tears. She mustered a calm demeanor from deep within her soul, took a deep breath and pushed the chair away from the table with her legs. Without a word she walked through the nearest door and onto Eaton Street.

Boldly, Ivy and Stump chuckled at the emotional destruction in which they had been complicit. Watching her walk away struck a nerve with Owen. Suddenly, he realized that he had done the one thing he knew that he never wanted to do; belittle someone. He never had appreciated being made to feel like a second class individual and promised himself never to perpetuate that undesirable trait learned from the only family he had ever known. Mob mentality caused him to disregard the lessons of a lifetime. It became clear that anger stoked by others endangered what was a promising relationship. If only he had allowed it to grow or die on its own. He looked at the one man he admired. Asa shook his head disparagingly. Owen questioningly shrugged his shoulders. The old man tilted his head toward the front door.

Without a word Owen stood and walked through the sea of tables, and onto the street. He made it outside in time to see Monica turn left onto Whitehead Street. To close the gap between them he began to jog after her. As he approached from behind he stopped running. It was evident she was still crying. Her shoulders shifted as she gasped for each breath. He felt worse. "Wait for me," he called out. Her pace quickened. "I'm sorry, Monica!" he said as he came to a stop. She continued momentarily, and then slowed her pace to a stop before turning and facing him.

"I guess I need to apologize too," she said.

Slowly, Owen walked toward her with what he felt were the only words he knew could save the fragile relationship. "I know that it's no excuse, but I was hurt very badly tonight when I found out you were a lesbian." Instinctively, he reached for her face to offer a gentle touch on her cheek for comfort. She drew back and he saw fear in her eyes. No words were needed to explain that she had been abused, and expected to be struck.

She brushed aside the concern in his eyes and asked, "Why?"

"*Why*?" Owen repeated, incredulously before answering the question. "Because I felt betrayed by you."

"Just because I am a lesbian and I didn't tell you, you feel betrayed? So, you obviously had expectations that I had nothing to do with."

Owen chuckled. "*Please*, Monica. Men and women have been coupling since the beginning of human existence. How could you not think that there was at least a slight possibility that I would want our relationship to become physical at some point?"

His explanation was one for which she had no argument. She smiled sheepishly. "I never did apologize. I'm sorry."

Owen smiled and held up his hands in surrender. "So, are we okay?"

"We're okay," she said.

"Can I at least walk you home?" he offered.

"I'd like that." She turned and began walking down Whitehead Street. Owen followed. He felt the need to comfort her, but had no desire to encroach on her obviously fragile psyche.

Passing mopeds made conversation difficult. The sidewalk narrowed at several points along their walk. Each time it did Owen allowed Monica to walk ahead of him. Showing her respect became paramount. Their connection became soulful. He understood that if she had endured repeated violence it would have numbed physical experiences while heightening emotional ones. Only then did he realize why his carnal lust seemed insatiable.

They approached Angela Street and looked both ways for any oncoming traffic. It was difficult to see due to the cars parked along the side-street. Owen leaned into the road to get a clear view. No cars were coming so he held out his hand. She placed hers in his and they crossed the street. When they stepped onto the curb they gently released their grasp and continued walking. His hand tingled as he realized their touch transferred more energy between them than he had ever known.

"I realize tourists are the reason we all have jobs, but I do wish they would outlaw those damn mopeds." Monica's observation came as a welcome relief to Owen. Their friendship was on the mend.

"They are annoying, aren't they?"

"You don't have to walk me all the way home," she said.

Her request stung. Parting ways before he was certain their friendship had been fully restored did not appeal to him. "We had such a good time talking last night that I hoped we could do the same tonight."

She hesitated. "Well, to be honest, I'm not real sure about having you over to my house."

Owen nodded his head in an exaggerated manner. "I certainly understand that. There is a park nearby where we can sit and talk, if that's okay with you."

She looked at him skeptically. "I don't know of any parks around here."

He smiled impishly. "I have a private park all my own and I'd love to take you there."

Feverishly she searched her memory of every street in the area, but could not think of a nearby public park. Faith was not a trait she gave away freely, but at that moment she realized he was worthy of it.

The couple crossed another side-street and continued down Whitehead. A few more blocks and they would reach the southern-most point in the United States, and there were no beach-side parks there. She had no idea where they were going. When they approached Olivia Street, Owen motioned for her to turn left. After several dozen feet he gently took her by the arm and led her between parked cars. Both looked each way and when the road was clear they hopped quickly to the other side. In front of them was a six foot brick wall with coils of razor-wire stretched across its top. Owen looked for signs of anyone who may spoil his plan. When the way was clear he reached up and tugged at a very specific place in the wire. Without much effort it parted, leaving a two-foot gap. He looked at Monica as he squatted and interlocked the fingers on both hands, creating a step for her. Without a word he tossed his head backward, motioning for her to go over the wall.

"Are you crazy? This is Ernest Hemingway's house," she whispered her insistence.

Owen smiled and murmured, "He, of all people, would appreciate the *cajones* it takes to do this." He motioned silently with his head, again.

She laughed, and appreciated the euphemism. The adventure intrigued her. No one was around so she stepped into his hand and he thrust her easily over the wall. Quickly, he followed. When they gathered themselves at the base of the fence, he motioned which direction they should walk. Lushly landscaped grounds gave way to an opening. A red brick pathway in the courtyard was bordered by gray gravel. Several varieties of hibiscus were in full bloom and colorful. Two benches bordered the trail. One was concrete with two two-by-twelve pieces of lumber for the seat and back. The other had an iron frame with four narrow slats of lumber that were mounted in an undulating fashion. That is where they chose to sit.

Reconciliation and a sense of loss filled the garden. Both were overcome with the desire to peel away the calluses that prevented them from experiencing the other in the purest sense. "I do owe you an apology, and I *am* sorry." Monica said. "I forget that I have a tendency to build a wall around myself, then you tried to comfort me and my reaction made the realization all too clear." He was not sure what to say. An apology would be redundant. His attraction to her had not waned. She sparked an aspiration to move beyond physical temptation and embrace an emotional relationship. In her was a quality he had never known, but found himself inextricably linked.

A gust of wind blew through the trees, and the large green leaves of the tropical plants rustled offering a much needed diversion. They both looked up and watched as the cool breeze brushed across their faces. She saved him from his conversational impotence. "This is really nice. How often do you come here?"

"This is only my second time."

"How did you find out about the hole in the fence?"

"I was having a frozen lemonade at the stand across the street while the workers were installing the razor-wire. That opening was where they were bringing together the last two sections. I could tell by watching they did not secure it properly. I gave it a shot one night and was able to easily break into the grounds," he explained in a satisfied tone.

"It would be so nice to have a little picnic. Some wine and cheese would be the perfect complement to the atmosphere," she suggested.

"And your lover, of course." Owen could not resist.

"Do you have a lover?"

Owen shook his head. "Do you?"

"Not at the moment."

"I guess we'll just have to entertain each other until we can hook up with someone else." The crassness of his words rattled his soul and he had no idea how to remedy what had already been said.

"This island is too small for either of us to hide from the circumstances that make us who we are."

Owen chuckled. "So how do we escape together? Leave Key West?"

She drew in a deep breath and released it before answering. "Neither of us can run. We've got to face all of our challenges, accept and defeat them. But, together we can do it." His silence spoke volumes. "There has to be at least one time you wished you had not run away from a painful situation."

The thought of Julia pained him more-so than it had in a long time. Not until he met Monica did he realize he had resolved nothing by walking out on Julia. In Monica he saw someone he thought could live up to her memory, but his future seemed hopeless. Pleasant thoughts of her were tainted by the memory of how he found her with Gianni. Intense emotional pain radiated through his soul and blanketed his psyche.

Monica saw his posture sink. "I can tell that you are thinking of a woman." When he did not reply she continued. "It pains you pretty bad, huh?"

"Yeah."

"I'm here for you." Monica was gentle in her tone. She reached out and rubbed him on the back. The stroke of her hand produced a ripple throughout his body like a wave of bright light on a still, black lake. It provided the desire to talk about the most painful time of his life.

"She was beautiful, sexy, intelligent … every superlative described Julia. When I looked into her eyes everything else became meaningless. We were inextricably drawn together. Every time we kissed I could barely distinguish her lips from the intensity of our passion."

"What happened?"

"I met her in Italy. I was there searching for the final resting place of my great uncle. I had some things to do one day that pertained to the search. She expected me to be gone all day. Well, I was able to wrap up what I needed to accomplish and hurried to her apartment to surprise her. I found her there with another man. I turned around and walked out."

"Just like that?"

He sat up, shrugged his shoulders and asked, "What was I suppose to do?"

"How about an explanation?"

Owen looked condescendingly at Monica. "I walk into the apartment of the woman I am dating and find a tall, thin, handsome, smolderingly sexy Italian man, and you think I should have stayed long enough to ask what the circumstances were surrounding their being together?"

"Exactly."

He laughed. "My life has been filled with questionable circumstances. I can't keep placing myself in situations where I am forced to consider what is right and what is wrong."

"Why is that?"

"Why is what?"

"Why is it that you can so easily walk out on someone you obviously cherish?"

The question was one he had never given much thought. What he did know was why it was so easy to give up hope for those who disappointed him. A clear distinction between that which should be treasured or forgotten did not exist for Owen. "I was orphaned when my mother and father were killed attempting to rob a bank. A local cop and his wife took me into their home. Bobby was a very angry man and Jenny knew how to deflect his rage onto me in order to save her own skin. I was beaten regularly by him; sometimes nightly." He thought about how recalling the loss of Julia had such an immediate negative effect on his psyche. "Monica, I suffer from depression and sometimes the least little incident can trigger it. I'm not sure if it's caused by being beaten down by my *father* all those years, or if it's because of how my brain is wired. What I do know is that the distinction between the physical and emotional is blurred. Sometimes I can't tell the difference in the pain."

Monica thought about her friend's admission. "Is that why you were so black and white with Ivy last night?"

"What do you mean?"

"He's either your friend or he is not."

"I consider him a friend."

"Then you should be able to stand by him no matter what. Last night you were ready to abandon him because he was drunk and acting like a fool. I'm sure there is something going on in his life that has caused him to lose control. *Now* is the time when he needs a friend who will stand by him no matter what."

At that moment it became clear to him. The desire to value relationships comes from within. It is not dictated by others. So much of his life had been controlled by those around him that he found himself rudderless and without direction.

Monica knew by the look on his face that something significant was happening. Another breeze blew his hair away from his forehead, exposing a scar that Bobby had bestowed upon him. She reached up and gently stroked its hard tissue with her thumb. The energy transferred between them was mystical. "I guess we all have our scars to bear," she said, smiling awkwardly.

Embarrassed to confession, Owen admitted, "That's the first time anyone touched one of my wounds and it didn't hurt."

Chapter Thirteen

Owen watched as the rod holding the ceiling fan above his head wobbled back-and-forth from the force of the spinning blades. His fingers were interlocked behind his head. A peaceful aura surrounded him like never before. No one ever cared for him the way Monica did. Not only did she engage his presence whenever they were together, she occupied his soul. For the first morning in many he did not wake up with a hangover. Talking had not afforded either the opportunity to imbibe. His mind was clear and he was well rested. They planned to meet for lunch at a waterfront restaurant, and he eagerly anticipated the opportunity to see her again.

As he walked her home not once did he debate whether to kiss her or solicit an invitation inside. Freedom from physical dependencies had heightened his yet untapped emotional capacity. Julia was the only other person who had been able to elicit such immense feelings.

His stay in Florence was extended by several weeks after he and Julia met. They traveled throughout Europe together. Owen smiled as he thought about an overnight train ride to Paris and how they slept in a double berth compartment. Uninterrupted conversation filled the evening. Dinner consisted of wine, cheese and a loaf of Italian bread. Every movement of her body created a spiritual sensation even as he recalled the long ago night.

An entire week was spent in Paris. Only two rooms were available in their hotel; one with two single beds, but it shared a communal bath. The room they chose had only one bed and *avec une douche*. Julia slept in the bed and Owen on the floor.

Each night when she emerged from the bathroom he feigned sleep while watching her walk. The nightgown she wore hung loosely about her body, touching it in only the most tender places. Without fail she knelt down and kissed him goodnight.

While viewing the Eiffel Tower from its base the couple gazed upward at the impressive structure. Owen remarked in awe at how magnificent the structure was and that it had been around for over a century. Once they ascended it, weakness shot through his knees as he realized that the structure was well over a hundred years old! Paris was amazing from that vantage point. The city stretched as far as the eye could see, but he never desired to look beyond the beautiful woman that accompanied him.

On their third day in town they wandered into a small grocery store and purchased an inexpensive bottle of red wine and a bag of pistachios. Both were placed in their backpack without regard until that night as they strolled along the banks of the River Seine. Several houseboats were anchored along the waterway. A spot where there were no obstructions offered the perfect place to sit and sample them both. While they sat a female Mallard duck waddled up to them and quacked loudly. Owen knew what she wanted, so he shelled several nuts and placed them on the ground in front of her. She quickly ate them. He continued to share until they were gone. Logic dictated the bird had been domesticated by all of the lovers that frequented the area, but part of him wanted to believe it was drawn to the energy that swirled around him and Julia.

A week in London was spent in a little hotel in Bryanston Court. The rooms were small and the cigarette smoke was noxious, but Owen would not have traded places with anyone. The Tower of London and its grounds exuded fantasies of princes on white horses and damsels in distress. Owen imagined being the king and Julia his queen. Her beauty and aura brightened the hallways of the dark, dank manor; while her smoldering features gave warmth to the otherwise dreary fortress. Its hallways wrapped their love in a sense that transcended the centuries.

When they returned to Florence she took him on a day trip to Rome. It was the crowned jewel of her country and a center of the civilized world. The city was a source of pride she wished to share with him.

Their trip across Europe had been fun and educational, but something about Rome instilled in Owen a greater sense of history and the struggle the human race had endured in order to survive. Strolling through the Forum and toward the Coliseum he looked at the woman next to him and *knew* that if he were on the path to meet his doom, as many had done before, he would be at peace knowing he had met the woman he would gladly give his life to save. Never had he recalled Gianni's insertion into their relationship without pain. It was different and odd, but for the first time he was happy for Julia. His search would continue, and knowing that she was fortunate to have found true love gave him hope.

Chapter Fourteen

Pleasant memories of Julia and the aura they created carried over to his lunch with Monica. He was first to arrive and secured a table on the deck overlooking the green waters that surrounded the island. A canopy of tightly strung piano wire crisscrossed, forming one-foot squares. It hovered mere feet above patron's heads and was meant to keep seagulls from begging for morsels. Owen perused the menu when Monica approached; not realizing she had arrived until he heard her pull a chair away from the table.

He looked up and greeted her. "Hello, counselor." She was not sure his characterization was meant as a compliment. Owen sensed her uneasiness. "I meant that as a term of endearment."

Skepticism was masked by a sly grin as she sat down and slid her chair under the table. "I want to thank you for the experience last night. I must say that I have never broken into a museum before. It was … *exciting*."

"You're welcome." He never thought of the Hemingway House as a museum. It was a place where he escaped the reality that was his life. The grounds were peaceful and offered an oasis from his troubled mind.

It was a hot day and sweat continually beaded on Owen's forehead. Every few minutes he wiped it away. A large blue umbrella mounted to a pole and secured through a hole in the center of their table provided shade for Monica. The sunglasses she wore mirrored his reflection each time he looked at her. He was not fond of his own image and averted his eyes whenever he caught a glimpse of himself. Monica's beauty prompted many visceral responses to the distorted figure that stared back at him. Forgoing comfort, he slid his chair away from the table and into the sunlight to enjoy her long, tawny legs that extended nicely from her neatly pressed shorts.

Monica silently perused the menu, aware of her friend's desire, but not acknowledging it. She appreciated the fact he knew there was no way they would ever make love, yet he could not resist. Looking upon her splendor was sustenance for him. She knew he would overcome his dependence on female flesh, but was unsure she had the intangible trait necessary to convert his badly damaged emotional core.

After they placed their order, each sat silently and gazed out over the undulating green water that lay before them. A small section of beach between the restaurant and the hotel next door where nude sun-bathers frolicked garnered their attention, simultaneously. Both momentarily suppressed gauche remarks that occupied their minds. Regardless, it did not take him long to overcome modesty and formulate a wise-crack. "Geez, would you look at the rack on that one." He pointed to a beautiful young woman wearing an orange bikini and whose skin was succulently tan. The fluorescent color of her bathing suit gave a wonderfully three dimensional appearance to her breasts.

Monica nodded in agreement. "Yeah, those are nice."

"I wish she weren't so damn young."

"Why?"

"Because then she'd have the guts to take that top off."

She challenged her friend. "Maybe you should go down there and convince her to do so."

He slid his chair away from the table and stood. "I think I might just do that." He looked at his reflection in her sunglasses and realized the man he saw did not have the courage to confront demons the beautiful, anonymous girl represented. He sat back down.

Monica wanted to continue their conversation from the night before, but she was unsure how to approach the subject without triggering her friend's depression. She had no idea his perception had changed, and that his time with Julia gave him hope that one day he would meet a woman he could embrace emotionally without fear of catastrophic consequences. "Tell me more about this woman you met in Italy."

Contrary to her fear, he happily asked, "What would you like to know?"

"What was her name?"

He laughed. "Julia."

"Julia," she repeated. "That's right. I like that."

"How old is she?"

Owen had to think for a moment about her age when they met and how long ago it had been. "Thirty-one?"

"Ooh, a younger woman. I like those, too."

Julia's ever-present aura provided him the encouragement he needed to speak freely about what she meant to him. "I'll never forget the first time I saw her. That day is etched in my memory." He wanted to peer into Monica's soul, but the barrier created by her glasses prevented the desired connection. "There was only one other time I felt so taken by a woman by simply laying my eyes on her."

"When was that?" Monica asked, cheerfully.

"The day I saw you for the first time."

His admission struck a chord deep within her. Not until then did she realize the full affect of not disclosing her orientation had on him. "I'm sorry that I disappointed you."

Owen felt the sincerity of her apology. He smiled. "You haven't disappointed me."

She smiled and dropped her head, chin-to-chest, and looked at the deck below her feet. "I hope I never do."

In an effort to keep their conversation positive he began sharing fond memories of Julia. "We happened into this restaurant one night. It was on a small side street in Florence. Julia had never been there so it was almost as if we were discovering this neat little place of our own, together. The waiter interacted so well with her. Who wouldn't? She was the most beautiful woman I've ever seen and I am sure he felt the same way. The dinner; the atmosphere; *everything* was perfect that night. It was so ideal one experience could not contain the energy that drew us back the next night. Our waiter was serving as the matre 'd that second night. He recognized us and told our server something in Italian that I could not understand. Julia said he was instructed to take good care of us. He did." Owen laughed. "There was one thing odd about that night."

"What's that?" Monica grinned, curiously.

"There was this guy who came in and sat down at a table that faced the front door, and his chair was placed against a column that was at least five feet wide. He was dressed in the finest Italian suit you've ever seen. It was beautiful. All the wait-staff doted over this guy. He showed them his new cell phone and they all thought it was the most wonderful device they had ever seen."

"Was he an actor?"

"No, or at least Julia didn't recognize him."

"Mob?"

He only responded with a nod and a smile. Suddenly, their happiness came to an abrupt halt, when he saw Monica's gaze fixate on someone approaching their table. Owen heard footsteps on the wooden deck, turned and saw Agent Melendez walking toward them. The man boldly pulled a chair away from the table and took a seat without being offered one. "Hey Owen." The agent's tone was smug. Owen glared at the man. The agent leaned across the table to shake Monica's hand. She took his hand in hers and returned the gesture. "I'm Agent Melendez with the F.B.I." he said.

"Monica," was all she offered.

"Are you two dating?" the agent asked, as he alternated the tip of his right index finger between them.

Before Owen could reply, Monica answered. "Yes, we are."

Owen looked at her curiously, not knowing why she lied. "Why are you harassing me *today*, agent?" He shifted a cold stare toward their unwanted guest.

"For the same reason I always have and will until you come clean."

"About what?" Monica asked.

The agent grinned confidently "I'll leave *that* discussion to the two of you."

As quickly as he had arrived, the man stood and walked away, disappearing around the corner of the building. Suddenly, Owen realized that at no time during that day had he worried about his treasure. That awareness was the result of his changing disposition. Fantasies of what might become of his life once again subjugated themselves to the reality that his future was in peril. Pervasive hope instilled by Monica could not pierce the cloak he donned to ensure mere survival.

Chapter Fifteen

That night Owen found himself at Mallory Square wandering through the tourists and entertainers. Monica had gone home after lunch. She had to work the next day and wanted a good night's rest. Boredom set in as he walked alone, but that was not because no one was with him. Most of his life had been spent without companionship. It was a fact that although the faces on the tourists changed from week to week, the atmosphere never did. For the first time the town in which he had chosen to live garnered the feel of a modern day Sodom and Gomorrah. True friendship helped him to understand there was something worth pursuing in life. What that was he had yet to decide. He sipped from his beer and walked through the mass of people who scurried about.

Continual brief meetings with Agent Melendez compounded his depression. It numbed his body. He was no longer sure if his life was interrupted by bouts with the disease or if his innate despair was interrupted by unwarranted hope. One thing he understood was his time with Julia was his brightest period. Happy memories withered in the psyche of a man who looked for negatives to provide the palette for his tainted emotional brush-strokes. He had no idea how to keep it from happening again, but knew he had to or face his own demise. Whether or not his reactions to the overbearing trials of life were physiological or environmental, Owen had no idea. Until he understood their cause he was doomed to continually encounter the cavalcade of warped characters that paraded through his life.

A group of young girls who were loud and obnoxious distracted him. Almost unconsciously, Owen focused on the one who lagged behind. When she saw his face in the crowd and how he looked at her she could not help but engage him with a wanton stare of her own. Her friends became disgusted at their instantaneous romance and left without concern for her safety.

As she spoke he imagined he was talking with Julia. When she told him she had been a cheerleader he wondered if they had pep squads in Italian high schools. She was from Louisiana and had twin brothers. Owen heard her name, but did not care to remember it. For hours she droned on incessantly about herself. Several times during the evening he found himself preferring an evening with Monica.

Their union was bound by a series of aimless laps around the square. The only stops made were for a trip to the bathroom, or to purchase beer. Neither had an overriding attraction to the other, but they stayed together throughout the night. Conversation waned the later it became.

An out of the way spot was where they chose to sit. Heavy petting neared a public carnal experience. Before taking her home he broached the subject of getting high with his friends. That notion excited her. They watched from afar as the group of entertainers coalesced on the planter where they gathered most nights. The fresh couple walked over and sat among them.

Saffron immediately offered an apology. "I'm sorry I burst your dating bubble last night, man, but I knew there was no way you were getting any from that girl."

"No worries." He didn't bother to introduce his date and no one cared. Associations were merely about convenience.

A joint was seemingly produced from thin air and passed from hand-to-hand for everyone to enjoy. When the drug took affect the mood lightened as their stress-filled lives became insignificant; except for the couple whose warped energy drew them together.

Bitterness was the only emotion Owen's date seemed capable of embracing. The inebriant made her belligerently obnoxious. Suddenly, she blurted out, "Is this all you people do every night? My Gawd! Get a life." She looked at Owen. "My daddy sold Cadillacs to *all* the oilmen in Louisiana … until he went bankrupt."

Suffocating dogma drove him into a greater state of depression than he had ever experienced. His longing for approval was met with crucifying looks from the others. After several minutes the girl realized no one wanted her around, so she promptly stood and walked to the other side of the planter and sat with her back toward the assembly. Owen watched as she lit a cigarette and then glared at his friends. He shrugged his shoulders and apologetically shook his head, unconvincingly. The others were direct with their disdain.

"That bitch is psychotic. Where did you find her?" Saffron asked bluntly. He did not respond for fear of upsetting his paramour. Although the purpose of their association was to dampen his emotional distress, she personified the caustic emotions that dwelled in the darkest recesses of his soul.

Dutch spoke for the first time. He exaggerated and softened his southern drawl to try and diminish the critical nature of his words. "Son," pointing to the woman's back, "that right there ain't nothin' but misery for you."

Owen heard and understood each of the warnings, but there was something about this woman he found intriguing. She was a strong and forceful personality; the kind in which he had been conditioned to succumb. He rationalized the fact she had not left to mean she was still interested in furthering their brief relationship. *Cute* was the best word he could find to describe her. She felt good in his arms. What Saffron, Dutch and the others saw as a pathetic cry for attention Owen mistook for strength of character.

Without a word, he left his friends, walked over to the woman and held out his hand. She placed hers in his and stood. Exhibiting pained disgust, she glanced over her shoulder at the entertainers as they walked toward his car.

During the drive to his house she opened up about how her father had been dependent on the oil business in Louisiana and when it went bust in the eighties he almost committed suicide. It was not the only personal story she shared. She had a child out of wedlock that was placed for adoption. The whole 'ordeal,' as she referred to it, was such an embarrassment to her family that they moved her into an apartment in New Orleans. There was no way the family would have survived the disgrace had anyone in the small town in which they lived found out. Her words were cold and emotionless, as though she were reading from a newspaper.

He looked at her as she sat in the passenger seat. Feeling his stare she turned and faced him. Her bucktoothed grin exploded from her mouth. It was awkward, yet appealing. Reaching into her purse she retrieved a cigarette, and pressed the button on the door-handle to roll down the window as she fumbled with her lighter. After inhaling deeply she leaned her head out of the window and blew smoke into the night. This woman seemed to have an endless supply of strange stories. Once again, Owen mistook her willingness to talk openly for a warm and caring personality.

Upon arriving at his house, he could tell by the look on her face she was impressed with its grandiose appearance. For the first time since the two met she was speechless. He got out of the car and she stayed in her seat. Her desire to be treated like a lady was obvious. Gladly, he obliged. With every passing moment he found himself increasingly drawn to her. She made him feel comfortable in his own skin. Pseudo reverence blinded him to the potentially destructive nature of their association.

As they entered the grand foyer, she stopped and looked around at the splendor of it all. Nodding her head reassuringly, she said, "I'll spend all your money!" in a sharp tone. Owen thought her comment was charming.

The woman walked over and sat on the leather sofa. Allowing her body to slide into the prone position she writhed in ecstasy. "Man, can you imagine your naked body on this?"

Owen smiled as he sat next to her. "There's no need to imagine."

She sat up, looked piercingly at him, and then stood. He leaned back against the sofa as she straddled his legs and sat in his lap. He placed his hands on her hips and tugged, bringing her closer. She fell forward, catching herself with her hands on the back of the sofa next to his head. They gently kissed. The shape of her mouth felt odd, and tasted of scorched tobacco. His hold on her was broken when she backed away from the embrace, stood and walked toward the entertainment center. Her approval was given with a nod as she found what she searched for in the C.D. case. To his surprise she maneuvered through the myriad of equipment in a deft manner and soon the house was filled with the evocative sounds of *Enya*. Something about how the singer's voice accompanied the music perfectly struck a nerve within him. It was tranquil, unlike any facet of his life. Many days were spent lying on the sofa, allowing her expressions to sooth the turmoil that engulfed his tenuous existence.

The convenient lover walked back toward him, slowly removed her shirt, and then her bra. Crawling back onto his lap, she leaned over and whispered into his ear. "This is the best music for fucking."

Even her vile words could not penetrate his attraction to her. There was nothing of substance about her, but she mirrored the essence of his outlook on life. Once again, material possessions defined the object of his desire. They were one, and his inability to apply the lessons life presented him prevented Owen from embracing the concept he deserved something far greater than fleeting riches. At a time when hope became a genuine possibility, he had never found himself so far from its embrace.

Chapter Sixteen

Owen awoke the next morning on the sofa. Its bolsters had been tossed onto the floor. The cushions had slid away from the back and he was pinned in the gap between them. His date was nowhere to be seen. Worry overtook him. He struggled to remove himself from his predicament and searched the house. When he saw she was not in his bedroom he checked the other four. There was no sign of her.

After securing the second floor he moved back downstairs and searched the office to no avail. Once in the kitchen he noticed the phone was not in its cradle. He removed it from the counter and placed it in its charger as he attempted to clear away his misgivings.

Suddenly, fear that she had taken his BMW engulfed him. Quickly, he ran from the kitchen into the hallway leading to the garage. A piece of driftwood hung on the wall and contained four hooks screwed into it. All of his keys were there. He opened the door, reached in and pressed the button on the wall that opened the garage door. His heart skipped a beat as his car took shape behind the gradually opening access. It was in the same place he parked it the night before. A heavy sigh of relief escaped as he pressed the button again to close the garage.

After closing the door he walked through the kitchen and into the living room. Bending over he began to pick up the pillows and cushions when the doorbell rang. *She must have locked herself out*, he thought.

An open entry revealed Monica standing on the front porch. She was dressed in a bikini that was barely hidden by a colorful wrap. It hugged her waist and was pulled up behind her neck where it was tied. She held a straw purse and wore a matching hat. Noting the look on her friend's face, she said, "I'm sorry to disappoint you."

He turned away and walked inside, leaving the door open for her to follow. "You didn't disappoint. I'm actually relieved."

"*Relieved*? What's wrong?"

"Nothing."

She closed the door behind her. "Could it have anything to do with that buck-toothed girl I saw leaving here?"

"You saw her?" Owen asked, urgently.

"Yeah. She was getting into a cab, and glared at me as she threw her cigarette out of the window toward me."

Owen was too embarrassed to respond. He continued picking up cushions and tossing them onto the sofa. His friend walked over, placed her purse on the floor, and began to help him clean up his mess.

After several minutes of silence, Monica spoke. "I took the day off hoping you and I could go out on the boat. You *did* invite me." He looked at her without responding. Urgency surrounding his treasure was compounded by Agent Melendez and the pirates. Suddenly she became an additional variable in the increasingly complex equation that was his life. His silence conveyed discomfort. "I could leave if you'd like."

"No!" he answered quickly, which made her feel better. "I just had something planned that I can blow off." The danger associated with Bahamian pirates knowing his dive spot meant the shipwreck was one place he would never take her. "Where would you like to go?"

"Is your boat fast?"

"*Oh yeah!*" he boasted.

"Then how about the Dry Tortugas?"

"Do you want to dive the reef?"

"Sure."

"Are you certified?"

"No, but you are, right?"

"Yes."

"Good. You can teach me what I need to know on the way out there." Monica was confident she could easily master the dangerous sport.

Although Owen considered himself an expert, the idea of diving with a novice did not appeal to him. "What about your fear of becoming shark excrement?" was the only deterrent that entered his mind.

"It's shallow water."

"That doesn't mean sharks won't be around." She did not respond, which gave him the opportunity to add to his objection. "I'm not real sure it's a good idea that you dive without certification."

Without hesitating, she challenged him. "I trust that you will tell me everything I need to know."

No one had ever shown faith in him. It disarmed, confused and left him no option. "You bet I will."

Readying the boat for the trip took less than thirty minutes. Although they could easily make it a day trip Owen erred on the side of caution and packed as though he would be gone for a week. Boxes and grocery bags containing provisions were placed on the cushions of the sofa below deck. When Monica went below she saw that everything was stored haphazardly. Disapproval was conveyed with a shake of her head as she began to stow everything in the various cabinets and cubbies.

It was nearly ten o'clock in the morning before they got underway. Owen masterfully maneuvered the boat into open water and engaged its engines, full throttle. The vessel skipped across the waves. Salty spray speckled their sunglasses and cooled their faces. Head-winds were strong. Owen stood at the console and pulled his Atlanta Braves baseball cap tightly onto his head to keep from losing it to a gust of wind. Monica removed her wrap and re-tied it more securely.

Finally, after being beaten repeatedly by the motion of the boat, she grabbed the stainless steel bar mounted to the dashboard, turned to her friend and yelled, "Can we slow down? We're in no hurry!"

Throttling down the engines he realized his trips were normally filled with fear. "Sorry. I guess we have a long way to go and I wanted to get there quickly."

"We could stay a week with all the stuff you packed."

He laughed. "I just want to be prepared."

"You see, you are a Boy Scout."

Owen shook his head. "I am *really* nothing like a scout."

The boat moved slowly as he sat in the captain's chair and propped his feet onto the console; occasionally steering with his foot. She seized the opportunity the silence offered. "Would you like to talk?"

"About what?"

"Well, the most important thing we have to discuss is you teaching me about diving."

He had forgotten about the need to instruct her. "Yes! Of course!"

He tutored her on the buildup of nitrogen in the blood stream and how that phenomenon occurred more rapidly the deeper and longer the dive. She was a good pupil and repeated each lesson to make sure she understood completely; impressing him like no one ever had. Trust had never been accepted by him. It scared him to realize his was being offered to her so readily.

Frightening prospects about their dive provided the perfect segue for her to ask, "Does it frighten you to dive with me?"

Owen looked out over the gulf waters and pondered her question. "No, but it scares me that I trust you so completely. I've never had that luxury. I'm not sure how to do it, or what will come of it." She hesitated to respond, which caused immediate embarrassment and he turned away from her and grabbed the wheel, gazing intently at the G.P.S. screen while steering the boat back onto course.

"It's not that you don't know how to trust, it's that you don't want to make yourself vulnerable."

Her words stung because he felt theirs was a bond like he'd never enjoyed before. "Why is it that I don't want to trust you?"

"Because if you did that would mean you would have to care about me. You can't care about me because you're looking forward to the day our relationship ends, aren't you?"

There was at least a modicum of truth to her statement. "I have no idea how to carry on a successful relationship. I don't know what to expect from someone, and what's expected of me."

She grinned at the ease in which the conversation played out. "You can stop with the tarts for one thing. This morning I come to your house only to be met by some woman leaving and looking like she had not slept all night." Owen smiled, embracing his night of debauchery. "Do you get satisfaction from nights like that?"

He burst into incredulous laughter. "Of course I do, and she did too." He responded, confident of his prowess.

Monica shook her head. "You're not a ribald person. You're an animal that doesn't know the difference between a meaningless physical act and the art of making love to a woman. It's no wonder you have no idea about the expectations of a successful relationship."

"Suppose you teach me," he said, glibly.

"Are you making a pass at me? You know that's useless, *don't you?*" Owen did not respond. Her next statement was intended to provoke a reaction. "I might consider it … just for your own good."

"That's very noble of you." He grinned. "But I don't need your charity. I do well enough on my own."

"Once again you've missed the point."

He grew tired of the challenging nature of their conversation and sat silently looking straight ahead at the expanse of water that lay before them.

To escape the tension, Monica went below and occupied herself by doing menial tasks that constituted nothing more than shifting provisions from drawers into cabinets and visa-versa. Owen saw her through the hatch and the imp within him burst forth. He shoved the throttle forward sharply increasing the boat's speed and watched as his friend's momentum shifted toward the back of the boat. Her feet pattered quickly along the floor as she tried to maintain her balance. Once she had done so he pulled back on the throttle, slowing the boat's speed just as harshly. Monica's momentum carried her the length of the galley toward the apex of the bow. She caught herself on the table mounted to the floor.

"Stop it!" she yelled from below. Owen laughed.

Upon reaching their destination the boat was anchored a hundred yards away from the reef; neither wished to damage the living organism. The water around the island was shallower than his normal dive spot. Owen made sure Monica was properly suited, and once again went over the hand signals they might need in order to communicate. Once he had all of his dive equipment on and appeared ready, Monica placed her mask over her face and the regulator in her mouth. Owen tapped on the glass, held his palm in front of her face and waved goodbye by repeatedly folding his fingers at the last knuckle. Smiling nervously she made her way to the platform on the back of the boat. She stopped at the edge and performed a scissor dive by keeping her right foot on the platform and extending her left over the water.

Monica released a burst of air from her Buoyancy Control device and sank toward the bottom. After equalizing, she rolled onto her back and looked toward the boat. A large shadowy figure moved aggressively toward her. The surface resembled a giant mirror reflecting the turbulent world above in an undulating two dimensional portrait. It was peaceful below the water.

When Owen reached her depth, the two swam hand-in-hand to the reef.

Coral extended from the ocean floor like an aquatic mountain range and the couple glided effortlessly over it. The palette of colors displayed on the reef was breathtaking. Crossing its apex, they descended quickly down the other side. Peering in opposite directions, Owen suddenly felt a great deal of pressure crushing his hand. Monica's strength was apparent in his pain. He looked over and saw unadulterated fear in her eyes. She pointed toward a hammerhead shark leisurely swimming along the sandy bottom at the foot of the reef. Bubbles exploded through his regulator as he laughed heartily. He held his palms up toward her and shook his head, assuring her that there was nothing to worry about. Stroking the palm of her hand with his thumb calmed her frayed nerves and gave her confidence to proceed in an unfamiliar world. Complete silence enhanced the peace she felt within, and the vibrant colors of the reef heightened every sensation.

Schools of fish gently parted when they approached; not concerned for their safety, but giving clear passage to those whose paths intersected ever so briefly. Tranquility engulfed each of their psyches and the security offered by the blanketing water allowed them to glide through an environment filled with encounters completely of their own choosing.

Their time submerged passed quickly and without mishap. Owen allowed Monica to climb the ladder and crawl onto the boat first. He helped her by gently pushing on her rear-end. She was strong, but there was a sense of chivalry in helping her lift the additional weight of the dive equipment.

It was nearly four o'clock in the afternoon when Monica emerged from the boat's cabin rubbing her wet, mussed hair vigorously with a towel. She had put on a pair of white shorts and a sleeveless denim polo shirt. Owen still wore his bathing suit that had been dried by the sun. He was shirtless.

"It's too late to get back before dark, isn't it?" Monica asked.

Owen looked at the bulky dive watch on his wrist and examined the sky, ascertaining the position of the sun relative to the horizon. "I think I can get us back in time." Disappointment was evidenced by the melancholy on her face. "What's the matter?"

She smiled unconvincingly. "I thought it would be nice to stay the night out here."

Owen furrowed his brow. "Then why didn't you say so?"

"I guess I was afraid that you'd want to get back to your life in town."

He could not believe she accused him of having a life. "I think it sounds like a great idea."

She became rejuvenated at the thought, and bounced downstairs. Disappearing into the galley she yelled back to him, "I'll fix dinner."

Owen spent thirty minutes securing the fore and aft anchors to prevent any mishaps. The VHF radio was tuned to the weather forecast and he listened for any indication of adverse weather. There were no such warnings. He turned the boat's running lights on to make sure they were working properly, and then switched them off to conserve the battery. When he was finished he made his way downstairs into the cabin. Tantalizing aroma from Monica's dinner preparation caused his mouth to water with anticipation.

"I'm going to take a shower," he said, passing behind his friend, who busily prepared dinner on the propane stove.

Owen left the hatch to the head open. It was a small room and the steam heightened his claustrophobia. Several times he caught a glimpse of Monica through the translucent glass in the shower door as she passed.

When he emerged he was clad in only a towel. Dinner was on the table, and she sat waiting patiently. They made eye contact and he asked, "Can I get dressed first?"

"Sure," she replied.

"Don't wait for me," he said, as he crouched and made his way into the aft birth.

After a couple of minutes he emerged wearing a pair of loosely fitting pajama bottoms and a t-shirt with a picture of a rather striking pirate captain on a wanted poster. It read, *Captain Coy Tull, Wanted for bigamy, piracy and other infractions too numerous and vile to mention*. Monica read the shirt and dropped her head, shook it and laughed. "Sit down and eat your dinner before it gets too cold, captain," she ordered.

"*Yes, dear*," Owen replied in an exaggeratedly meek voice as he sat across the table from her. On his plate sat a nice juicy steak encrusted in pepper. "Where did you get steak?"

"There were two in the freezer," she said. "They must have been left over from some romantic dinner cruise."

He shrugged his shoulders, not remembering when he brought the meat on board. "What do you call it?"

"Steak au Poivre. It literally means steak with pepper," she explained, as Owen placed the first bite into his mouth.

"Mmm. This is good."

The two ate and talked. Conversation amounted to nothing more than innocuous chatter. In that time they finished a bottle of red wine and opened another.

After dinner they took the second bottle on deck. It was placed in a wine-bucket between them as they sat on the bow and used the windshield as a back-rest. The gulf waters were dark and the moonlight's reflection shimmered across its surface. When the second bottle was gone Owen went below and quickly retrieved a third.

Their minds as well as their inhibitions were loosened by alcohol. The sky was clear and the stars were abundant. With her next to him the sordid details of his past did not seem as ominous to his disposition. Freedom from emotional barriers afforded him the opportunity to say anything to her without fear of reprisal. Suddenly, their bland conversation became very personal. "Have you *ever* been with a man?" Owen asked.

His question took Monica by surprise. She felt the sincerity of his inquiry and it gave her strength. "I was raped by several men when I was twenty years old." The memory that was once very painful she forced herself to speak about like it was nothing more than a moment in time.

"I'm sorry," he apologized. "I certainly did not want to bring up any bad memories."

"It's okay, *really*."

As quickly as he had rushed to his apology, he expounded upon his question. "So, was that the only time you've been with a man?" The alcohol shattered his sensitivity.

She laughed. "Yes," then explained further. "I never told you why I left Venezuela. I left because every man in my town was taking it upon themselves to *convert* me into a heterosexual. They are so threatened by lesbians."

"Who?"

"Latin men. They're wired for one thing and one thing only ... sex."

"Except the gay ones."

Monica laughed. "Yes, except the gay ones." Their examination into her personal life provided the opportunity to delve into his. "Why do you cavort with women the way you do?" When he did not answer immediately she explained the genesis of her question. "The woman that left your house this morning; you can do much better than that. So, why do you lower yourself to her level?"

He thought for a moment. "It's a challenge?" he replied, unsure of himself.

"You don't even know why. That's *rich*!" She threw her empty hand into the air in disgust.

Owen was offended. "Wait a minute! What do you expect me to say?"

"I want you to tell me how you can speak so eloquently and with passion in your voice when describing this beautiful woman you met in Italy, yet wallow in the gutters with countless women of dubious morals?"

"Because I don't care about them." Owen's answer came across as flippant, but he was sincere.

"You don't care?" Monica repeated.

"Why should I? If it wasn't me it would be some other poor sap."

"Sap," she repeated. "You really don't have a very high opinion of yourself, do you?"

He thought for a moment. "Why would I?"

"Stop answering my questions with a question. You're beginning to piss me off."

Owen thought about returning to his berth, but felt compelled to finish the conversation. "In order to care about something you have to be impressed with it. In order to care for someone you have to know unequivocally that person is trustworthy and has your best interests at heart. People aren't made that way."

"You're blaming *everyone* for your inability to commit?" Monica's confusion confounded him.

"Of course. This is the point to where we have evolved, right?"

She thought, momentarily. "You're going to have to help me understand."

"Okay. You want personal examples? How about people who sleep with their cousin's wife or girlfriend? That is *very* personal and it happens all the time." When Monica did not answer, he continued. "I'm just playing the cards that were dealt me."

"So what is it that you are attracted to in these women?"

"That I don't have to see them, or to deal with them for more than one night."

The directness of his answer shocked her. "So, you don't think you're capable of carrying on a relationship for more than one night?"

"I don't want to. Don't you get it? There will always be someone there to destroy what you've worked so hard to build with very little effort, like kicking over a child's sandcastle."

She had no idea how to respond. There was a lot of truth in what he said. Then it came to her. "You must see *something* in these women?"

"It's purely physical."

"Like your relationship with your father?" She paused. "You carry on relationships exactly the way you wish you could have with him; getting just what you needed from him; basic simple needs, but if you ever sense you have an attraction that is more than physical, with any depth to it, you'll have nothing to do with that person.." He still said nothing. "I guarantee you there are good people out there who are worth knowing … worth loving."

Her insistence triggered something deep within him. Suddenly his tone became compassionate. "I just remembered a dream I had last night while sleeping on my sofa."

"Tell me about it."

"I was at a reunion. It was an odd gathering because there was no rhyme or reason why any of these people were there, especially me. I mingled through the crowd talking with everyone. There were hundreds of people there and I knew them all. I would walk up to someone knowing who they were and begin a conversation, and then on to another. Some of them were family, some were people I had gone to school with, or team-

mates from little league. The odd thing was that I did
not recognize a single one of them, physically. I knew
their voices ... I knew their souls, but did not recognize
a single face in the crowd. I remember feeling very
anxious until Julia walked up and sat down next to me.
She hooked her arm in mine, held me tightly, and all the
worry I felt dissolved immediately."

Chapter Seventeen

The *Pirate's Local #69* was crowded. Owen sat amongst strangers feeling isolated. Uneasiness filled his psyche as people walked by and stared at him. He would have taken a seat at the bar if he knew no one would be coming. Someone always showed up and in anticipation he leaned all of the chair-backs against the table to reserve their seats. It was a weekday and he should have anticipated his friends would be at work. For an hour he sat alone, drinking.

Tourists packed the city. All of the bars on Duval Street were filled to capacity. People were spilling out of them and wandering onto side streets looking for a place that offered a cold drink and space in which to enjoy it. The *Sixty-Nine* offered just that. Not a single face in the crowd seemed the least bit familiar to Owen. Normally, that did not bother him, but something was missing. His thoughts were consumed with Monica and the nights they spent talking. It left him wanting more. He had no idea what they would talk about, but knew he could say anything to her. Having someone like that in his life left him craving more. His past seemed like a distant memory, and his perspective focused on the future. He searched the crowd for any sign of Monica. There was no reason for her to be there, but he could hope she would continue to help him along his newly found path to enlightenment.

The crowd grew and Owen was forced to move his chair closer to the table. Passages between tables became narrow as people filled every available space.

Just as the thought of leaving entered his mind a familiar face emerged from the crowd. Her name was Lorraine Connor. She was of diminutive stature caused by the polio that riddled her body as a child. She walked with the aid of a cane and the pain she felt in her legs was evident on her face. It was a struggle for her to move freely, but she was aware the alternative was much worse. She knew as she aged what strength she had in her legs would diminish, confining her to a wheelchair for life. Regardless, her spirit was indomitable. Owen did not notice her until she passed right by his table. Before he had a chance to call out to her, they made eye contact. When she recognized him a smile crossed her face that was so infectious it brightened his mood.

"Hey, Lorraine! Have a seat." He motioned with his hand toward the chair nearest her.

She plopped her exhausted body down. "It's getting harder for me to get around, Owen."

"Can I buy you a drink?"

"That would be nice," she said, as she situated herself comfortably in the chair. "I'll have a Vodka Gimlet, please."

Without a word he stood and squeezed himself through the mass of bodies between their table and the bar. Lillith saw him and moved toward him without hesitation. There were no pleasantries exchanged between the two. She was too busy and he knew it. Once the drink was placed on the counter in front of him he made his way back to the table.

"Thank you so much," Lorraine said, as he handed her the drink across the table.

They met a year earlier and always enjoyed each other's company, but never had the chance to talk one-on-one. "Where's Bob?" he asked.

"He's coming later," she replied. "Today is our anniversary."

"Congratulations!" Genuine happiness filled his soul. "How many years have you been married?"

"Thirty eight." She grabbed her lower back with her hand. "Just the thought of that many years makes my back hurt."

He laughed. Her cheerful disposition gave his life perspective. Never once had he ever heard her complain about being dealt a bad hand. The two talked across the table for an hour. She boasted about her two sons, and shared stories of the ups and downs of her marriage to Bob for all those years. Never once did he get the feeling she would change a single moment of her life.

"So, Owen, do you have a steady girlfriend?" Lorraine asked.

He smiled. "Not yet, but I'm hopeful."

Ignoring all of the chatter that she had heard about his lifestyle, Lorraine added, "Well, I'm sure you will find a girl who is lucky to have you."

After a few more pleasant exchanges between them, Asa appeared as if he had emerged during a mitotic process from the mass of bodies that created a human wall around the table. He pulled a chair away from the table and sat down placing the bottle of beer he held in his hand between his legs, and said nothing.

"Asa, do you know Lorraine," Owen asked, as he motioned toward her with his hand.

He nodded at Lorraine. She answered the question. "Asa and Bob worked together for years on the boat."

Owen cocked his head to the left. "Hmm, it's odd that I never met Bob on the boat."

Within the next hour several more friends made their way to the table, but it wasn't the usual group. Stump was there, of course. Carmen was a fiery Latina who wore her hair tightly in a bun on top of her head. The brunette was Nancy. She had breasts so large any man would realize the burden of being made to carry them around. Jacqueline was a freckly red-head who was impeccably dressed. She had her hair done in a French braid that was tight against her head and the base of her neck.

Everyone sat and talked loudly in order to be heard over the crowd. At times as many as three conversations were carried on at once. Owen and Asa took part in none of them. They were amazed these women could actually carry on discussions as they shouted over each other.

Then Stump drew Owen into the conversation. "Hey man, whatever happened the other night after you chased after that lesbian?"

Owen was offended. "Don't call her that." His affection for her was unmistakable.

Stump looked astonishingly at everyone at the table and said loudly, "Well, isn't she a *lezz bee un*?"

Calmly, he replied. "Yes she is, but you are using the term to separate her from the rest of us, and that's not right."

Stump drew her head back and once again looked at everyone at the table, then asked, "You slept with her didn't you?"

"No. But I've gotten to know her and she deserves my respect."

"*Respect*?" Stump looked incredulously at him. "Are you the same guy that I go to the Bahamas with and does God knows what with God knows who?"

"I am that guy, but when you meet someone special like Monica your outlook changes. I hope that one day you meet someone special."

Ignoring his verbal jab, Stump continued her assault. "That's your fantasy, isn't it, to nail a lesbian?"

Jacqueline interjected, desiring to move the conversation away from the confrontation, "I have a fantasy for you," by making it all about her.

Asa leaned forward against the table and listened intently. Stump sat back in her chair and glared and Owen, who rolled his eyes and looked into the crowd as he sipped his beer.

Once Jacqueline realized she had everyone's attention, she shared her fantasy. "My husband and I are at the Oak Bar in the Plaza Hotel in New York. It's late and there are only a few people left in the room. It's by no means crowded because I don't think I could handle that ... personally. He lifts me off the stool and places me gently on the bar. Then he slowly undresses me and we make love right there."

"Can anyone else join in?" Carmen asked, eagerly.

Proudly, she answered, "Nope. They can watch all they want but no man can touch me except my husband."

Stump leaned forward again with her arms on the edge of the table and looked at Jacqueline. Her interest was piqued. "Who else would like to share?" She looked at Asa. "What about you, Asa? You told us that your wife told you what her fantasy was. Why don't you share it with us?"

He shook his head. "There's no way I'd betray my wife's trust."

"Well then, tell us what your's is?" she insisted.

"You weren't listening the other day, because I told you then that her fantasy *was* mine."

Stump became disgusted. "You're no fun old man!" She then turned toward Carmen. "How about you, sweetie?"

Carmen dropped her head down and peered at everyone over the top of her glasses. "Does this fantasy have to be something you've never done, or can it be my ultimate fantasy that I *have* done?"

"As long as it's your ultimate fantasy, it doesn't matter whether or not you've done it," Stump answered without hesitation.

"The top of the Empire State Building," Carmen answered.

Everyone was quiet as they envisioned her naked and making love to a man with New York's skyline as the backdrop. Owen asked, "What time does the observation deck close?"

Sassily, she responded, "Man, that thing is open until two a.m."

"Was it late at night?" Stump asked.

"Pretty late."

"Was there anyone else up there?" Jacqueline inquired.

"A couple of people came and went." She paused. "I think there was another couple doing the same thing we were. They came around the corner and saw us, which I thought would have scared them away, but later on we ran into each other again and exchanged guilty smiles."

"Did you have an orgasm?" Asa asked, bluntly.

"Of course! Why?"

"No reason, except that I know a lot of women would have a hard time relaxing in that situation."

As she was so apt to do, Stump pressed Nancy, "What's your wildest sexual fantasy?"

"Five guys," she answered without hesitation. "I want to feel their strong hands all over my body and to be desired by them."

"Jesus Christ!" Stump exclaimed. "It would take thirty men to cover those breasts with their hands," she said, pointing to Nancy's chest.

"You got that right, girl," she replied playfully as she held them from the bottom and bounced them twice.

Owen listened to every word and for the first time in his life such impetuous conversation did not appeal to him. Of all the stories that had been told the one that meant the most to him was the one that was not. Asa's refusal to divulge something so very personal was his first lesson about how a gentleman should conduct himself. The value of his mentor's decorum was not lost on him.

Stump searched the faces at the table, associating a fantasy with each until her eyes fell on Lorraine, who had not told her story. "Alright Lorraine, it's your turn."

She wiggled her short body, moving toward the edge of her chair so she could lean onto the table and see everyone's face as she spoke. "Bob has been a very good husband to me for thirty-eight years. He's been a great father to our sons. I want nothing more in life than for *one night* to have the perfect female body for him. I would lay on our bed with a big red bow and tell him, 'it's all for you.'" She paused. No one said a word. Everyone at the table felt extraordinarily selfish as they thought about how their fantasy compared to Lorraine'-s. When no one spoke, she added one more detail. "Oh, and Bob is wearing a loin cloth."

There was much to learn from this person who was nothing more than a mere acquaintance. Owen knew how circumstantial their meeting had been, but in the short time they spent together Lorraine taught him something he had never known. Although her desire was physical in nature it was grounded in humility and sacrifice for the one she loved. He had always lived his life trying to satisfy his own needs. What he realized was they had been nothing more than basic desires. The high regard in which Asa and Lorraine held their spouses was a skill Owen was not sure he possessed. It was obvious they worked hard to preserve relationships they cherished. Intimacy's quality was innate and the desire to embrace completely honest love thrived within Owen. His once singular perspective focused on the multiple layers of his being that lay dormant for most of his life. Recognizing depth of emotion for the first time opened a completely new world to him. Knowing who he had to thank for that awakening solidified his love for her.

Chapter Eighteen

It would be the last time Owen strolled casually down Duval Street heading toward Mallory Square searching aimlessly for something to fill the void in his life. His legs were unsteady; feeling the effects of the alcohol he carelessly consumed all afternoon. The street was crowded and the further west he traveled the denser the foot-traffic became. Faces in the crowd seemed a generation younger. He stepped onto the street to avoid an oncoming throng of young people who were drunk and unaware of obstacles around them. Hopping back onto the curb after they passed he continued his journey toward the square.

Quickly, people entered and exited his field of vision as thoughts passed in and out of his consciousness. Alcohol exacerbated his depression and he desperately tried to make sense of a lot of things that had happened during his life. It confused him that his friends were seemingly unwilling to allow him to be himself without being made to endure their ridicule. Why could he not have a friend who was a lesbian?

Asa and Lorraine were not a part of that characterization. It was the first time he ever witnessed such devotion to one's spouse. Their level of commitment provided them peace. He realized his reaction to the situation was as tumultuous as his life had been.

Monica had been the best friend he had ever known, but their relationship could grow no more. That realization fueled his despair.

When he got to the square it was filled with people. He made his way to the kiosk where he regularly bought beer. Once he had done so, he walked through the crowd stopping occasionally at each entertainer's make-shift stage. Acknowledgement of his presence was with a wink or some other familiar expression. Discovering treasure freed him of a lot of burdens. He appreciated not having to rely on anyone to make a living and he appreciated his friends who could make it solely on their talent. There were no pretenses between them and their audience. If someone did not like what they were watching they could walk away without paying; no guilt, no pressure. He admired that freedom.

After an hour Owen found himself in a very familiar position, leaning against the railing at the edge of the square, looking out over the bay. His forearms were against the top bar and held his beer in both hands above the water.

A dapper looking gentleman approached, stopped next to him and assumed the same position. The stranger also had a drink that was held in the same manner. He was handsome and dressed impeccably, wearing starched shorts and a polo shirt that appeared new. Owen glanced at the man and they exchanged smiles. Although he appeared healthy, something about him seemed unnerving. He was gaunt and his skin sagged on his pale face.

"Hello, friend." The man spoke in an engagingly smooth voice. It exuded a groomed quality.

"Hello," Owen returned the greeting.

The man extended his hand. "I'm Roscoe Russell."

"Owen Taylor," he said, as he took the man's hand in his and shook it firmly.

"What kind of work do you do?" the man asked.

"I'm a lawyer," Owen responded, not knowing why he chose to lie. The only explanation could be that he was tired of being alone, and wished to be a part of something greater than himself.

"Me too!" the man exclaimed.

A chill ran down his spine as Owen worried the man would expose his fib once they talked business. "Where do you practice?" Owen asked, nervously continuing the conversation.

"In a small town in the panhandle called Erstwhile."

"I've heard of that town," Owen responded. "I grew up in a place just like it."

The man turned and coughed violently. Owen winced. "Where do you practice?" the man inquired.

"Here, in town. I have a small office on Caroline Street."

"I'd like to come by and see your setup."

Owen nodded and smiled. "You do that." He paused. "But I won't be in until Monday."

The man shook his head. "I'm leaving on Sunday."

"Too bad."

Roscoe sensed Owen could be trusted and talked about things he would never knowingly discuss outside of the profession. "I just settled this case for a client of mine that I should have put a lot more effort into."

"Why didn't you?"

He laughed. "You know how it is, we all have to look out for one another, right?"

"Sure."

"The opposing attorney had done a favor for me in the past so it was time to return the favor."

"At the expense of your clients?"

"You got it, friend." Suddenly, familiarity with this man became unpleasant. The stranger continued his confession. "The other attorney, myself and a mediator cooked up a good looking mediation hearing that we choreographed like a frigging Broadway show."

Owen did not respond as the man took a sip of beer. After a few moments he asked. "Have you got a wife?"

The man grinned widely as if he had some sort of patent on the subject of women. "No. My best relationship is with a woman in France. I do a lot of work overseas."

Bawdy desires of his own blinded Owen to the arrogance of the man's statement. Sympathy overtook him when he noticed the man suddenly went flush. "You don't look too well. Are you sick?"

The man reached into his pocket and pulled out a prescription bottle. He shook it and the contents rattled. Roscoe smiled. "Darvocet, my friend."

Suddenly, it became a game for Owen. He wanted to draw more information out of the man. "Do you have a client who prescribes that for you?"

"Not any more. I have a thirty-eight foot fishing boat. One day I fell from the ladder as I climbed down from the crow's-nest. I broke several vertebrae and that's when I discovered the magic of these beauties." He shook the bottle again.

Owen slid a little closer and lowered his voice to a whisper; attempting to elicit information. "Doesn't your addiction to those pills impair your ability to provide your clients with the best legal services?"

Smugly, Roscoe responded, "No way! I'm the best attorney in Erstwhile. I'm handsome and deserving."

"Deserving of what?" Owen asked in a very soft, non-threatening tone.

"Deserving of the title."

"Which title?"

"*Attorney.*"

In the face of unsubstantiated conceit, Owen's legal career became authentic. "It is great to be looked upon favorably by everyone because of the profession we are in, isn't it?"

Roscoe smirked. "Attorneys aren't looked up to by anyone outside the profession. It's up to each of us to derive personal satisfaction from the career we have chosen."

Owen nodded his head satisfactorily. "So it's like a Zen thing, right? Inner reflection has brought you to a self-satisfied state."

Roscoe shook his head, condescendingly. "*No.* I measure the worth of my practice the way a Wall Street banker would; how much cash can I extort from my clients."

"*Extort?*"

Still believing he was talking with a member of his professional fraternity, he leaned toward Owen and whispered. "I had this client once who I convinced she had signed a standard A.B.A. contract for a tort case. I dragged the case out for five years. She was an absent minded tart. When she finally *remembered* signing the contract, I dictated the terms to her. Of course, they were much more in my favor than the standard A.B.A. contract."

Owen was shaken back into reality. Somehow he found it in himself to thrust disgust upon Roscoe without apportioning any to himself for his own indiscretions.

The men bid adieu without fanfare.

Owen continued his journey through the promenade, buying beer after beer until the night grew late. He scoured the crowd for women who appeared to be alone. The later it became the easier it was for those who looked for a night of pleasure to spot each other. Desperation doesn't have a reflection. It is sensed by those who seek it, but cannot feel it within themselves.

When the festivities were over the entertainers gathered near one of the gun turrets removed from the USS Maine after its sinking in Havana's harbor. Owen decided to join his friends.

"Are you still dating that lesbian?" Saffron asked.

"No, but we *are* good friends," he huffed. "Her name is Monica, by the way."

Dutch silently rolled the joint that would be shared by everyone. His dirty white hat was all that could be seen as he held his head down looking at the papers and baggie of pot in his lap. From underneath it his boastful voice emanated, "I've got a little something here that will unwind the shorts that the both of you have knotted up your arses."

"Is that the Jamaican stuff, mon?" Winston asked.

"No. This shit is from the good 'ole U.S.A. Straight from the University of Mississippi's garden."

Winston shook his head. "Mon, let me tell you; those mountains in Jamaica is good for growing more than the best coffee in the world, if you know wot I mean."

Again, Dutch's voice came from beneath his hat. "You know Owen, maybe that's what your problem is, you need to get high more often. When you made that statement about looking for the uber-lover, whatever the hell that is," he exaggerated his southern accent, "you were high. Now, having been married myself, more than once, I can honestly say the best way to endure such pain is to be high, *all of the time*. Medicinal marijuana is what they call it and that's why they grow it at Ole Miss." He raised his voice to make his point as he looked from under his hat directly at Winston. "And that's why we are smoking it tonight!"

Winston held his hands up, defensively, surrendering to Dutch. "No worries, mon. Just spark it, pass it, and I'll smoke it."

That is exactly what Dutch did after running his tongue along the edge of the paper and pressing the cigarette closed with his fingers. It made its way around the group, hand-to-hand, and back before Saffron pulled out a roach-clip, and finished it off. Once the first was gone there was another to take its place. Few words were exchanged as everyone waited in silence for the effects of the drug to alter the realities that trapped them. The effect Owen experienced was the same as it had always been; an exacerbation of his depression, which dragged him down physically. It elicited a variation of the question posed to the group at the *Sixty-Nine*. "What's the worst thing you've ever done?"

Silence blanketed the group until Saffron asked, "Who are you asking?"

Owen blinked his burning eyes as he stared at her. "*Everybody*," he answered as if it were blatantly obvious. "Would you like to start?"

She looked at the faces in group. There was not one person she did not feel some sort of kinship and decided to answer the question honestly. "I've killed someone."

"Is that why you are here?" Owen asked.

"In a round-about way, I guess it is."

"Who was it?" Dutch asked.

She shook her head. "I don't even know the name of the person I killed."

The momentary silence that followed was interrupted by Owen. "What were the circumstances? Was it self defense?"

"It was an abortion."

No one spoke. There was not a person there who would judge her for her actions, but no one wished to comment on such a divisive subject.

"What about you, Dutch?"

The senior member of the group removed his hat by pinching the rim between the thumb and forefinger of his right hand and scratched his head underneath it with his free fingers. Many years of life had passed and he methodically filed through the decades in his memory, searching for the single worst thing that even he could not believe he had done. "Hmm," he tried to buy time to think, "I'm gonna have to think a little longer about that one. I'm sure whatever it is has been repressed deep into my psyche by now."

"Fair enough," Owen said. "Winston, how about you?"

"Well, mon. I must say that I am guilty of the same thing that the pretty young Saffron is guilty of, only I know who I murdered." He paused while looking at everyone, all of whom eagerly awaited his response. No one seemed willing to push for answers fearing they themselves would be pressed. Winston drew a deep breath before continuing. "I had a friend who was sleeping with my girlfriend. There was nothing I could do about it at the time … until the country's elections came around. Politicians in Jamaica will arm people in order to win them over. My friend just so happened to be a member of the opposing faction. When I saw the opportunity, I took it."

"You killed him, just like that?" Owen asked.

"Even better, mon. I waited until the two of them were together and got 'em both. All in the name of the political process, right mon?" He took a long, exaggerated drag from the joint.

"Geez, I don't think I could ever bring myself to murder anyone, much less two people," Owen said just before realizing how his words might be received by Saffron. He looked at her and held out his hand holding back any comment that she might consider making. "Not that I think what you did was murder, because I don't."

"Have you ever cared for anyone so bad it hurts … I mean *really hurts* when you realize that she is playing you the fool?" Winston asked.

Owen thought about Sara. "I did once, a long time ago, but she wasn't worth the effort."

"Well, my friend," Winston countered, "I hope that one day you will find a woman who can bring that kind of emotion out in you. That is the *best*," he said in a breathy voice, "kind of love … but it can be deadly. Beware of it if you do find it."

Dutch held up another joint. "Do ya'll want another one?" A smattering of *Yeses* and *uh-huhs* cluttered the conversation. The group enjoyed it in silence until it was gone.

"What's the worst thing you've ever done, Owen?" Dutch asked.

Owen wiped the sweat from his brow and slung it off his hand onto the ground in front of him. "I'm afraid I can't compete with Winston, so it's probably not even worth mentioning."

"Oh yes it is," Winston said.

Owen looked at Dutch and Saffron who both nodded their heads. "I don't want you all to think less of me."

"Come on, mon. Quit stalling," Winston insisted.

"Okay, here goes. I once made love to a married woman inside her house while her teenage kids were home." He hung his head and stared at the ground beneath his feet.

"You need to get out and live a little, boy," Dutch exclaimed.

"Yeah, on a scale of one to ten, I'd have to give that one a five," Winston added.

Owen looked at Saffron. "What about you? What do you think?"

"That it was your wife and your teenage kids you lame bastard."

"I'm not old enough to have teenage kids."

"Yes you are!"

"Okay, but it wasn't my wife and they weren't my kids." He paused. "If you could have seen this woman you wouldn't have been able to resist the urge either. It was the best sex I ever had."

"Now that says a lot!" Saffron exclaimed. "Knowing your prowess, that woman needs to be told how you feel, it would make her day."

Owen smiled. "She dumped me. She doesn't care."

Dutch could not resist making the obvious observation. "Why would you want to marry a woman who was cheating on her husband?"

"Because it was the best sex he ever had," Winston answered for Owen.

Dutch looked from Winston back to Owen. "So you could have been true to this woman knowing what you knew about her?"

Owen laughed. "Hell no. A buddy of mine picked me up down the street from her house and we went out that night."

"'Went out' means you got laid again that night, right?" Saffron inquired.

They all shared a laugh, before Owen added, "I *used* to be something."

Dutch shook his head. "Your reputation hasn't dropped off considerably since you've been here."

Saffron couldn't help but add her opinion. "You know, Owen, there is a lot more to having a successful relationship with a woman than great sex."

He looked deeply into her eyes and spoke in a caring, sensitive voice that dripped with sarcasm. "I'd like for you to show me how to be a better man so that when Mrs. Right does come along I'll be able to recognize it."

"No you don't. All you want is to nail me like these other two assholes." She pointed to Dutch and Winston.

"Do tell," replied Owen.

"No, I have not slept with them. They wish they could, though."

"Whew!" exclaimed Dutch. "For a minute there I thought I had done something that I couldn't remember, and sister I would want to enjoy the memory of sleeping with you every day for the rest of my life."

The groups laughter was interrupted when Owen pressed Dutch for his story. "So, Dutch, you've had plenty of time to think. What have you got for us?"

Without hesitation, he started. "I grew up in a house where there was no such concept as responsibility. Because of this, when I got married to my first wife I continued to date other women. I never felt like I was doing anything wrong. It was something to do and it felt good. When we got divorced I continued that family tradition and allowed our kids to slough-off responsibility and it drove my ex-wife crazy. Maybe that's why I did it."

"Is that the best you can do?" Owen scoffed the same disapproval he endured earlier.

Dutch's look was solemn. "I think that's the worst thing I could have done to my kids. I didn't realize it then, but I do now." The words came from deep inside his soul and everyone knew it. No one said anything, allowing him to elaborate if he wished. He did. "My older brother was an alcoholic. He was thirty-eight years old and laying on my parent's sofa everyday watching Braves' baseball games and reading novels. At night he would drink himself into an absolute stupor. After forty years of never holding him to a standard, my folks finally told my brother he needed to find himself. He moved out and went to Montana. He met a girl and they shacked up together. Well, he got really drunk one night and got into an argument with her and he ended up killing her." Dutch shook his head. "Damned if that pattern didn't repeat itself. My boy, who I never held to a high standard ended up doing the same damn thing about ten years ago." He looked at the others. "That's when I decided to move down here. I needed to escape and live out my days without being faced with it every time I went to the post office or the grocery store."

"I guess we all have some pretty deep wounds, huh?" Owen said, rhetorically. His statement was met with the nodding of heads.

It was late and everyone sat in silent self-reflection. Hearing the stories caused each of them to examine their life's paths. Each wondered whether they could have handled themselves differently and how would it have affected the outcome of their lives.

Owen's attention was diverted when he saw a woman pass by the group. She was an older woman who had obviously once been very beautiful. Her miniskirt was too short to hide her beefy thighs and her ample bosom billowed from the top of the vest she wore. There appeared to be nothing underneath that would inhibit the quick exposure of the flesh beneath.

"Excuse me," Owen said, as he stood and walked toward her.

She turned and took a long hard look at him. "Were you talking to me?"

"No, I've been wishing for you," he responded. Incredulous looks grew on the faces of his friends. Saffron rolled her eyes, Dutch dropped his head and shook it in disbelief, and Winston and Jack grinned.

"What exactly is it that you wish?" she inquired as she walked toward him.

Without hesitation he replied, "I have been wishing to meet a woman with the *tightest* body I can imagine, and tonight appears to be my lucky night." His second lie that night stung, but only briefly.

"Appears?"

"I don't want to seem overly confident."

She looked Owen over, and liked what she saw. "A man such as you has a right to be confident."

He smiled as he realized his latest conquest was well under way. Deception surrounded him and was embraced as a means to secure that which satiated desires. It would take a crisis for him to understand there was no scale to measure hypocrisy. What he did not realize was that one cannot apply critical analysis to others without placing himself under the same scrutiny. Ignoring one's own faults by accepting those of others will only doom those who do not face reality. Terminating the vicious cycle in which Owen found himself meant he had to disavow all he had known without destroying his hope for a bright future. Knowing the right questions to ask constituted only half the means necessary to convert experiences into discoveries. The pain associated with growth had the potential to become unbearable to those who don't have the courage to change.

Chapter Nineteen

On the drive home Owen learned that Gloria was a psychologist and her husband worked for a start-up pharmaceutical company in Coral Gables. The revelation she was married did not faze him. He was numb to human behavior and resigned himself to play the game as well as he could.

He opened the front door to his house and she walked inside, through the living room and onto the pool deck, removing her clothes as she went. Watching her as she walked, it was obvious her body had seen better days. Loose skin hung and jiggled with each step. Reaching down, he grabbed the slightly present roll around his waist and pinched it between his fingers and the heels of both hands. He could not deny he was aging.

His gaze returned to Gloria who struck a pose at the edge of the pool before diving into it. Regardless of her age, she was still a pleasant sight. Owen watched from the living room as her head bobbed above the water as she swam the breast stroke. When he realized she wasn't interested in coming inside he joined her.

Gloria made no bones about wanting to spend the night frolicking under the stars. Regardless of the difference in their ages Owen remained eager to oblige. As they swam together the two performed an impromptu *pas de deaux* in the water, swimming around focusing their wanton stares on one another without coming together. They gazed at each other with hungry eyes and wry smiles, but neither made a definitive move. When he decided the time was right he swam slowly toward her from the deep end of the pool. She backed away until she reached the steps, then turned and negotiated the incline on her way out of the pool. Owen watched her skip giddily down to the dock behind his house. He smiled as he followed her, slowly. The fact they were both nude and could easily be seen by his neighbors never crossed his mind. His focus was on what he could do to please her and make this an evening she would never forget.

When he reached the end of the dock Owen found her lying on her back staring up at the stars. The night was clear and heavenly bodies were abundant. She had one leg flat against the deck, and the other was drawn close to her bottom with her knee in the air. Her hands were folded behind her head providing a makeshift pillow. It was obvious she needed protection against the hard lumber of the deck so he turned and walked to the boathouse.

Inside was a large air mattress he used as a float. After inflating it with an electric pump, Owen carried it down to the dock. By then Gloria had gotten up and taken a seat on a bench. He placed the cushion at the water's edge, and with a slight motion of his head invited her to join him. She did.

Sex was different with Gloria. A tight embrace meant to heighten intensity was muted as her skin slid across her frame. The firmness of her breasts and ass had long since waned, but were still pleasurable to the touch. Nothing about her was novel. Encounters with women had always possessed a breezy, fresh quality. Although he struggled with his enthusiasm for her, somehow he found the experience curiously erotic.

Much to his relief the night passed quickly.

Owen awoke to the sound of boat motors rumbling. The sun was high in the sky, and on the mattress next to him laid Gloria. They were both still naked. He was overcome with an extraordinary sense of self conscience. For a man who had spent most of his life not caring what people thought of him, he worried his neighbors would not appreciate that he and his date were lying naked on his dock for everyone to see.

He rolled over, laid on his side propped up on his right elbow and looked down at her. The woman he saw before him was not as attractive as he remembered. For a brief moment he considered making a dash for the house. He would then bring her clothes to her. Owen pondered the lesser of two evils; leaving her alone, briefly, or making her run to the house for all to see. His decision was based on which action appeared more chivalrous.

Sensing that no one was watching he ran toward the house, alone. As he passed the pool his path was diverted into the the guest house where he kept a change of clothes before remembering he had to go to the main house and retrieve Gloria's clothes. So, he darted out of the smaller room. As he closed the sliding glass door behind him, Owen heard a man's voice coming from somewhere down the canal, "Woo hoo!" His brief hesitation had exposed him.

After donning a pair of shorts and a t-shirt he picked up his date's clothes from the floor in the living room, and calmly made his way to her. When he approached he saw that she was awake and sitting up. Her legs were tucked tightly against her body with her arms wrapped around them. Owen sat next to her. He handed her the clothes.

"Thank you," she said, as she took her garments from him.

"I debated whether or not to wake you."

"I appreciate that."

"Did I wake you up?"

"No, the man who hollered at you did."

"Sorry. I tried to get into the house as quickly as I could, but I guess it wasn't quickly enough."

"I know," she replied, reassuringly.

His developing curiosity for what life meant drove him. Intimacy with Gloria was sadly mistaken for a meaningful connection. "Can I ask you a personal question?"

"Of course," she said, as she lifted her butt off the dock resting on her feet and shoulder blades while pulling her skirt over her hips.

"What is it that you want out of life?"

"Hmm," she thought aloud. "Well, I enjoyed last night. So, I'd have to say to continue to get as much enjoyment out of life as I can before I die."

"What about your husband?"

"What about him?"

"Do you ever feel guilty that you cheat on him?"

"Not at all."

"Why not?"

"He's more focused on his work than he is me. I leave him to develop the next great cure for cancer, and he leaves me to my devices."

"Does he know what you do when you come down here?"

"I think he does."

"How?"

"Because I talk about how much fun it is in the Keys and I talk about how much partying I do, and I tell

him he is never welcome to come down here with me."
Owen laughed softly as he shook his head incredulously. "*What*?"

"So you're trying to drive the man crazy?"

"What do I care how he feels? If he's not man enough to accept the woman I am, he's free to leave any time."

He ignored her question. "So, he knows what you do with your spare time. What does he do with his?"

"He coaches little league baseball, and we don't even have any kids in the league. There is no other connection he has with those kids other than wanting to coach them. Isn't that *pathetic*?" Pangs of guilt echoed through his body like sonar. It became obvious to him that he was party to loathsome behavior. Gloria read the concern on his face. "What's the matter, hun?" she asked with an excessively condescending tone.

"You perplex me. Apparently you have the *Man of The Year* for a husband and yet you treat him like dirt. And, to top it off, you're a frigging psychologist. I would think that you of all people would be overly sensitive to the intricacies of human interaction."

Gloria stood and began to walk away. She stopped and glanced at him over her shoulder. "Look, sweetie, if it's not you nailing me it'll be someone else."

Owen watched her walk to the house and as she vanished through the sliding glass door. He realized that if Monica had shown up the night before he never would have met Gloria. The woman he considered his friend had become more than that. It was new to him, but no less obvious. In Gloria he saw a decaying shell of the woman she had once been. There was only one way for him to avoid suffering from the reversal of roles that would expose the mortal nature of his existence. Only by killing his ribald outlook could he ever hope to escape his flesh starved bonds. One night spent with his aging sexual partner provided the opportunity to finally understand that although he was free of commitment he was no less guilty than those with whom he chose to associate.

Chapter Twenty

His body ached like never before as Owen ran down the shoulder of A1A. He pushed himself harder than in the past. Sweat oozing from his pores carried years of toxins, both physical and emotional, and he wanted them gone. No matter how desperately he inhaled, he could not seem to satiate the need for oxygen his lungs demanded. Coral and crushed shell ground beneath his shoes with each step. His sunglasses did not adequately protect his eyes from the sun's rays. He squinted behind them to filter out the glare. Nothing prevented him from veering off course and onto the highway several times. Each time he overcorrected toward the farthest edge of the shoulder. Sweat dripped into his eyes and stung. He wiped away perspiration by removing his glasses and rubbing his face on his shirtsleeve. Futility seemed to be the only product of his effort.

Several times Owen thought he heard the hum of oversized tires on the highway behind him, but a vehicle matching the vision he conjured never passed. Curiously, he glanced over his left shoulder and saw a brightly painted yellow Jeep. A black Bimini-top was stretched between the top of the windshield and the roll-bar. The front glass was awash in sunlight and appeared more like a mirror than a window. He had no idea who it could be. He feared Agent Melendez was making a move against his treasure.

His legs burned as he pushed harder. The slightest incline was met with determination to speed his pace rather than as an opportunity to succumb to the weakness that inhabited his psyche. When there was only a mile left Owen tasted bile as it bubbled into his throat. He turned once again. The Jeep was no longer behind him. He breathed easier until it occurred to him to turn all the way around and run backward. Only then could he see the vehicle on the shoulder of the road. Who drove it was indiscernible. Brashness overtook him and he motioned with a wave of his left arm for the person to follow as he turned and ran. They obliged by accelerating and closing the gap between them.

When the familiar opening in the Mangroves became visible Owen picked up his pace. No matter the outcome of this encounter, he was determined to show no weakness. An innate strength of character he never knew existed drove him.

Owen reached the break in the shrubs and darted between them without removing his shoes. He sloshed through the water and made his way toward the driftwood where he spent many mornings contemplating life. Once there, he dropped down behind the log and waited for his adversary to appear in the breach. While he peered over the log he gently ran his hands through the sandy bottom looking for a weapon he could use against this person. It was not a sharp piece of coral or a jagged conch shell he wanted, but a specific implement. A man-made weapon had been wedged between the ocean floor and the piece of wood after someone took a shot at him. The tips of his fingers tingled as they brushed across the familiar shape. A smile brightened his face as he pulled it to the surface. He gripped the handle with his right hand and the sheath with his left. Owen then slid the stainless-steel knife out of its case. Its blade was eight inches long and glistened in the sunlight. He placed the case in a notch in the driftwood and held the dagger down near his hip, out of sight.

He heard the crush of gravel on the road's shoulder as the Jeep came to a stop outside the entry to his sanctuary. He watched the opening intently without blinking for fear he may miss a glimpse of his pursuer. The bushes shook as whomever it was grabbed branches for leverage. *This asshole is too sloppy*, Owen thought. *It'll cost him dearly*.

A figure appeared in the space between the limbs. It was difficult for him to get a good look at the person as he laid low behind the log, not wanting to give away his position. Suddenly, he heard a splash in the water. There was no movement for what seemed like an entire minute. Owen's heart began to pound. He worried his strength was no match for the eventuality of death he faced. He took deep breaths to calm his nerves and get used to the idea of what he had to do to survive. Slowly, he rose just enough to see a familiar figure wading toward him. The stream of urine that left his body warmed the water around him and evidenced his relief.

"I should not have taken my shoes off," Monica yelled toward him. "These fucking rocks are killing my feet."

He waved her over as he stood and then plopped onto the log. "There is a sandy bottom over here," he called out.

She slogged through the water, holding her shoes and socks above the surface. When she reached the log she sat down to his right, placing her shoes to her left. She pulled her feet up one at a time and rubbed away the pain.

"Why did you follow me here?" he asked.

"I was going to your house when I saw you running out of your neighborhood, so I followed you."

"Couldn't you have pulled up next to me and said something?"

She shook her head. "I didn't want to interrupt your workout."

Sarcastically, Owen replied, "*Thanks, a lot.*"

Monica noticed the knife in his hand. "Is that for me?"

"If you weren't you, then yes."

She shook her head as she looked out over the green and blue waters of the Atlantic Ocean. "One of these days you're going to tell me why you're so paranoid."

"Why were you coming to my house?"

"No other reason than to visit."

He plunged the knife into the log to his left, and stared out over the water as she looked at him. She searched for an indication of relief in his face, but not until he violently thrust the knife into the wood did she understand just how scared he was. Restlessness emanated from her friend and she grew to understand its deep seeded nature. Her attraction was not physical, but she knew she was willing to do anything to help him.

"As I watched you run I could see how you pushed yourself."

Owen nodded.

"You don't see that kind of determination from most people," she added.

He looked at her and smiled. She returned the gesture.

"I can tell that deep down you really *do* care." Monica desperately wanted him to open up to her.

"Care about what?"

"Yourself."

"And?"

"That's the first step to being happy with who you are."

"You think I'm not happy?"

"I think you're avoiding something. I don't know what it is ... *commitment*, maybe."

"Commitment to what?"

"A woman?" Owen said nothing and she continued. "No matter how brashly you conduct yourself, you're obviously steadfastly determined to make your life better."

He thought about the night spent with Gloria. Everything wrong in his life entered his consciousness; Agent Melendez, the Bahamian pirates, and the potential loss of his livelihood.

Monica knew exactly what needed to be done, but was unsure of just how to go about getting Owen to open up his mind to an existence that was so foreign to him. Never had he been able to trust and he was not trustworthy. She searched her mind for the one thing that would give him the personal enrichment he deserved; then it came to her. She slung her left leg over the log and faced him, "Do you remember the night you asked me if I had ever been with a man?"

"Uh-huh." His response was muted for fear she would hold his lack of discretion against him.

"The next night I sat at home, drank four bottles of wine and cried myself to sleep on my sofa. The only reason I awoke the next day was because the sun's heat radiated through my window and baked the side of my face. You forced me to re-live the most traumatic experience of my life, over and over that night."

"I … I'm sorry!"

Monica smiled. "Actually, it was the best thing that's ever happened to me, and I should thank you for opening that door into my psyche. I realized my outlook on life was colored by that one incident, and I alone allowed it to happen. The men who set out to control my sexuality … my physical being, ended up controlling me from that moment forward. When I introduced wine into the equation death became a welcome alternative. But once I had retreated so deeply into myself that my body no longer functioned I was forced to grab onto my own soul for mere survival. There I found the person who knew how to fight for *everything* I want out of life. No longer would those assholes influence me into being something other than who I am. I'm sure that's why I didn't tell you I was a lesbian the night we met. People's reactions have prevented me from expressing myself for too long. No more."

Owen had no idea how to respond, other than a simple, "You're welcome."

She chuckled. "You've given me my life back. That is more valuable than any department store gift."

"So, now what?"

"I am going to repay you whether you want it or not."

"How?"

"The way I see it, you and I have a lot in common. We both have a great deal of scar tissue covering … even burying our souls so deeply we've lost touch with them."

Owen smiled. "And you're going to help me get in touch with mine?"

"Are you skeptical?"

He hesitated briefly. "Uh … yeah, I am."

"You're so jaded you don't even know how to recognize the person within you that would make the most difficult choice for the right reason. I do, and I see it in you."

"So, what's the most difficult choice, and the right reason?"

"Death and someone you'd rather not live without, but for whom you'd make the ultimate sacrifice for their happiness. It's the most selfless act imaginable."

He shook his head. "I'm definitely not there, and I doubt I ever will be."

"Just come by my house tonight at eight o'clock."

"What's going to happen at eight o'clock?"

"Something you will enjoy." She smiled at her friend. "It will revolve around the physical desires you embrace."

For a man who enjoyed the company of women, hearing her utter innuendo frightened him. He had no idea how to react. Monica was one of the most beautiful women he had ever known and just looking at her piqued carnal urges within him. He had finally gotten past, and learned to control them. *Now she wants to make love!* He thought. "How do you suppose we accomplish the self actualization of Owen Taylor?"

"Just come to my house at eight o'clock tonight."

Owen smiled, "You can bet your ass I'll be there."

Chapter Twenty-One

His afternoon was filled with anticipation. Owen had not been nervous about a date since the first time he took Sara to the Dairy Queen to share a chili-dog and hot fudge sundae. He kept telling himself there was no way she would let him make love to her. Each time he convinced himself of that, primal urges took over. Desire welled inside him until it became palpable. In his imagination the smell of her hair was fruity and her skin was soft to the touch as he ran his hand down her flank and over her hip. He salivated at the thought of satiating his desire for her. Wrapped tightly together and holding each other as they lay side-by-side, he rubbed the arch of his right foot inside hers. It was soft and tender, or so he imagined.

Then it occurred to him she may be interested in a prolonged relationship. Maybe she needed to clear the air once and for all that she was not a lesbian. He had not bargained for that, and it would have been too much for him to handle. His emotions oscillated and he considered not showing up. Rationality was the victim of his arrogance.

Nervousness churned his stomach as he focused on the pleasure of making love to Monica. She would be like no other woman he had known. Memories of women he experienced during his life were examined in order to give her a night she would remember forever. Somehow he began to believe what he was feeling was love, an emotion he had very little experience with and never recognized. Everything a man could possibly desire in a woman she had, but most importantly she wanted to be there for him. He found it comforting.

Joy gave way to revenge as he wished Sara were there to witness his happiness. Owen had become a millionaire through self determination and a fierce independence, and it was in spite of her. Pleasure was driven by anger, but he did not recognize how deeply it was seeded within him. Surface emotions were the only ones he felt. Mere recognition of what motivated his actions provided the impetus to change his life.

Melancholy blanketed his outlook as he wondered if he was the kind of man who could be true to Monica. After Sara there had never been any reason to worry about such drivel, but as he thought about his family he realized he was not cut from a tightly woven cloth. His soul was threadbare and weak. *How can someone so filled with fear possess character?* He had not gone back to the shipwreck since his encounter with the Bahamian pirates. Instead, he had thrown himself into the other half of his life; drinking and cavorting. He was disgusted with what had become of his life and once again thought of canceling the date.

The undulations of his emotional state peaked once again as he thought about how he had stood up to Agent Melendez, not allowing himself to be bullied. Owen could think of no better way to rid himself of the man other than leaving Key West without a trace. If he and Monica were about to get serious there was no way he could risk losing her like he had Julia. His psyche sank once again as he realized that maybe he should cancel their date. A trip to the guest house to check on the bag of coins stashed in the intake would satiate his craving for tangible proof of his worth.

When he entered the pool house he did as he always had; went straight to the kitchen drawer that held

the screwdriver. He then walked to the grate and removed it; slowly unscrewing the screws and thinking to
himself, *one day I will get an electric screwdriver*.

Once he removed the cover he looked at the
duffle bag. It was flat and obviously empty. A wry smile
crossed his face. No longer would he worry about dis-
posing of his treasure. Owen reached into the vent,
grabbed the bag and slid it toward him. He unzipped
and pulled it open using both hands. The smile on his
face grew as he peered inside. Barely filling the bag
were twenty six bundles of one hundred dollar bills
bound by currency straps. On each was printed,
$10,000, and through them all a line had been drawn.
Handwritten below was, *$9,000*. The person who acted
as Owen's fence cared enough to bundle the money in
increments that would not raise suspicion at the bank.
Worry that his riches would draw attention was justified
the day Agent Melendez arrived at his doorstep. It appeared the game of chicken between the two would
come down to which one would flinch first.

When the time came to get ready for his date,
Owen took great care in deciding how to present himself. After a shower he dressed in front of a full-length
mirror, and chose a well-pressed pair of shorts and a
lavender polo shirt. His primping came to an end as he
slid his Rolex over his hand, onto his wrist, and folded
its clasp together. The need to show Monica he had
enough money to take care of her for the rest of her life
was important. His watch was the most subtle way of
communicating that fact.

Owen stopped what he was doing and posed in
front of the mirror. For the first time ever he saw that
the skin on his throat sagged. He slapped it with the

back of his right hand hoping to bring it taught. Sensually, he made eye contact with his reflection.

When he arrived, Owen stood outside Monica's house for several moments before pressing the doorbell. Anticipation welled in his stomach as he waited anxiously. He listened for any sign of movement and impending entry.

Once he pressed the bell the door opened without any apparent aid. Nothing could be seen between it and the frame. He placed his hand on its handle and pushed it open gently. Standing four feet away from the entrance stood Monica. She was dressed in a pair of old, faded jeans that had large, thread-tattered holes in both legs; exposing her brown thighs. She wore a sheer white top that failed to conceal the fact she was not wearing a bra. Owen said nothing as he stepped slowly over the threshold and moved toward her. Just before he reached her, Monica turned and walked away. Calmly, he changed direction and moved toward the sofa where he sat with his legs crossed.

"Would you like something to drink?" she called from the kitchen.

Owen did not wish to have alcohol numb his experience. "Water, please."

She emerged from the kitchen holding a large glass of white wine in her right hand and a tall glass of ice water in her left. When she reached the sofa she handed the water to him without saying a word, and sat at the opposite end of the couch.

After sipping from her glass Monica placed it on the coffee table. They leaned against the sofa's arms and faced each other. At first all either could manage was a grin. Owen resisted the urge to examine the artwork that was her body. He appreciated how beautiful she was, and noticed her strap-laden high heels and that her toe nails were neatly manicured. It was obvious she had taken great care to look fantastic. He thought about how close he had come to not showing up. *What a fool I would have been.*

"There's really no reason for us to do this boy-girl dance," she announced.

"What's that supposed to mean?"

"I told you that I was going to give you the tools necessary to heighten every sexual experience you'll have for the rest of your life."

Owen furrowed his brow. He did not remember her saying that, but it sounded good to him. "I thought you said that you were going to bridge the gap between sex and being a self actualized person."

She nodded her head in a conciliatory manner. "Okay, but I still meant what I just said."

"Sounds good to me," Owen said, sliding across the sofa, toward her.

She leaned over and lifted her glass from the coffee table in order to stop his progress. His desire ached within him, so he reached out and caressed her thigh. She sipped from her wine. He looked deeply into her brown eyes and wanted her to look deeply into his soul. She placed her glass back onto the table and looked caringly into his eyes. "We are going to do this my way if you don't mind." She sensed the effect she was having on her friend. "There is something in you that I've never seen in any man."

Owen smiled.

She continued. "That's the only reason that I am about to do what it is that I am about to do."

Words escaped him. Monica stood and walked toward her bedroom. When she got to the door she turned and motioned for him to follow; which he did, eagerly. When he entered he saw a queen size bed with its headboard positioned angularly in the corner. On it was a large knitted blanket with two large red squares and two black ones. The similarly colored shapes were arranged in opposite corners.

"Red or black?" she asked.

Owen was not sure what she was asking, but he answered her anyway. "As Stump would say, 'always bet on black.'"

She walked over to the bed and before sitting down asked, "Do you want the head of the bed or the foot?"

"Foot," he replied, with a bit of trepidation.

Dutifully, she sat on the black square near the headboard, and pointed to the black one opposite hers. Without a word he crawled onto the bed as she folded her legs and sat in a Yogic meditation position. "You can't move into my black square and I can't move into yours. The red squares are open game, but you can't occupy the one I'm in."

While she established the rules, Owen's mind went berserk as he tried to figure out how they were supposed to make love without touching each other. "How are we supposed to make love?" he finally asked.

Monica grinned. She had not known before that moment how she would break the news to him. "We're not going to make love."

His heart sank. The ache and desire to touch Monica and hold her in his arms slowly waned. "So what are we supposed to do here? Play chess? I'm not going to be your pawn."

"Oh, you'll thank me after the night is over."

"So, what *is* going to happen tonight?"

Monica chose her words carefully. She did not want to lead him on any further. It had been necessary to do so, because his emotions needed to be raw for her to accomplish her goal. "You can do anything you want. You can ask me to do anything you want me to do, but we cannot touch each other. I can ask you whatever question I want to ask and you have to answer me honestly. Likewise, you can ask me any question you want and I have to answer you honestly."

"I may be getting the cart before the horse, but what am I supposed to get out of this little exercise?"

She smiled. "I believe that humans, as individuals, are not complete unless they have that special someone in their lives. We have a need, a desire, to experience something that is not of our flesh; something spiritual. The catch is that we have to relinquish control of our bodies to allow the spiritual to enter our consciousness. Once it does it becomes much easier to live as a being that understands the value of those around us." She looked into her friend's eyes. "Make sense?"

"Right up until the part where we don't make love."

"What part of 'I'm a lesbian,' don't you understand?"

"The part that got me over here under the guise that it was a date."

She pointed at him. "And that's exactly why I did it. You think that all dates have to end with sex. You have that part down, and I'm sure you're good at it, but I'm going to teach what it means to be a true friend. Only when you have a true understanding of what your woman wants and desires can you be the forever love for which you yearn."

"Forever love? That's not something that I've ever desired."

"And there's your first lie. You cannot lie to your forever lover. That will ruin *everything*."

"Okay, so who is my forever lover?"

Without hesitation Monica answered, "Julia." When he did not respond, she added, "I see the look in your eyes when you talk about her. I think that is one of the reasons that you are so special. Not many men would admit they never made love to a woman they desired so much, and lost."

For the first time he saw himself possessing the same trait he admired in Asa and Lorraine's relationship with their spouses. Denying the feeling Owen nonchalantly reached down with his right hand and undid the clasp on his Rolex, removed it, and leaned over and placed it on the bedside table. "I'm not in the square without your permission, am I?" he asked, sarcastically.

"As long as I'm not in the square you're okay."

He finished what he was doing and returned to his black square. "So, what would you like me to do to get this party started?"

"I'm not real sure," she admitted.

Astonished, Owen asked, "You thought about this extravagant scenario with you and I on the same bed, without touching each other, and you haven't thought about your first request of me?"

She furrowed her brow. "I kinda guess I thought you would be the first to make a request."

"If you want me to, I will."

"Go ahead."

"Take off all your clothes," he challenged, expecting her to balk at his request.

Without a word, she swung her legs off the bed and planted her feet firmly on the floor with her back toward Owen. Slowly, she removed her top. Once it was off she dropped it onto the floor beside the bed, and proceeded to remove her jeans. She was the only woman he had ever seen who was more beautiful in her natural state than when clothed. When she turned and resumed her position on the bed he began to unbutton his shirt. "No! I didn't ask you to do that."

"Don't you want me to?"

She shook her head incredulously. "What part of …"

Owen finished her sentence. " … 'I'm a lesbian don't you understand.' I know. I know." Regardless, the view of her nude body caused many emotions to thrive within him. Her flawless skin begged to be touched and her breasts felt firm and tender in the caverns of his mind. The more he imagined them together the harder it became to refrain. He had no idea what she wanted to accomplish, but was willing to play along.

For forty-five minutes the two sat, mostly silent. An occasional smattering of conversation concerning something altogether trivial filled the void. Owen spent most of the time staring over the headboard and through the window at the palm tree outside swaying in the cool island breeze. It was the only way to combat growing mad with desire. Monica sensed she was losing him and knew he was thinking of something other than developing a connection between them. "Don't you want a love that will fulfill your needs for a lifetime?"

"That'll never happen," he answered.

"Why not?"

"That kind of love is not out there."

"You don't think so?"

"No."

She furrowed her brow. "You don't think it's possible that a man and a woman can love each other unconditionally for the rest of their lives?"

Owen thought carefully. "I'm sure there are couples who can do it, but it's just not in the cards for me."

"Why not?" She desperately wanted to draw out the demons deep within his psyche. Only then could he slay the beast that grew within him.

Owen's posture sank. He felt the darkness of his depression taking over. The thought of getting up and walking out grew until he had one foot planted firmly on the floor. That's when he looked into Monica's eyes and saw something. Walking out was what he had always done, and she deserved more. Instead of leaving he paced about the room with his hands clasped behind his back. Unpleasant memories filled his mind; many of which were so trivial they were not worth mentioning. That was until he realized they were together because he valued her opinion. Once he composed himself he returned to the bed. "I've had three people in my life who I would consider best friends."

"Do you keep in touch with them?"

The smile that crossed his face was filled with melancholy. "That would be impossible." He could not bring himself to mention the circumstances of why they were no longer a part of his life.

"Why is that impossible? Have you gotten into arguments with them?"

It pained him to say the word, but he did. "Suicide." As the word escaped his breath an overwhelming sense of relief blanketed him. Only then did he realize he had never faced any of their demise.

Such a tragic tale was not one Monica had anticipated, but she knew he needed to understand how all of his experiences made up the man he was. "Will you tell me about your friends?"

"William and I grew up together. Our mothers were friends and we were born two months apart. When my mother was killed his mom became a surrogate for me. She couldn't afford it, but she scraped together enough money to buy me a new pair of jeans whenever I needed them." Owen stopped. "I think that's the first time I remember realizing how important money was to survival."

"So, what you got out of your relationship was that you never wanted to be poor, right?"

Owen nodded his agreement with her assessment. "I'm sure that's why Bobby was always angry. He never had any financial stability, and took it out on Jenny."

She said nothing. He would have to come to the realization on his own that it was not money that William's mother had given. It was a piece of herself.

They lay side-by-side for several minutes ignoring the rules of the game. His other two friends, and the circumstances surrounding their lives and deaths were not discussed. Instead, Owen thought about his treasure and how it had alleviated all of his problems. With the great sense of being he felt, his question was puffed with benevolence. "What about you?"

"What about *me*?"

"Are there any burdens you need to shed?"

Monica lay silently staring at the ceiling, thinking about his question. In her twenty-eight years there had been many disappointments, but none that she considered monumental enough to share. "I can't think of anything other than your average, everyday life lessons that sting."

"Tell me what it's like to have a family who cares."

"Cares about what?"

"Cares enough about your well-being that they don't attempt to extort your self-esteem."

The smile that grew on Monica's face was filled with warmth. She stared at the ceiling. "That's the one thing I cherish about my relationship with my parents; I can go to them and say whatever is on my mind, and I *know* the advice they give me is in my best interest. It's always been like that between us." She rolled her head over on her pillow and faced him. "What is it that you wish you could change about your relationship with your family?"

Without hesitation, he answered, "I wish that my parents had not been killed and that I had them with me today."

"What about your ... adoptive parents?"

He took a deep breath and exhaled. "The most valuable lesson they taught me was that when things go wrong the best thing to do is run." He thought of how he had left Julia so abruptly. Monica did too. She knew he had more to say, and allowed him to do so when he was ready. "My father's anger was so passionate that the least little thing set him off. There was this one time, when I was eight years old; I was sitting on our sofa eating a piece of toast with peanut butter and jelly on it. My sister came and sat down beside me. She started crawling all over me and I dropped the toast. It landed gooey side down on the couch. Bobby was sitting in his favorite chair across the room and saw the whole thing happen. He got up, and as he walked across the room unbuckled his belt. He yanked me up by the arm and held me so that my feet weren't touching the floor. With his other hand he pulled his belt off." Owen shuddered at the memory, "I can still hear the sound of that belt slapping against his waist as it was being pulled through each of his belt-loops. He beat me mercilessly. It was so bad that I spun as I dangled from his grip. He hit me pretty much everywhere from my knees to my stomach."

"That's awful." Monica quivered, as she vividly imagined each strike upon his flesh.

"And that was just one time. That was what I had to deal with growing up."

"You don't strike me as a violent person."

Owen rolled his head over and looked at her. "Thank you. I've tried not to perpetuate that family tradition."

"I think you've done a good job."

He returned his gaze to the ceiling above. "I do worry that if I ever find myself in a situation that I *need* to be violent I won't be able to because my passion for life has been beaten out of me. I'll probably end up dead because of it."

"There's nothing wrong with walking away."

"I know, but what will happen when I won't be able to walk away?"

Monica did not have an answer for her friend, but she was curious how all of his experiences had affected him collectively; which she summed up with one simple question. "When was the last time you felt truly loved?"

He knew the answer immediately, but hesitated in order to downplay the importance of a memory he embraced in detail in his conscious mind. "I'm not sure how old I was, but I can remember tossing a baseball with my dad before he died. So, I must have been four or five years old. It was late and we started in a park. As it grew dark we moved under a lighted gazebo. I could sense that he didn't want our time together to end. I've never had anyone else convey that feeling to me." It was the only time he shared the story he held dear and recalled daily. Owen felt like he never had before. It was a sensation that he was no longer alone. He knew he could count on his friend. Owen rolled his head over again. When he did, she did the same. They looked into one another's eyes and he reached over and gently stroked her cheek with his thumb. There was not a word that needed to be spoken. His simple gesture communicated how much she meant to him. For the first time in his life he was able to do so without ulterior motives. His feelings for her were so genuine that he was totally oblivious to the fact that one of the most beautiful women he had ever known lay naked beside him.

Chapter Twenty-Two

The next morning Owen awoke to find he was lying askew on Monica's bed. She was nowhere in sight. He sat up and shook away the cobwebs associated with a good night's sleep; something he had not experienced in quite a while.

Placing his feet firmly on the hardwood floor beneath him he stood as erect as his body would allow. He held his arms above his head and stretched mightily until he felt his bones crack and his muscles twinge. Once he was done he dropped his arms and they gently slapped his hips.

When he opened the bedroom door the pleasant smell of coffee wafted inside. Saliva filled his mouth as he inhaled the aroma. He shuffled into the hallway and realized that Monica had removed his shoes and socks. It brought a smile to his face to know that she cared enough to make him comfortable. When he got to the kitchen he found her busily preparing breakfast. She wore a pair of shorts that had a silhouette of a mermaid stitched onto the bottom. He leaned against the door frame and watched her. She looked at him, smiled, and continued her task without saying a word.

Whatever facades that were once between them had been destroyed and made him feel like a totally different person. Never had Owen realized the power of honesty, but it made perfect sense to him. *Not until someone knows you completely can they trust you completely*, he thought. That fact may have been known by every other person on earth, and being the last to know did not make him any less grateful for the information.

Without a word he walked to the dining room table. Monica had placed the morning paper on it, which Owen picked up and spread flat on its surface. Slowly he turned the pages, searching each headline until one garnered his attention. It was a story about Mel Fisher's Museum. The thought of his shipwreck and the circumstances that surrounded it normally would have caused him great angst. Instead, he thought about the wonderful secret he kept, and how he had someone with whom to share it.

Owen quickly flipped through the pages searching out the marine forecast. He read the prediction for the following days. Conditions were perfect for a trip on the boat that day. Then he recalled Monica's hesitation to dive. *She did really well at the Dry Tortugas.* Still looking down at the paper, he called into the kitchen for Monica. "Would you like to take another trip out on the boat today?"

"That sounds nice. How long will we be gone?"

"I have a special place that I'd like to show you, and we won't be back until late tonight."

"Cool! Sounds like fun."

Not until her response did he realize the depth of her trust in him. He picked up a pen that was lying on the table and wrote the G.P.S. coordinates on the front page of the newspaper. Never had he written down or communicated them to anyone other than the voice in his head with whom he carried on numerous conversations throughout the years. Trusting Monica felt natural. He folded the newspaper to a quarter its size with the numbers exposed, and nervously he slapped it against his leg as he walked into the kitchen.

Monica looked up and smiled at him, again. An unequivocally serious look flashed across his face. "What's the matter?"

"Don't ever recycle this paper," he said as he held it up for her to see. Owen pointed to the coordinates. "This is where I am going to take you today. It is a place that holds quite a treasure."

Monica banged the spatula she held against the side of the pan and placed it on the counter. She wiped her hands on a dishtowel as she walked toward him. Her gaze dropped to the numbers on the page and then back to her friend. They looked into each other's eyes and connected with the soul that each felt responsible. She knew he was serious about what he told her. The information answered her questions about how he was able to maintain his lifestyle. "That's where we are going today?"

Owen nodded. "We won't be back until after dark. It will take quite a while for us to get there."

"Or, we could spend the night on the boat again," Monica suggested.

"Yeah, that would be nice." Owen's thoughts were not of pleasurable experiences, but the opportunity it would provide them to make a second dive the next day; and the additional treasure they could retrieve. "We are going to make a dive of about a hundred feet. Are you okay with that?"

Monica backed away and returned to the stove, and the eggs that required her attention. Hesitantly, she answered, "I guess so, if you think I can make a dive like that, I trust you."

"I *know* you can," he reassured her, as he closed the gap between them. She looked up from the skillet into his eyes. In them she saw reassurance. Gently, he reached out and stroked her cheek. His touch was no longer meant to withdraw physical pleasure without of-

fering anything to fill the void created by self-indul-
gence. Its purpose was to instill trust and connect the
energy of two living beings with the intent of enhancing
a bond that would continue to grow.

Chapter Twenty-Three

After breakfast they drove to Owen's house. He felt like a kid excited to share his secret fort with a new friend. Monica's anticipation was built upon tattered nerves. She tried to liken one hundred feet to something she encountered in daily life. Owen sensed her nervousness and explained everything she needed to know to make a dive like that; and the necessity of a ten foot stop. And, as she had done before, Monica asked intelligent questions. Giddiness escalated within him the closer they got to his house.

It took less than an hour to prepare the boat and gather necessary provisions. Owen switched on the motor while Monica stowed supplies below deck. Exhaust gurgled in the brackish water.

Habitually, Owen reached toward the throttle to grab the St. Christopher necklace Julia had given him. His heart sank when he realized it was no longer there. Ritualistically, he kissed it for luck each time he set out for the wreck. He shook away his disappointment and laughed at his superstitious nature before bumping the throttle with the heel of his hand; engaging the motor in reverse. Slowly, the boat moved into the channel. When it was clear of the dock, he reversed speed and moved past homes that lined the canal before heading into the gulf.

He navigated the waters around the Keys speedily and recklessly without concern for who might take note of his boat and its seemingly urgent path into the open ocean. The long ride offered the opportunity to once again think about how he left Julia. Opportunities lost had driven him to vow that when another presented itself it would not be squandered. Sharing his secret with Monica was meant to fill that void.

The boat skipped across the waves and Monica's nerves became fatigued. She worried about her ability to make such a difficult dive without professional training. Life for her had been a struggle against a homeland she loved and missed. The horizon she stared at had an endless and eternal quality that represented a great deal of uncertainty. She wondered whether or not she could see the actual spot on the globe that was their destination, or did it lay beyond her perspective. "What awaits us out there?" she asked, pointing in front of the boat.

Owen smiled. "A treasure that will make life worth living for us both."

She nodded her approval, and then asked a more ethereal question. "What do you think awaits us after death?"

Owen shifted his gaze sharply from the ocean that lay ahead to his friend. "Why are you so gloomy today?"

She shrugged her shoulders. "No reason. We have a long way to go and it's definitely a worthwhile subject … among friends."

He returned his attention to the waves that effortlessly tossed the boat. "I've never really been a big believer in Valhalla, if that's what you're asking."

"I'm not sure what you mean."

He took a deep breath and exhaled. "I guess what I'm trying to say is that I don't believe that to get into heaven, if there is one, that it's conditional on the accomplishments of one's human self. The vision of my

God is one that loves all and forgives all, which is something we have not been able to do."

"*We?*"

"Humans," he answered. "We do everything in our power to segregate each other into neat little categories in order to define the kind of person we think they are. It doesn't matter the kind of person *we* are." He stopped and looked at Monica. His glance was met with a curious look. "Take Ivy, for example. He spends much of his day denigrating everyone he meets without the same credentials he possesses."

"And, your point?"

"My point is that somewhere, buried deep inside him is a truly good person, and when he dies I choose to believe that my God will accept him regardless of the many he has refused to acknowledge. That good person will survive forever among all others."

"I like your sentiment," she hesitated, "but I must say that I find it odd coming from you."

"Why?"

"Because … as un-accepting as Ivy can be, you are equally accepting … of other men's wives into your bed. That makes you a hypocrite, in my book."

Owen nodded. "I understand."

"*And?*" she insisted.

Owen throttled down the boat until it simply drifted aimlessly in the water. He swiveled around in his chair and faced his friend. "I've thought a lot about that. Before last night my response would have been that if it wasn't me it would be someone else, so I might as well enjoy the pleasure of their infidelity. You opened up a lot of old wounds for me, and that has allowed me to see things more clearly than I ever have before." He paused. "Not until recently have I come to understand that I suffer from depression. I'm not sure if it's caused by being beaten into an emotional fetal position by the only father I ever knew or if it's how my brain is hard-wired."

Monica interjected, "They have medication for that."

Owen shook his head. "I can't do that."

"Why not?"

"There have been suicides linked to anti-depressants."

"But that is such a small percentage of people who use them."

"One is too many. Besides that, if I were on anti-depressants now, I would not have the benefit of clarity you've brought to my life. I'm afraid it would have masked the breakthrough I had last night as a result of our conversation."

"Which is?"

"After we talked last night, I lay awake for quite a while thinking about my life." Owen held both hands to his chest. "I now realize that because of my depression I am attracted to gregarious types because they provide a balance for me. They are the court jesters in the halls of the dark, dank castle that is my mind. I've had three friends who committed suicide. They were all very outgoing, yet volatile people. I can remember being inebriated most of the times we were together ... and if we were all four together, man!" Owen's tone shifted from that of an excited discovery to a more somber one. "It's not that I don't love them, because I do, and I miss them terribly. I wish I could tell them what I now understand. It may have helped save their lives." A tear rolled over Owen's lower eye lid and down his cheek. He quickly wiped it away with his thumb. "I thank God that you were able to be the kind of person that I was incapable of being for my friends."

Monica was stunned. "That's the greatest compliment I've ever been given."

"Good, because I was afraid I'd never be able to show you how much you mean to me," he said, as he shoved the throttle forward once again, engaging the boat's motor and propelling them forward. He maneuvered it left and then right as he read the G.P.S. coordinates attempting to get the boat back onto the course that would take them to his shipwreck.

Nearly two hours later, Owen throttled down the motor in the exact spot he needed to drop the bow anchor. Hurriedly, he stood in his chair and stepped one foot onto the dashboard as he launched his weight forward over the windshield. Quickly he walked to the anchor-locker, opened it, grabbed the anchor and tossed it overboard. He gave it time to sink to the ocean's floor; watching the anchor line disappear over the bow. When it stopped moving he tied it to the cleat before carefully making his way back over the glass and into his seat. He engaged the engines in reverse and slowly backed the boat. When the line became taut he shut down the engine and looked at the GPS. Ocean currents kept the boat hovering over the wreck.

When Owen removed his shirt and began to put on his wetsuit he asked Monica one last time, "Are you sure you're ready to make this dive?" She nodded. It was obvious she was nervous. Her curiosity provided the drive to perform such a dangerous task. Treasure had a way of distorting vigilance. "When we get to the bottom I want you to look for a mesh bag. It'll probably be buried under a foot or two of sand, but I'll show you where to look."

She nodded. Her arms and legs felt numb as she put on the wetsuit he had given her to wear. When she was finished he helped with her buoyancy control device and tank. Monica breathed through the regulator and found the air to be cold. Chills ran down her spine.

Once she was suited and ready to go Owen put on the rest of his equipment. This was the first time in over a year he made a dive of significant depth with a partner. It felt good and his excitement could hardly be contained. He gave a *both thumbs up* signal and they moved to the diving platform. Owen went into the water first so that he would be there to help if she needed it. He held a nylon rope that was tied to one of the aft cleats. It would secure the mesh bag. There was no way he would allow it to be left behind, again.

Owen held Monica's hand as they descended into the darkness. He made the trip as slowly as he could for her benefit, but knew they needed to be quick about their business. When the white sands of the ocean floor came into view of their flashlights, a moray eel quickly slithered into an exposed hole in the hull of the ship that protruded from the bottom. Owen quickly surveyed the territory and pulled on his friend's hand, guiding her to the spot where he wanted her to look for the bag. He knew she must be terrified, so he stopped and looked into her eyes. She appeared relatively calm, but he asked her anyway if she was okay by pointing to her and then giving the *okay* sign by encircling his thumb and forefinger. She nodded and he breathed a little easier.

The spot where she needed to search was communicated by making digging motions with his hands above the area. Once she began, Owen swam away to look in another spot.

Monica waved her hand gently over the ocean floor generating a small current to move the sand and create a crater. Her approach led to murkier water and diminished sight. With every breath she became more uncomfortable, bordering on claustrophobia. When the sense of urgency became too great she stopped brushing away the sand and plunged her hands into the ocean floor. She desperately wanted to surface.

While digging she frantically looked around for Owen. He was nowhere to be seen. *Surely he would not leave me alone down here*, she thought. Her breathing became quick and short, but she was not deterred from the task at hand. She dug deeper and deeper, while moving her hands away from the center of her search. Disappointing Owen was not something she would allow to happen.

Monica plucked her left hand from the sand and held the gauge that dangled from her buoyancy control device. She had been under water for over thirteen minutes and knew time was short. Just as she began to feel like a failure something brushed past her pinky. Fear kept her from grabbing it outright. Slowly she slid her fingers over what felt like a piece of metal. She maintained contact, but dug vigorously into the sand until she was able to wrap her fingers around whatever it was. Tugging mightily did nothing to budge her find.

Suddenly, a tap on her shoulder frightened her. Monica rolled over onto her back and saw Owen. He held out his hands, palms up, questioning the luck with her search. When her fright dissipated she realized she had not let go of her find. Relief overcame her. She took Owen's hand and forced it into the sand next to hers. He dug as she had until he felt what he knew to be his mesh bag. The smile on his face grew so wide it caused the mask's seal to break away from his face. Cool ocean water rushed in before he had a chance with his free hand to secure it once again.

He pulled with all of his might. The bag was heavy and buried in the sand. It wiggled slightly, but he persisted and it began to slide toward him. Monica tapped him on the shoulder. She motioned to her wrist that they were running out of time. He nodded by quickly bobbing his head. Frustrated, he acknowledged the obvious. Monica pointed to the ocean floor vigorously and waved it away. She wanted to leave the bag, but Owen would have none of it. He shook his head forcefully. There was no way he would leave it again.

Owen pointed toward the nylon rope that was swaying in the current a few yards away. He wanted her to retrieve it, and she did. Without loosening his grip he removed his fins. He then sank his feet into the sand on either side of the treasure. When he had done so, he reached down with his free hand, secured both to the handle and pulled using every ounce of leverage he could muster. To his astonishment the bag slid out of the sand relatively easily.

Monica handed him the loose end of the rope and he tied it to the handle, making so many knots upon knots that there was no way it would come loose when they pulled it to the surface. Once he finished, Owen took a deep breath and pushed it out through his regulator. The mass of bubbles rose toward the surface and the two exchanged smiles filled with satisfaction. She could not resist reaching down and holding the bag in her hands, massaging the coins between her fingers. Owen reached down and grabbed her left hand. When she looked at him he pointed toward the surface with his thumb. She nodded, let go of the bag, and the two began to swim toward the boat.

The journey away from the depths was joyous. Monica was no longer scared and the satisfaction Owen felt was palpable. Dutifully, he watched the instruments that hung from his equipment to make sure they were not ascending too quickly in their fervor to get to the boat. A couple of times they looked at one another and grinned uncontrollably.

Owen's elation quickly shifted to worry as they neared the surface. There were two boat hulls hovering on the surface of the water. Monica had not noticed it and he questioned whether he should alarm her. He did nothing until they got to the ten-foot stop. They drifted at the depth while Owen tried to develop a plan to get on the boat safely. The pirates would not leave before murdering all witnesses.

Thoughts raced through his mind until his concentration was broken when he saw the bag of coins ascending toward the boat. When it passed the couple Monica saw it too. She quickly looked at Owen and then toward the surface. There she saw the two boats. He saw the panic in her eyes before she began to swim quickly toward the surface. There was no other choice. He followed her.

When he reached the dive platform he took off his mask, tossed it over the side, and wiped away the saltwater from his eyes. He saw three Bahamians; one of whom held Monica by the arms from behind. His mask had landed at the feet of another man, who held a rifle with its butt against his hip and the barrel pointed skyward. Owen unbuckled his vest and allowed it to slide off his shoulders, sinking to the depths below. He knew that if he had any chance of saving his friend he had to be free of all encumbrances.

Reluctantly, Owen climbed into the boat. One of the men grabbed him and shoved him toward the helm. On the deck at the third man's feet was his bag of coins. The apparent leader, the man with the rifle, saw that Owen was looking at what he considered his find.

"Nice bag of coins, huh?"

Owen acknowledged begrudgingly with a nod, and looked at Monica. There was a peace he sensed about her. Maybe she was simply relieved to breathe through her nose. Regardless, her demeanor had a calming effect on him, until he realized she might be in cahoots with the pirates. She appeared too calm. He was so nervous that it felt as though his legs would collapse beneath him at any moment.

"Take the wetsuit off the girl, mon," the leader of the gang instructed the man who held Monica by the arms. "She might bring quite a price in the black market."

Black Market, Owen thought. *They really are going overboard trying to make it look like they aren't all in this together*. He looked into the faces of each of the men. None of them looked the least bit familiar to him. The two underlings wore side arms that were holstered and locked down with a leather strap. Appearing to be the most immediate threat was the leader. He had scars on his face that seemed to physically manifest a psyche that was equally damaged. He was jittery and sweat streamed down his face. The man paced back-and-forth in the small space between the boat's stern and its helm, much like a caged lion contemplating his next move to ensure survival. Owen saw that his finger held the rifle's trigger in a manner that was much too precarious for him to try to disarm the man. He looked once more at Monica. There was no way he could rely on her, and for his own safety had to count her as one of the bad guys. *She will be taken out last*, he thought.

The man holding Monica was wispy, yet wiry enough to present a threat to anyone who crossed him. She was spun around by her arms so that she faced him. He smiled at her through rotten teeth that were brown like his skin. She turned away in disgust. The leader sat on the edge of the boat and watched as his compadre unzipped the wetsuit she wore. When the zipper was just below her navel the man grabbed its open collar and pulled it over her shoulders and down to her waist. She stood helpless with nothing but a stringy bikini top to offer protection from physical and emotional abuse.

It became apparent to Owen by the men's lustful stares they had never seen her before. Each of them was drawn in to her beauty and Owen saw his opportunity to strike while their minds entertained fantasies. Slowly, he slid his right foot backward to plant it at the juncture of the deck and the wall. He planned to spring toward the leader and disarm him before he had a chance to lower the barrel of his gun.

Just before making his move, the leader hopped off the edge of the boat and announced, "There will be time for that later. We need to get rid of the man," he said as he lowered his gun and pointed it at his intended victim. When he turned to face Owen something caught his eye. "What's that, mon?" the man pointed toward his dive belt. His hand shook and his manner was edgy. Something silver captured his attention.

Owen looked down. Hanging over the belt was the St. Christopher pendant that Julia had given him. Rather than spend time below gathering Spanish Pieces of Eight, Owen wanted to find the charm he had always used to guide him safely in his travels.

"I threw that overboard the last time I was on your boat." The man walked toward Owen, reaching for it. Instinctively, Owen reached down and grabbed the necklace and held it tightly to his waist. The man lowered his gun and pressed it into Owen's chest, pushing him backward and letting him know who was in charge. Owen held the charm tighter as rage grew within him. He thought about how Bobby made him grovel for the most basic of necessities, and how Jenny never came to his rescue. Living on the fringe for so long had colored his outlook on life and he realized that, with Monica's help, life was not disposable. A week earlier he would have faced death and accepted it. The instinct to survive had never been stronger. He *knew* there was something greater that awaited him. What that was, he had no idea, but the desire to seek out experiences beyond the physical overcame him with a fury.

He lunged and grabbed the barrel of the leader's rifle, then tried desperately to yank it from the man's hands. His grip was too tight. A chill ran down Owen's spine as he realized he had provoked the man and was unable to disarm him. Determination to fight until the very end cloaked him like a shield. Owen pushed the barrel of the gun skyward as he bull-rushed him.

The thug who held Monica at bay stepped back, planted his foot on the deck of the boat and lunged into her with a punch across her left cheek. She quickly collapsed onto the deck. Owen pushed the leader against the edge of the boat and had an advantage as the man leaned backward precariously over the water. He turned and saw the man who hit Monica kicking her ribs repeatedly. Owen pulled the rifle and the leader back into the boat. He had given up his advantage to try his best to take aim and shoot the pirate who was killing the only true friend he had ever known. The two men struggled mightily with the rifle, Owen desperately tried to hold a steady aim, and the leader tried with equal determination to disrupt him. Just as Owen felt he had a bead on the man, he felt a crushing blow to the back of his head. Desperation caused him to squeeze the trigger. The sound of the rifle reverberated across the water as Owen fell to the deck. He heard the leader yelling at one of his underlings. "You kill her. Take the damn gun out of its holster and shoot her right between the eyes."

Through blurred vision Owen saw the silhouette of a man walking toward him and holding the rifle across his body. He knew he had to rush the man again. It was his only chance. He gathered his feet under him and acted a bit more dazed than he actually was in hopes of not exacerbating the man's edginess. Just as he lunged at the man with every ounce of energy left in his body, Owen heard the distinctive click of the gun's firing mechanism. His momentum shoved the man backward and over the side of the boat with ease. The man let go of the rifle as he waved his arms in the air trying desperately to regain his balance as he fell overboard.

Somewhat astounded at his good fortune, Owen stood at the edge of the boat holding the rifle. Before he had a chance to gather himself, he realized that the man who was ordered to kill Monica was moving toward him. He held an aluminum gaff and raised it high over his head, then swung it swiftly downward, toward Owen. Pain radiated through Owen's extremities as he held his left arm up to absorb the force of the blow. Instinctively, he drew his arm into his body to protect it from further damage. The rifle fell to the deck between the two men.

The pirate looked at the bent gaff he held in his hand and tossed it overboard. He drew his gun from its holster and took aim at Owen. Monica struggled mightily against the pain of broken ribs and a crushed jaw as she pivoted on her side in order to swing her legs around and trip the man. He fell, but held onto the gun. While he gathered himself, Owen reached for the rifle and pointed it at the man. He refused to fire it, shaking his head as he stared intently at the man imploring him not to fire his weapon. "Jump over the side of the boat and you can live."

Without a word the man scurried to his feet and did just that. Owen and Monica were relieved to witness his acquiescence. He stood, holding his arm tightly to his stomach, and walked backward reaching for the captain's chair as he watched Monica closely. When he felt the chair behind him he spun it on its pedestal and sat so that he faced the rear of the boat where she lay.

"Are you okay," he asked.

She shook her head. "I can't breathe," Monica replied, in a shallow voice and through clinched teeth.

"I think my ribs are broken and I'm sure my jaw is too."

Owen had forgotten about the third pirate, but realized he must have hit him when he pulled the rifle's trigger. While the thought of having killed someone seeped into his psyche, Owen saw the hands of the pirate leader grabbing the side of the boat as he tried to pull himself aboard. He stood and walked slowly to where the man was; held the rifle firmly against his ribs with his good hand and pointed it at his head. It was obvious the man was filled with evil, and the only thing the other two were guilty of was not having an adequate spine. He mourned the one man he had been forced to kill, but this was not a man. If he did not shoot him Owen was certain that the man would live to terrorize others. A great sense of satisfaction came over him as he pulled the trigger and watched blood explode from the man's forehead. He walked to the edge and watched as the pirate's lifeless body sank into the water. Owen threw the rifle in behind him, and thought about how he might see him again if he ever came back to the wreck. He looked at his arm and could tell it was broken. It would be quite a while before he came back, if ever.

"Hey, Mon," a voice called. Owen walked to the stern of the boat. He saw the second man treading water. He asked, "Can I get in my boat now?"

"Wait until we're gone!" Owen barked.

"Mon, can you leave now, *please*? My arms are getting tired."

Owen smiled, nodded and then walked back to the helm, stopping to pick up a machete. Quickly he hopped on top of the bow and cut away the anchor rope. The boat drifted while he walked cautiously back toward the controls. Once there he stopped and removed the Saint Christopher medal from his belt and hung it around the throttle lever. In one swift motion, he turned the ignition key and shoved the throttle forward sending the boat bouncing on top of the late afternoon ocean waves toward the nearest hospital on Stock Island.

Monica was silent the entire trip. Her skin became pale and clammy. He worried several times that she had died. Remorse was an emotion he never understood, but he knew that he was responsible for her, and if she died he would never be able to forgive himself. Only then did he realize his animalistic rage had given way to an unyielding passion like he had never known. Guilt overcame him as he realized the contempt he held for those who chose a life based upon greed could be employed when describing him. Voracity for possessions that merely held physical value could no longer be ignored. He would have gladly traded his life for all that it provided, but when his avarice nearly killed Monica he understood their relationship meant more to him. Desires that were once carnal and mortal became spiritual and eternal.

Chapter Twenty-Four

For weeks Owen stayed by Monica's side as she lay in a hospital bed. The blow to her face had broken her cheekbone, and she had two broken ribs. Owen's left arm bore a cast that stretched from his hand over his elbow and midway up his bicep. Lasting physical effects were not expected, but his emotional strength had never been more formidable.

At first, whenever Monica's parents came to the hospital, they looked upon him with a jaundiced eye. They blamed him for what happened to their daughter, and he did too. On the fourth day when the couple walked through the door and saw him and his disheveled appearance, they realized he had been by their daughter's side the entire time. It became apparent that was more than could be said of them.

Each time Monica stirred Owen rushed to her side to make sure she had everything she needed. Without hesitation she assured him what happened was not his fault. Time progressed and he gave of himself like he never had before. Being responsible to her brought more satisfaction than he had ever experienced. His epiphany could not be ignored. When he questioned Monica's loyalty, death became acceptable. Complete trust between them took on a life of its own. It was something that needed nurturing and effort, but its significant potential for growth proved intoxicating. Their relationship was the first he was certain would continue to grow. She would be in his heart forever.

When they arrived at the hospital Owen had given a statement to the police. Monica was in no condition to do so. Several facts were omitted from his story, including the existence of the shipwreck and the death of two of the men who attacked them. He assured the officers the men would run back to the Bahamas and not venture near that part of the ocean for a long time; a place several nautical miles from where they had actually been attacked.

Every time the two spoke as she lay in bed he reminded her that there was no wreck and no one died as a result of the assault. She resigned herself to smiling through teeth that were wired shut.

It had become the custom for him to sit silently and allow her parents to speak in their native tongue when they were there. During their first visit he offered to leave the room so they could have privacy. Monica insisted he stay. After her mother's realization of how much Owen cared for their daughter she made her wishes known with a forceful, "*Sientate!*" He had no problem translating her command and returned immediately to his cot.

Stump, Ivy and Asa all came to visit. Visitors that Owen did not know showed up from time-to-time. They were mostly women who smelled of patchouli; none of whom paid him much attention.

On his last day spent with her in the hospital he sat at the edge of his cot trying to shake away the grogginess of a fitful night's sleep. Owen was tired of hospital food and for the first time thought of leaving so that he could get a decent meal. His cast kept his arm permanently bent, and he wanted desperately to feel the freedom of straightening it.

The sound of the door opening startled him. He looked up expecting to see the doctor or one of the nurses. Monica rolled her head over on her pillow to see her mother coming through the doorway. Blanca smiled at her daughter as she walked toward Owen. She held a large brown paper grocery bag, which she reached into and removed a quilt. Its pattern was colorful and distinctly Spanish.

"¡*Hice este edredón sobre todo para usted*!," she told Owen as she handed it to him.

He took the blanket from her and looked at Monica, hoping she would translate. Through clinched teeth she pushed out each word in order to annunciate. "She made it," Monica drew in a breath, "especially for you."

Owen's throat became tight and a chill ran down his spine. No one had ever shown him such personal gratitude. He tried to thank Blanca, but the tears that flowed from his moistening eyes made that impossible. Senora saw that he was deeply touched, which brought a smile to her face. She reached out, patted his shoulder and then walked to Monica's bedside. Owen held up the quilt and admired it as the two women carried on a conversation in Spanish. Her mother did most of the talking.

After Blanca left the overwhelming urge to talk to Monica about what she meant to him welled within Owen. He needed to develop the ability to communicate in a personal manner and he had rehearsed what he would say several times. He watched while she finished her dinner, which consisted of yogurt through a straw and something pureed.

Owen stood and walked to her bedside. She smiled at him and he returned the gesture. He grabbed the railing on the bed with his right hand and held it tightly. Her smile disappeared and a look of concern replaced it. He shook his head. "There's no reason to be concerned." She smiled her acknowledgment, and relief. He continued. "You asked me the night we were at Hemingway's house what was it I was looking for in a relationship, and I gave you some lame answer. To be honest, I don't even remember what it was. What I do remember was the disappointment I felt from you. That hurt, because I had no desire then and will never wish for you to think less of me." Monica reached up, grabbed his hand and squeezed. Without allowing her gesture to deter saying what he had on his mind, Owen continued. "There was a girl I knew in high school." He smiled. "The funny thing is, she had the same name as you."

In an attempt to lighten to mood, Monica pushed the word, "Rojas?" through her wired teeth.

Owen laughed. "She was one of the most beautiful girls I've ever seen, she knew exactly what she wanted from life at a very early age. I think that scared me."

"Why?" Monica asked.

"Because one of the things she wanted was me." He gathered himself before continuing. "I knew there was no way I could live up to her standards. She would have expected that I go to college and graduate and get a job where I could wear a buttoned-down collar and a pin-striped suit. That's just not me."

"So why are you thinking about her now?"

"Because she was the one person I knew at such a young age that had it all together. It's taken me until now to realize that. Monica knew it at sixteen. Instead, I have relegated myself to the job of relationship garbage man. I pick up the broken pieces and salvage whatever I need from them and toss them into a greater trash heap.

A lot of people would say that I did what I did on the boat because I was able to tap into the anger that I carry around within me. I *am* angry at my parents for dying while robbing a bank. I'm angry at Bobby for treating me the way he did. I'm angry that Jenny never had the guts to stand up to him. But, I know deep in my heart I did what I did because I love you more than life itself."

Monica strained to return the sentiment. "I love you, too!"

"I owe it all to you, because it feels damn good to have someone in my life that I care so much about."

"So, what about my question?"

Without hesitation he answered, "I want a woman who is as passionate about our relationship as I am. I want someone who will hold me to the same standard you have. I want someone who I can be completely honest with and she will know that she can be honest with me knowing I won't be judgmental, only supportive. I know that if I can find a woman that special, the energy around us will swirl and bind us together for eternity."

Monica squeezed his hand again and did not release the pressure for several minutes. For a brief moment she wished she could be that woman. But she knew they could never be together. Sadly, the odds were stacked against them, and they knew it.

The deep emotional connection between them was broken when the door opened. Neither looked up, assuming it was someone who regularly stopped by to check on Monica.

"Well, isn't this sweet," a man's voice said. They both looked up and saw Agent Melendez walking into the room wearing a wide grin on his face. He walked over to where Owen stood, grabbed his arms and pulled them around behind him. The agent bound his right wrist to the cast on his other hand with a zip-tie and proudly proclaimed, "You may have fooled the locals, but I know exactly what happened out on the ocean. I've got the bodies to prove it."

While leading Owen out of the room Agent Melendez looked over at Monica and said, "I hope you feel better."

She never felt more helpless.

Chapter Twenty-Five

Owen settled into the car ready for the long ride to Miami. The agent took a left onto A1A, driving toward the nearest FBI field office. He still did not understand why the agency was interested in a shipwreck. Two Bahamians killed in international waters might fall within their jurisdiction. Feverishly he looked for a way to escape his predicament, like a cat in a cage. The door handles had been removed; his hands were secured behind his back; and Agent Melendez had a nine-millimeter pistol holstered on his belt.

Looking out over the green-blue water of the ocean he wondered if he would ever see that landscape again. A great deal of remorse came over him for killing those two men, but he knew he acted in self-defense. Surely Monica would testify on his behalf, as would her mother and father.

Giving up on any realistic chance of escape Owen slouched, dropping his head onto the seat. Peering through the window he saw power-poles that lined the highway and an occasional palm tree pass into and out of his vision. Quickly he slid up in his seat when he recognized a grouping of trees as the car headed north. His suspicions were confirmed as the car passed in front of his neighborhood. He looked at the gates and immediately craved the security they provided; staring into the subdivision until the car went over the Barracuda Channel Bridge. The vehicle climbed over its summit and Owen looked back through the rear window and searched the coastline for his home. He found the waterway just before catching a glimpse of it just inside the mouth of the canal. Once the house was out of sight he slid back down in the seat and closed his eyes. He could not bear to face what lay ahead.

Nearly an hour later Owen felt the car turn, leaving the smooth asphalt road in favor of a sandy, uneven surface. He wrestled against his weight in order to sit up. Once he had righted himself Owen looked around and saw nothing but a sea of palmetto bushes, with an occasional scrub-oak rising above abundant palm fans. The trunks of trees were twisted and gnarled, appearing as though their growth had been inhibited by repeated hurricanes. He turned and peered through the rear window and saw nothing but the white dust that had been thrown into the air as the car traveled speedily down the road.

Scooting toward the front seat he looked through the windshield. In the distance the road met the beautiful blue-green waters of the gulf and continued parallel to the shoreline from there. His eyes traced what he thought would be their path. Peering over the low-lying shrubbery his eyes fell on what appeared to be an old boathouse. It was dilapidated and situated at the end of a dock that was in need of repair. Owen fell back into his seat. He knew it! This man was not an FBI agent, but someone who wanted to steal his treasure. The only person who could have ratted him out was his fence; a man who he trusted for years.

"So, what's your real name?" Owen asked from the back-seat.

The man looked at him through the rear view mirror. "Luca Antonelli."

Great! It's the friggin' mob. I'll never be seen alive again, he thought. "Why did you use your real name around town, and not keep up your FBI front?"

The man laughed. "That was stupid of me," was the only explanation he offered.

"Hey, Friend," Owen hoped that by being cordial the man would grant his wish. "Can you do me a favor?" The man looked at him in the mirror again, and he continued. "After you kill me, do you think you can shove a Spanish Piece of Eight in my eye socket so that it won't easily come out?" It was the only way he knew to communicate his ultimate demise to Monica; if his body was ever recovered.

The man laughed and said nothing. Owen thought there may have been a nod in his expression. He desired closure for Monica.

Owen's heart pounded through his chest as the car came to a stop at the boathouse. Luca got out of the car and moved toward the rear door. He opened it and Owen slid to the other side. Luca laughed heartily. It was apparent the hit-man enjoyed this part of his job. He tried to tap into the rage he had weeks earlier, but the confinement of the sedan did not allow for him to gather any momentum. Luca leaned into the doorway and Owen thrust his legs outward as quickly as he could, delivering a blow that sent his captor tumbling backwards onto the sand. He stood and gathered himself before walking back toward the car.

"I am about to stop being so nice," the man announced. He reached in and grabbed Owen by the leg, then dragged his captive out of the car and dropped him onto the road. "It doesn't feel too good now does it?" He then proceeded to pick Owen up by the collar and drag him across the dusty road, down the length of the dock and into the boathouse.

An oily fifty-five gallon barrel sat in one corner with a length of chain hanging over a rafter above it. The structure appeared unable to withstand his weight. He began to plot his escape. It would be easy for him to jump into the water among the confusion of the collapsing building. He looked for a place of refuge once he escaped. It all seemed too risky. "Don't you want to know where the shipwreck is?" Owen asked.

The man shook his head and smiled as he dragged a stool by hooking one of its legs with his right foot. Once he had it positioned in front of Owen, he reached over and grabbed his shoulder and sat his captive firmly onto it. "I want to know … what you know … about the patriarch of your family."

"He's the biggest asshole I've ever met," he replied.

The man punched Owen in the face. Blood trickled from his nose. "What the hell was that for?" he asked, just before realizing that Luca was talking about his great-uncle. "Oh, you mean the uncle that died in World War II, right?"

"He did not die in the war."

A burst of laughter through his nose sprayed bloody snot over his mouth. "Okay, whatever you say. All I know is that to my family he is dead. You may know he is alive and dealing in stolen artifacts, but I don't." The man slapped Owen across the head. "*Jesus*, would you stop with that? You're the one who told me the man is a criminal."

"In Italy family is everything. Don't talk about your uncle like that."

Owen rolled his eyes and looked away. He became more confused and had no idea how to react. "Of all the hit men in the world, I had to get the one with a strong sense of scruples," Owen blurted out, sarcastically. "I don't suppose you'd consider me a member of your family for a day and let me go, would you?"

"*Ti vuole conoscera.*" The man told Owen in his native tongue that he was not there to hurt him. His sadistic nature enjoyed watching his captive squirm and wriggle. He gambled on the fact that Owen's knowledge of the Italian language was rudimentary at best.

"Huh?"

The man smiled. With confirmation of Owen's inability to speak the language he confessed everything … in Italian. "*E stato preso in prigiona duranta laguerra dei fasciti.*"

Owen couldn't help but laugh. "Whenever you want to have a discussion in English let me know." He stood and walked over to the open end of the boathouse that overlooked the gulf. For a moment he thought about jumping into the water, but sensed the man was not going to kill him.

Luca continued; speaking toward Owen's back. "*Quando era liberato, e rimasto in Italia.*" When the words left the man's mouth he saw Owen's shoulders slump in frustration. Luca's sensibility overcame him. He walked toward his captive and removed a knife from his pocket. He unfolded it, exposing the blade. Luca reached out, cut the zip-tie, and placed his hand on Owen's shoulder. Gently he turned him around and the two men faced each other. Luca confessed, "Your uncle did not die during the war. He was held prisoner by the fascist regime. When we lost the war your uncle was set free. He decided to live out his days in Italy."

A chill rattled Owen's body and he walked slowly toward the stool. He sat down again and placed his head in his hands. "How does he know about me?" Owen asked, as he stared at the floor of the boathouse.

"When you were in Florence several years ago word came that an American was looking for the final resting place of a relative that had been killed in the war."

"Why didn't he come get me then?"

"He was not sure you were one of *his* relatives." Luca took a couple of steps toward Owen. He spoke in a reassuring tone. "I promise you that from the day he learned of your presence in Florence he had his avvocati working on finding you and making sure the two of you were related."

"What does he want from me?"

"He'd like to meet you," Luca answered incredulously. "Wasn't that the purpose of your trip to Firenza?"

Owen nodded. "Yeah, I guess I was trying to connect with the only family I ever romanticized about. I've been looking for answers all of my life."

"Now you can have them."

Owen sat contemplating everything he had been through since this man introduced himself as Agent Melendez. It was enough to turn a man's stomach and make him want to puke. "What was all this Agent Melendez crap?"

A sheepish look grew onto Luca's face. "I'm sorry about all that. But, you see, I've never been to Key West, and your uncle works us pretty hard on the olive plantation. When I got the opportunity to come looking for you I wanted to make a vacation of it."

"Why weren't you honest with me?"

"Because if I had been up front with you, you would have wanted to leave right away to meet your uncle, and I would have had to go with you. Besides, I had to make life in Key West uncomfortable for you."

"Not necessarily," Owen responded.

Luca laughed. "Tell me, do you feel like catching the first flight to Italy right now?"

Owen laughed too, and nodded his head; until he thought of Monica. It was the first time in his life he had someone to consider when making such a monumental decision. The depth of their relationship was supported by the realization that if Luca had not played his juvenile game of cat-and-mouse they never would have met. "Why all the drama in the hospital room? You didn't have to put that damned zip-tie on me."

Luca's mood turned solemn. "Your uncle is an elderly man. He has been without his American family for most of his life … for nearly sixty years. He would not tell you this, because your uncle would never be so pretentious to make a decision like that for one of his children, Italian or American, but he secretly wishes that once you get to Italy, you'll never leave. It was my job to give the appearance that you had left Key West for good without disclosing why."

"Why would anyone care if I moved to Italy?"

"Having seen some of the people you associate with, no one would. However, your uncle is a private man and does not wish to have any other relatives become aware of his life in Firenza." Luca sensed that Owen was unsure of this newfound family. "I can assure you that you have many cousins who are anxious to meet you."

For a man who had never counted on the warmth of a family, the revelation Luca presented made him almost giddy with anticipation. "Where do you fit into the picture?" Owen's question did not translate well, and he saw confusion in Luca's eyes. "Are you a relative?"

"Ah, yes. I am a nephew by marriage. Your aunt … your uncle's wife is my mother's sister."

Owen sat silently and tried to wrap his mind around all of the changes in his life. In an effort to give him time to think, Luca walked to the end of the dock and gazed out over the water. None of his experiences prepared him for the revelation of a large family filled with people looking forward to meeting him. His existence had been one of distancing himself from his past in order to avoid its dogmatic sway. Monica's influence helped him view the opportunity to meet the man he was named for with optimism. Elation was replaced by melancholy when he realized he would have to leave behind the only person to whom he was bound emotionally for a tenuous connection that was only defined physically.

Chapter Twenty-Six

Owen drove Luca to Miami to catch his flight to Italy, and assured him the message he would soon follow was one that could be delivered with confidence. He watched his Italian cousin board the plane and yelled to him that as soon as he got the cast removed they had a date to settle their score. The Italian laughed and waved away the threat as he disappeared down the jet-way.

The doctors told Monica it would take at least six more weeks for her ribs to heal. When he got back to Key West, Owen drove straight to the hospital and had her discharged. He resolved to do whatever was needed for her to convalesce at his house. What originally had been guilt became honor.

Traveling to Italy became a less attractive proposition as he and Monica grew ever closer. No one there needed him. Staying in Key West meant he could be there for her. He knew she would never allow anyone to be accountable for her, yet he had a strong desire to be responsible to her.

Many tasks were required to allow her to navigate around the house in her wheelchair; all of which were expeditiously completed.

Weeks passed without any discussion of the trip Owen promised Luca and his great uncle would be taken. Several times the thought of taking Monica crossed his mind, but knew she belonged with her family. His life as a loner was one he embraced, but found himself facing the reality of relatives in a far away country. Desire to know them grew concurrently with his affection for Monica.

After a couple of weeks Monica developed the strength to propel herself in her wheelchair. It hurt Owen to know she was weaning herself of the need to have him around. One afternoon he walked into the den and found her sitting next to the sliding glass doors; staring out over the canal. He walked over, stood next to her and looked in the same direction. There was nothing unusual outside and he realized she was in a far-away place. Just before he turned to walk away, she asked, "So what happened to that bag of coins we fished off the bottom of the ocean?" without removing her fixated stare.

Owen smiled. "I honestly don't know. I haven't thought about that in weeks."

"Where was it the last time you saw it?"

He pointed toward the boat that hung from its lift. On the day he hurried Monica to the hospital, he had taken the time to attach the lift's hooks to the cleats and tightened them just enough so the boat would not drift away. Not until he returned from his adventure with cousin Luca did Owen raise the boat to a normal height. "The last time I saw the coins they were on the deck of that boat, lying next to your mangled body."

"Do you think they're still there?" He reached down and grabbed the handle on the sliding glass door, pulled it open, and stood aside. She wheeled over the track, onto the deck, and made her way around the pool toward the lift. Owen walked into the guest house and turned on the electricity. He joined his friend at the boat, reached up and grabbed the lift's switch and turned it to the *down* position. They waited patiently while the vessel slowly descended. Once it was low enough Owen stood on his toes and looked over its edge. No discernable reaction drove Monica to the point of exasperation. She slapped him on the leg. "Come on, asshole. Are they there or not?"

He remained calm, looked down at her and smiled. "They're there." Owen climbed inside the vessel as it moved lower, grabbed the bag with both hands and tossed it onto the ground next to his friend. Once he crawled out of the boat and turned the winch off, he reached down and hoisted the bag. The two moved back into the house. Monica wheeled herself over the threshold and stopped in front of the coffee table where Owen placed their treasure.

"What are you going to do with all that?" she asked.

"Do you want it?" When Monica did not respond, he offered it again. "You can have it *all* if you want it."

She sat silently thinking of everything she could do with the money. Thoughts intoxicated her. She could afford to bring her aunt from Venezuela. That would make her mother very happy. Sobriety quashed her fiscal inebriation. "How do you turn all of this into cash?" she asked, as she waved her hand over the coins.

"I have a man who takes care of that for me." Owen smiled as he recalled accusing him of divulging their secret.

"What are you smiling about?"

"Nothing," he responded, still smiling and shaking his head.

"How much do you think is here?" she asked.

Owen squinted his eyes and looked at the coins. "I'd say about three million dollars, maybe more."

"Imagine the things you could do with that much money."

He nodded. "What do you plan to do with it?"

Monica shook her head. "I can't take this money. It's not mine."

He pointed to her ribs. "You've earned it more than I have," he said, as he held up his cast.

She shook her head again. "I know what you're trying to do. You're trying to absolve yourself of any responsibility for this treasure."

"And I thought I was trying to do something nice for the only true friend I've ever known," he responded, sarcastically.

"Hey!" Monica exclaimed. "You never did tell me what happened with you and that FBI agent? And don't think of avoiding the subject this time."

Owen rolled his head back avoiding the glancing blow of her question. It was a subject he did not want to broach with her, yet. "He let me go."

"*What*?"

"It was a case of mistaken identity."

Monica looked skeptically at her friend. "What is it?"

"What is what?"

"Ah-hah! Whenever you answer a question with a question that means you're hiding something. I've known you long enough to know that."

Owen plopped himself onto the sofa, sat forward and looked his friend squarely in the eye. "Back in nineteen forty-three my great uncle was shot down in the Mediterranean while fighting during World War II. He is the man I was named after. His body was never recovered. A few years ago when I went to Italy to connect with that part of my heritage ..."

"How were you going to connect if they never found his body? Did you suspect he was buried somewhere over there?"

"No. It was more like a pilgrimage for me. There's always been something inside me that knew there was more to life than what I had been brought up to accept and I always thought my great uncle was the key to that discovery." Frustrated by the sound of his words, Owen blurted out, "I'm not really sure what I was trying to accomplish."

Monica shook her head in disagreement. "I think I understand exactly why you went and I would have done the same thing myself. That's when you met Julia, right?"

He nodded. "Through the miracle of the internet I was able to make contact with a man who flew in the Army Air Corps with Uncle Owen. He gave me the exact coordinates of where his plane went down. I rented a boat for a day and went to the spot and prayed to him and asked for the strength to be the man I need to be ... that I know I can be."

"What has that got to do with the FBI agent?"

"As it turns out, there is a reason they never found my uncle's body." He tilted his head portraying disbelief. "It turns out he's still alive."

"*No way!*"

"Way! And that FBI agent is actually a cousin of mine who was sent by my uncle to get me to come to Florence."

For someone who had a keenly developed skill to appear as though nothing fazed her, the revelation

Owen would be leaving felt like a punch in the gut to Monica. Her first instinct was to ask if she could go, but before the words came from her mouth she knew that was not possible. "Are you going to go?"

"I'm thinking about it."

She fixated her eyes on the coins. If she made eye contact with Owen she knew she would begin to cry. Suddenly the analgesic effect of the joy she shared with him left her body and the pain in her ribs and jaw returned. She slumped in her chair under the weight of her disappointment. Owen recognized the melancholy through the black-and-blue traces on her face. His psyche sank with hers and they sat silently, depressed at the realization their relationship might have reached its conclusion. Finally, he confessed his need. "I have never felt like I was a part of a family until I met you and your folks." Her head was slung low against her chest as she sat in her wheelchair. "Now that I know I have a family I *have* to go and at least get to know them."

Monica nodded. "I know. I was the one who took on the task of reforming your ribald ways. I just didn't count on becoming attached to you the way I have."

"You make me sound like a puppy."

She lifted her head and looked at him. "You know what I mean." He nodded, and she continued. "It's just that there is something between us that is intangible and I don't know how to describe it."

"Hope," Owen responded. "I've never felt about anyone the way I do you." He thought about the questions he had on the boat, and knew that they were caused by never having known anyone he could trust. Those doubts about Monica had nothing to do with her.

"I may have had my doubts at times, but that was because of *me*."

She nodded. "Trust is an overused word, but I agree with you. We should come up with a word of our own to describe it."

"How about invigorating?" Owen asked. "Every time I am around you I feel as refreshed as the first time I saw you. It's almost like there is this self-sustaining energy around us that will never wane." The joy in his voice was quickly tempered by the realization, again, that this relationship was doomed. He worried he may have said too much. "Do you feel the same way?"

"Yes," she said, as a huge grin grew on her face.

"What?" Owen asked.

"I just realized that I know the exact moment that my trust in you was complete."

"When was that?"

"When I took off all my clothes in front of you." They both laughed. "I was so afraid you would jump my bones."

"Why did you do it?"

"Because I knew that was the only way I could make my point with you. The only way you would able to ever look at me as more than a sexual object was to force you to see me as just that, while having a meaningful conversation."

"It worked, because I haven't thought about having sex with you since that night."

"Good!"

The two sat silently contemplating their lives together. Finally, Owen had to say what was on his mind. "The one thing I'm having a hard time getting over is that it is so good between us, but now it has to end. It just isn't fair."

"I know, but your family in Italy can give you something I can't."

"What?"

"They can give you a future and help restore your past." The profound nature of Monica's statement helped him understand that he needed to approach his trip with enthusiasm. After a few seconds she slapped her hand on the arm of her wheelchair. "I've got it." She pointed to coins on the table in front of them. "We can take that and give someone a future."

"Great! Who do we help?"

She sank in her chair. "I don't know."

"Someone deserving, and someone who won't squander the opportunity."

"Agreed … and it has to be anonymous. That way there will never be any uncomfortable feelings."

Owen furrowed his brow. "That's a pretty tall order. Where are we gonna find someone who fits all of those characteristics?"

Moments later Monica raised her head and looked at her friend. "It doesn't have to be one person. It can be several, right?"

He looked at all of the money that lay on the table, pursed his lips and drew the corners of his mouth downward. "Sure."

Without hesitation, she added. "Who are the people you have the most respect for?"

"Other than you?"

"Other than me."

He thought briefly. The answer was obvious. "I'd have to say that my friends at Mallory Square are some of the most genuine, unpretentious people I know … Winston, Saphron, Dutch, and Jack."

The smile on her face grew. "Exactly! Just think what a million dollars would mean to each of them?"

"How do we give away that much money without them knowing where it came from?"

Monica pointed to the bag on the table. "We split these coins into equal portions and drop them in their change buckets while they're performing."

Sadly, Owen conceded, "That won't work … unless they have someone who is willing to buy them. And even then, they won't get market value for them."

"Okay," not to be deterred, she countered, "You convert these to cash and we get cashier's checks from the bank, put them in envelopes and drop them in their change buckets."

"Why don't we anonymously open bank accounts for them? Aren't you afraid someone will steal the checks from them?"

"Not at all. Besides that, I want to see the looks on their faces when they open the envelopes."

"So much for anonymity."

"We can do it!"

At that moment money ceased to provide the only security he had ever known. It lost its tangible qualities along with the affluence it provided based merely on faith. Basic needs were replaced by ethereal desires. Belief in others began to seed in a fertile psyche that was once barren.

Chapter Twenty-Seven

Fewer people were at the square that night, but the atmosphere was more stimulating than it had ever been for Owen and Monica. They could barely contain the excitement for the deed that would change the lives of the donors of wealth as well as its recipients. Scratching and clawing for everything had been the only way Owen knew how to survive in a world he viewed as patently unfair. In the years that he salvaged a vast fortune from the shipwreck his opinion of the inherent inequities of currency had not changed. It had become a necessity for the exchange of goods and services needed for survival. Those who controlled it wielded the mammon with precision to separate themselves from undesirables. Never once had the enjoyment of his treasure extended beyond the tactile; until that night.

Monica had accomplished something neither he nor Spanish Pieces of Eight could. Owen had never been so agreeable to giving away so much of what he had allowed to define him. He clung to his tenuous prosperity; coveted it; and even considered dying for it. When the time came to lay his life on the line it was not for the safety of his treasure, but a selfless act in which he was prepared to exchange his life for the safety of someone he loved. His relationship with Monica had taken on a more ethereal quality. The transition had not been effortless. There had always been an innate desire to search out a better life. He knew it could be accomplished regardless of the environment he grew up in, or that in which he placed himself. Monica helped him realize the search was not an external one. It had to come from within. Purposefully, she had not told him in so many words. He had to come to that conclusion himself, and he had. Of all his adventures, none provided the enthusiasm and anticipation he felt as they made their way through the square seeking out their beneficiaries.

Owen pedaled a mountain bike that had, until that night, hung from an oversized hook mounted to a ceiling beam in his garage. Behind it he pulled a chariot purchased at a garage sale. It had never been used, but was the perfect manner in which to carry Monica. She felt better, but tired quickly. The carriage was made for a child, and her diminutive frame fit perfectly in its narrow confines. At her feet rested a silk bag with a tie-string, tightly drawn. It held four envelopes, each with a cashier's check for a million dollars.

Given the square was so sparsely populated, it would be difficult to sneak the dowries into their friends' tip buckets without being noticed.

Owen circled, watching each position like a hawk; searching for an opening in which to swoop unnoticed. Winston had to be first. He had been known to get frustrated and pack-it-in for the evening if the crowd was not there. Owen maneuvered to a corner far away from where his Jamaican friend set up for the evening. He appreciated how the entertainers shifted positions each night so that the promenade took on a completely different feel. Their respect for one another strengthened his desire for benevolence.

Winston attempted to attract an audience by walking on his hands around the edges of his stage that was marked by a rope laid along the ground. When few people responded he quickly sprung to his feet and walked toward Saffron's area adjacent to his. Owen saw agitation in his face and body. He rode in a large exag-

gerated circle waiting for an opportunity. Winston pointed toward his props, apparently asking Saffron to
watch them while he went to the restroom. After she
agreed, he quickly ran down a passageway and disappeared into a public bath. Leisurely Owen directed the
bike toward the vacated area. Monica reached into the
silk bag and retrieved the envelope earmarked for their
first recipient.

Saffron continued trying to attract a crowd of
her own by juggling three shiny scimitars high into the
night's sky. It worked perfectly that her gaze was directed skyward as the two stopped in front of the tip bucket; into which Monica nonchalantly dropped a check. In
a cautiously fluid motion Owen steered the bicycle
away and rode as if his movement had not been interrupted. They kept a surreptitious eye on the tip bucket
until Winston returned.

Saffron successfully gathered a crowd and examined each approaching face, which prevented Owen
and Monica from conferring their gift upon her. His
path was never direct, and he changed direction by
maneuvering in several large circles. The choreography
of their benevolent ballet shifted toward Dutch.

Moving toward their friend they realized how
difficult it was to tell where Dutch's eyes were focused
because they were hidden under the brim of his ever-
present hat. Owen's heart sank when he saw the man's
head tilt back exposing a stare directed at him and
Monica. The three exchanged waves and smiles. Their
compassionate waltz moved away with ease.

Desperation intensified knowing that with so
few tourists in the square they would stand out. Regardless, fear did not dampen their giddiness. So what if

they got caught! Certainly they preferred anonymity. Lack of it would cause a strain and create expectations where there were none. Pure gifts are those without the presumption of obligation. Desire to be stealth bene-factors motivated them to carry on their charade with increased vigilance. Owen maneuvered the tandem completely out of the square and behind an adjacent hotel. He thought it was best to remove themselves from the consciousness of their objectives.

Something neither had considered caused Mon-ica dread. "Owen, we have to get back in there. What if Winston opens his envelope?"

"They usually don't do that until the end of the evening as they smoke a … cigarette. I've been with them a few times and that's always been the M.O." He did not want to admit to the use of drugs. "You're prob-ably right, though. We can't count on that being the case tonight. All of those nights we spent together were very busy and that was probably the first time they had the chance to count their tips." With that, Owen re-versed course and made a hasty entrance into the square. He quickly scanned the three remaining targets for the one most vulnerable. Dutch was well into his routine and Ralphie, his dog and fellow cast-member, was at his side. The canine walked a tight-rope during the show, which required Dutch to turn his back to the crowd as he coaxed the dog along the narrow rope. The trick was easily accomplished, but in the name of show-manship his prodding was done for effect.

Out of respect, Saffron, Winston and Jack stood at their respective stages watching as he continued his show. They looked out for one-another and never tried to steal audience members. It presented another problem, however. Would the others see Owen and Monica as they bestowed their good fortune onto Dutch? "Monica, can you get out and mingle with the crowd without too much pain?"

"I'll try," she responded.

He slowed and then stopped behind the line of people that populated the breadth of Dutch's proscenium. After getting off the bike he made his way around it to help Monica stand. After she squeezed her way out of the chariot she realized she had left the envelope in the bag. Without thinking she leaned over to pick it up. "Shit! That hurts," she exclaimed as she grabbed the side-car to prevent herself from falling.

Owen leaned over and held her by the shoulders as gently as he could. He felt for her and could not believe the words that came from his mouth. "Can you try not to draw any attention to us, please?"

A burst of laughter exploded from his friend, which hurt as badly as bending over. Unable to say anything she stood with Owen's help. He bent over, retrieved the silk bag, removed the envelope earmarked for Dutch and handed it to her. When Ralphie began his walk his master turned his back on cue. Monica seized upon the opportunity, walked over and squatted down, avoiding bending her ribcage, and dropped the envelope in the glass fish bowl he set out to collect tips. When she stood and turned she noticed Owen was shielding her from the other entertainers. Slowly, Monica crawled back into the chariot and Owen mounted the bike, and once again resumed their sweeping ballet.

Owen steered in a direction that took them away from the last two beneficiaries. He imagined it being much easier to swoop toward the next target when the time was right.

Just as he had ridden clear of Dutch's stage, the entertainer finished his show and the crowd moved, herd-like, toward Jack. As he steered toward Jack, Owen noticed Winston was packing everything into a canvas duffle bag. Nervously, he watched as the gymnast picked up his tip bucket. If the only thing inside was the envelope surely he would remove and open it. He stared unconsciously, worried what Winston may do. Much to his relief, he picked up the bucket by the rim and turned it over, dumping its contents into his carry-all without discretion.

Most of the onlookers migrated toward Jack's area. Witnessing this phenomenon he quickly mounted a twelve foot unicycle that was the centerpiece of his show. An extreme sense of balance allowed him to crawl up the seat post while his assistant held a foot on one pedal. The control he exerted over the contraption as he wriggled his body over and past all of its impediments was a feat in-and-of itself. Owen looked over his shoulder at Saffron who did something surprising. Her patrons had moved to Jack's stage so she laid her swords down and walked away. Owen quickly maneuvered the bicycle past the crowd in front of Jack and swerved to a stop right in front of Saffron's tip container; a replica pirate hat turned upside down. Monica quietly placed her envelope inside, and Owen slowly pedaled away, returning to Jack's show.

When he stopped and held his hand out toward his friend, she removed the last envelope from the bag and handed it to him. It was difficult for her to contain the smile that manifested the pleasure of sharing such a noble undertaking with her friend. Owen walked into the crowd and made his way toward the front. He fell into the shadow of a large man and waited. A portion of Jack's act was spent juggling flaming torches while maintaining control of the unicycle. Excitement ebbed as he shifted his position to avoid being spotted as Jack moved about the makeshift stage. It was regretful Dutch had seen them, but it was equally imperative the others not. There could be no common sighting to connect Owen and Monica to the cash.

Jack hovered twelve feet above the crowd and announced, in his raspy voice, "This is what an Ivy League education will get you." The crowd laughed, hooted and clapped.

When Jack's eyes turned skyward Owen bent down and gently squeezed himself between the legs of the people in front of him, reached out and placed the envelope into his chest.

Nonchalantly he slid back through the crowd, got on the bike and leisurely pedaled away. He felt as though he was exiting a stage as he left the square. The two did not say a word to each other. Each chose to capture their feelings in silent reflection hoping to never lose them to the passage of time. Throughout his life Owen had been made to grovel, cajole and steal when necessary, simply to secure basic human needs. With Monica's help his perception of a thriving existence moved away from the physical. His burdens had been lifted and his emotional state was just as free.

Chapter Twenty-Eight

On the same day Owen's cast was removed he was scheduled to fly from Key West to Miami and then on to Rome. Eagerly awaiting family never seemed plausible in the world he created for himself. Procrastination caused him to rush about making sure everything had been taken care of before he left. Monica was given temporary power of attorney to handle his affairs while he was gone. She drove him to the airport in his BMW. The trip was made in silence. Melancholy blanketed them both. He told her to merely drop him off at the terminal. Monica insisted she come in and give a proper send off and planned to enter short-term parking.

Owen nervously rubbed his left arm. The cast no longer masked his anxiety. His thoughts centered on meeting a man he thought had been dead all of his life. Leaving Monica in order to see his uncle caused a great deal of angst. Relationships were no longer dispensable. Theirs was one he did not want to end.

Few thoughts were expressed as they made their way inside for Owen to check into his flight. Once the mundane tasks associated with air travel had been completed the awkwardness of his eminent departure grew. They lingered in silence at the entrance to security until the last possible moment before he had to board his flight. Reluctantly, he reached out and took her hand in his. Gently he squeezed it. A simple non-verbal statement of his feelings for her was all he could muster. She appreciated the sentiment and returned his expression. At the moment reserved for lovers who were saying goodbye, their clumsy feelings disappeared when they noticed four familiar people moving toward them; each of whom wore huge grins. Dutch, Saffron, Winston and Jack made their way eagerly toward the pair. It was not lost on him that the people he considered friends were the ones who showed up to offer their well wishes.

Immediately, the ugly distrust that had been ingrained in Owen's psyche surfaced. "You didn't tell them it was us who left the envelopes for them, did you?"

Monica looked at him incredulously. "Of course not. I'm the one who has to stay here with them." She paused, and then confessed, "I did however tell them that you were leaving and the time of your flight."

Owen put his arm around her and squeezed. "I'm sorry."

The group stopped, and Dutch extended his hand. "I hope you have a safe trip, friend." Owen took the man's hand in his and they squeezed firmly as they smiled at one another.

Dutch backed away and Saffron approached. She handed him a little doll. "I've had this since I was a little girl. It has always brought me luck."

He smiled. "Thank you." Her sentiment was surprising, as well as refreshing.

After Winston and Jack offered their well-wishes everyone stood in silence. Owen tried to dissolve the uneasy situation by telling them, "You all don't have to stay here … if you don't want to."

"Aw, hell," Dutch replied, "We wouldn't dream of missin' seeing you off."

"I appreciate it. I really do," Owen said, sincerely.

"Hey, mon," Winston held up his finger. "Has anyone told you that we each got a check for one million dollars?"

"No way!" Owen said, in a convincingly excited tone.

"Can you believe that?" Jack added. "You wouldn't know anything about that, would you?"

Owen pressed his lips together, drew down the corners of his mouth, and shook his head. "I'm touched that you all came to see me off." He changed the subject to deflect the nervousness he felt.

Several minutes of silence grew more uncomfortable with every passing second. With each announcement that blasted through the intercom he listened intently, discouraging questions about his friends' new-found fortunes. Monica touched him for the sake of being able to do so before he left. It was either a pat on the back, a soft punch to the hip, or a grab of his arm. Goodbyes had always been difficult for her. Owen never dealt with formalities; choosing to leave whenever the time seemed right. An emotional fjord surrounded him. On one side he had a group of friends he cared for, and on the other the chance to embrace a family he had never known.

As the time drew nigh, Owen knew he had to face the great unknown that lay ahead. Many questions to which his uncle had the answers shot through his mind. Life had taken on an eternal quality. He finally understood if he could become part of something greater than himself, his influence would transcend generations. Whether or not he had anything to contribute would become apparent soon enough. His thoughts were interrupted by the announcement he had been waiting to hear. The small commuter plane would take almost no time to load. Monica made the first move. She reached up and put her arms around his neck and squeezed. It was a hug like he never experienced before; filled with warmth, compassion and longing. The three men each took turns shaking his hand, and then Saffron finished off the pleasantries with a hug of her own.

"I'll be back soon enough." Owen choked as the words got stuck in his throat; which he loudly cleared to mask his emotion.

Monica looked him squarely in the eye. A tear rolled down her cheek. "You won't be coming back." She smiled through her melancholy.

"And why not?" Owen inquired. Something within him needed to be convinced he would see Key West again.

"When a man becomes devoted to a family, he will never leave them."

"Maybe I shouldn't leave, then."

She shook her head. "We'll always be your friends, but we're not what you've been searching for your entire life."

Owen looked at the others. Each wore a forced smile that conveyed their agreement with Monica. He bent over, picked up his carry-on bag, and looked into his friend's eyes once more. "But that doesn't mean that I cannot love you, forever." He turned, walked away from the group and toward the security checkpoint. When he placed his bag on the conveyor belt to be scanned, he looked back. "I will always love you."

She nodded as another tear streamed down her face. "I love you too, Owen."

He walked through the checkpoint, into the gate area, then turned and looked through the window separating the two. Everyone exchanged a wave and smile. A lump grew in his throat and chills spread throughout his body.

The sun reflecting off the tarmac was blinding as he emerged from the building and made his way to the waiting plane. He drew in a deep breath and let out a heavy sigh as he reached the bottom of the portable stairway. Something inside made him look back. Never had he concerned himself with those he left behind. It had always been best to move forward out of fear of suffocating in the dense, dogmatic pall that hovered over the only family he had known. His feelings for his friends were too strong.

When he reached the midpoint of the steps, he quickly scanned the landscape of Key West's tiny airport. Disappointed, he turned and continued toward the plane until he heard his name being screamed from the horizon behind him. He turned and spotted five figures standing on the observation deck on top of the terminal. All of them were waving vigorously, and Monica added several jumps to exaggerate her enthusiastic farewell. None of them had to make that effort. They chose to do it. When Owen realized that no one from the *Sixty-Nine* came to see him off it pained him. His relationship with each of them was based on the group's dynamic. That barrier would not allow for a free exchange beyond the facade each member maintained. Owen appreciated the sincerity contained within his connection to each of his friends who wished him well. No matter how hard he fought he could not hold back his tears as he boarded the plane.

236

Sunsets at the Piazza de Michelangelo were meant to be experienced by lovers. Owen and Julia spent three nights there during their brief relationship, but there was no beautiful woman with him. Couples were scattered about; some embraced; others simply held hands; while still more engaged in kisses. They were all so into their passion the only person who noticed their activity was Owen.

A train brought him to Florence the night before. Luca left a message at his hotel for them to meet at the piazza. It was not a long walk, so he strolled leisurely over the Ponte Vecchio where he stopped for a pistachio gelato. He arrived early to view the sunset. Its life giving energy was not lost on him.

He held his arms out side-by-side and snickered at the difference in skin tone and the atrophy that caused his left arm to diminish in size. The significance of his meeting overtook his silly thoughts when Owen realized he was thinking about everything but the man he was about to meet. He was his maternal grandmother's brother. Everyone in his family thought this man had been dead for over fifty years, and Owen was the only one who knew differently. Maybe there should have been some pride he could glean from that fact, but his nerves would not allow him to feel anything other than anxious.

Stories of adolescent girlfriends who swooned at the sight of his uncle filled the younger man's mind. He tried to recall the names of the ladies who told him the stories, but it was useless. Owen thought he could use them as an icebreaker. One person he had a clear recollection of was his grandmother, Sue. She was a woman filled with pride; always impeccably dressed and well kempt. There was a kindness in her gaze that made him feel safe as a boy. Closing his eyes he imagined her sitting next to him. He inhaled the pleasant smell of her violet lotion. Memories ran deep and were there for him to enjoy. Not until that moment did he realize her influence was still with him. Disappointment radiated from his soul at the awareness that until that moment her positive impact had been ignored.

The sun set over the horizon, but it did not disappear into the river as he remembered during his nights there with Julia. It all seemed less magical. *The time of year is different*, he thought.

Florence was no less beautiful. Rays of light illuminated the city from behind the horizon and made the buildings appear bright orange. Everything was so beautiful; the Duomo, the Ufizzi, and the train station with its uniquely baroque architecture. They could all be seen from his vantage point.

Day turned to night and Owen continued to wait patiently. Some lovers left, but most stayed embracing the sunset as the beginning of their evening. The lights of the city took control of the night sky. His thoughts were as far from his reality as the horizon, and it was too dark for him to notice the elderly gentleman that approached from behind. The man made his way around to the front of the bench.

Rubbing his left arm as he stared out over the city, he was startled when he heard his uncle's voice for the first time. "Owen?"

Shaken from his daydream, he looked up and saw a man with a healthy head of silver hair. The skin about his face was loose and sagged, but he was still

238

quite handsome. He repeated the elder man's question. "Uncle Owen?" They laughed at the relief they felt.

"May I sit?" the old man asked, as he pointed to the spot next to his great-nephew.

"Of course," he said, as he slid along the bench to make room.

The man held out a frail, boney hand. Owen held it to support the man, but was impressed with the strength in his uncle's grip. "Do you work out?"

The man laughed. "No. We all have to pitch in at the olive plantation."

"Do you sell them in a market?"

"No. We make olive oil that we ship all over the world."

"I'd like to see that sometime."

The man's laugh was possessed by a devious overtone. "Oh, you will experience it alright."

Brief silence was broken when the younger man asked. "So what now? Can I take you to dinner?"

The man shook his head. "No. There's too much commotion in a restaurant. I want to sit and talk with you."

"About what?"

"I want to get to know you, and I want you to get to know me." He paused. "And then I want to explain to you why I did what I did to our family … and apologize."

The younger man leaned back in order to straighten his waist so he could shove his hand into his front pocket. "First," he pulled something from inside, "I have to give you this." He reached toward the man and flattened out his hand. Removing the item from his nephew's palm he held it in front of his face. The light was dim, but he could make out the shape of a Purple Heart. He ran his thumb over the three-dimensional bust of George Washington, then rolled it over and looked on the back. Inscribed there was, *For Military Merit, Owen Albert Franklin*. He was speechless. The elder knew the gift was meant to bring closure to an ugly situation, but he could not help feeling the magnification of his betrayal. The young man saw the consternation on his uncle's face. "I wasn't trying to do anything other than returning something that belongs to you."

"I know." The man nodded.

"Your sister gave that to me."

"Tell me about her," he said, as he dropped the medal into his shirt pocket.

Owen felt the old man's action was a little too curt; that he should treat the item with more respect. "She was the most important person in my life until her death. She taught me how to stand up for myself when no one else would."

His uncle laughed. "That's exactly how I remember my older sister."

The nephew became agitated as he recalled how his grandmother convinced herself that her brother was still alive. "You know, every time there was an unexpected knock at the door she was positive it was you, only to be disappointed each and every time. For all those years she knew you were still alive, and we all just shook it off as wishful thinking." Owen's tone increased. "She was right!"

"That's why I need to apologize," the man answered. He shook away his despair. "My only hope to repair the damage I've caused is to give whatever time I have left to you."

Owen sensed that his uncle felt horrible, which made him feel guilty. In an effort to lighten the mood, he quipped, "And that nephew of yours, Luca, he's a riot … a regular Jack Benny."

"Yeah, he told me what he did to you. I gave him extra chores around the house as punishment." The man leaned back and pointed over his shoulder. "He's waiting in the car. He wanted to come see you, too."

"Should we go now?"

Shaking his head, the uncle replied, "No. There will be too much confusion at home and I still want us to get to know each other first."

"I think Luca knows just about everything there is to know about me."

"You're probably right." He paused. "Is there anything you'd like to know about me?"

"I'm sure there are many questions I'll ask when the time is right. But, the only one I can think of now is, why? Why did you abandon your family without so much as a letter letting them know you were okay and that you had decided to live out your days in Italy?"

The old man's face soured with memories of the circumstances that brought him to the Mediterranean nation. "After my plane crashed I was fished out of the ocean by a German U-Boat. They transported me to the nearest port where there was a prisoner of war camp. Eventually I was shipped to a camp in Avezzano. I labored there for over a year until Italy signed an armistice with the Allies in September of 1943. I made several friends while I was a prisoner. One of them was a man named Gianni Politzi. He lived in Brooklyn, but was born in Italy. At night he would tell us stories of Tuscany and its beauty. We were all able to escape our predicament by dreaming we were surrounded by the beautiful scenery he described and not in a filthy, stinking barrack. Well, when we were set free I slipped out of camp without checking in with U.S. Army Air Corp officials. I guess after that I was listed as Killed In Action. That really didn't bother me too much. There was no-one waiting for me back home."

"Why do you say that? My grandmother certainly missed you."

The old man stroked his chin as he thought. "There were some very ugly things said between the two of us before I left for the war. We had a great grandfather who was the only surviving brother of four who fought in the Civil War. The only reason he was spared was that his three older brothers told him he was too young to fight and sent him home. Your grandmother always remembered what a tenuous existence ours was. She tried to play that same role with me. It didn't work. We sat up in bed late at night talking about me joining the Army. She pleaded for me not to go and I insisted that I had to fight for our country. I wanted to fly planes in the worst way." He laughed. "I got my wings taken away once for flying under a bridge in Texas where I trained. I knew the Army Air Corp needed me though. I was cocky as hell." His mood turned solemn. "That brashness almost cost me my life."

The nephew looked upon this man who was so willing to share of himself in a new light. "You still haven't answered my question."

"Sorry. I guess I got side-tracked by memories." He paused. The answer to this question was one he had thought about for almost sixty years. "Have you ever felt like no matter how hard you tried, you just didn't fit into certain circumstances?"

"Of course."

"That's how I felt in our family. There was something innate telling me there was more to life than the environment that surrounded me. It turned out that what burned inside me was passion for life. Italy brought that out in me. After I got out of Avezzano I headed north toward Florence. I spent several weeks enjoying the culture and *everything* it had to offer, I knew I had to get a job, and went to work on an olive plantation. There I met the most important person I've ever known."

"The owner?"

"Better! The owner's daughter, and my wife of fifty-six years. She instilled in me an understanding of family like I had never known before. *Man*, the Italians have a zeal for family. When someone cares for you passionately, returning that love becomes almost effortless." He turned to his nephew. "Owen, I sincerely hope that one day you will find the perfect woman. I don't think too many couples actually find their ideal mate, but I know that I have." The man recognized the longing look in his nephew's eyes as he stared across the river at the city lights. "Have you already found that person?"

The younger man shook his head without altering his stare. "There is someone very special in Key West who taught me a lot about myself. She helped me understand that everything happens for a reason and whether it's bad or good we can always take something constructive from all of our experiences."

"She sounds very special. You should bring her here. I'd love to meet her."

He avoided the issue of why they could never be a couple. "You know uncle, sometimes no matter how good it is, it's just not meant to be."

"I understand … believe me, I understand."

Over an hour was spent discussing parts of their lives that were significant as well as trivial. It was the first encounter experienced by the younger man in which he allowed his energy to immediately connect with someone, and even more so with a person he desired a lasting relationship. Their positive auras came together and formed the purest of connections. It was a bond that had been fashioned decades earlier, and was never once broken. Neither would ever doubt the other's sincerity.

Chapter Thirty

Luca drove the two men toward the estate. They sat next to each other in the back seat and continued the conversation started at the piazza. Topics centered on major events of their lives. A connection formed as each man envisioned the other inside their own circumstances. Good-natured banter concerning the happenings in Key West was exchanged between Owen and Luca.

The drive took nearly an hour on roads that wound through the hills of Tuscany. Luca maneuvered the car onto the long driveway that led from the main road. Owen was taken by the beauty of it all.

A full moon on a cloudless night provided enough light for him to see the driveway was lined on both sides by Italian Cypress. Luca drove around a large stone fountain in the middle of a courtyard, and stopped in front of the main house. It was one of several structures on the estate Owen saw from the back seat. All of the buildings were constructed of the same stone of varying sizes. They appeared centuries old and conveyed lasting strength.

Luca dutifully hopped out of the car and made his way to his uncle's door and opened it. The frail old man struggled to get out of the car. Owen watched, wondering if he should help with a gentle push from behind. Luca grabbed the man's hand and gently pulled him from the vehicle. Owen got out and met them at the rear bumper.

"Luca, you go into the house and make sure everyone is here for dinner. I'm going to take Owen to the warehouse and show him around." The old man commanded. Without a word the Italian nephew made his way inside.

Owen followed his uncle as he walked across the courtyard, past the fountain and toward a building with the same façade as the others. The only distinguishing characteristics were three large wooden warehouse doors that gave it an industrial feel.

The old man scooted through a small side door after opening it and his nephew followed. He reached over and turned a light switch. Several aged implements covered the warehouse floor. Exposed conduit provided the tale-tell sign electricity had been installed long after the building was constructed. Without saying anything the old man led Owen to a machine that was round with a basin shaped like a funnel. At its top were four large wheels made of granite; each was secured to an axle at its ninety degree points. His uncle pointed to the contraption. "After we've removed all the sticks, twigs and debris from the olives, we put them in this mill and grind them into a paste." He looked seriously at his nephew. "We don't de-stone the olives. That reduces your yield."

"How do you separate the olives from the waste?"

His uncle laughed. "Until about ten years ago we did it by hand at a long wooden table with raised sides to keep the olives from rolling onto the floor. They almost mutinied on me. That's when I agreed to upgrade our operation. Now we have a machine that acts like a sieve. There are several different mesh screens. The first series allows the olives to drop away from the large pieces of trash. The next series removes the smaller debris while leaving the olive." The old man sauntered to another machine. "Once the olive paste is ready we put it in here." He pointed to a large hopper attached to the side of the mechanism. "We feed the paste in while a centrifuge separates the meat from the oil." He pointed to a chute on the opposite side from the hopper. "This is where the oil comes out. We save it in large kegs until it's time to bottle." When Owen had no questions the old man moved to a long wall next to the door where they entered the building. Wooden shelving units covered its length from floor to ceiling. They were completely filled with boxes imprinted with the name of the plantation. "In each of those boxes is six bottles of some of the finest extra-virgin olive oil in the world."

"You must get a great sense of pride from your work."

The old man smiled. It warmed his heart to have his great nephew there. He reached out and placed his arm around his shoulder. "Come on. Let's go inside and get some dinner."

The two men walked out of the warehouse and across the courtyard. When they passed the fountain, the young man asked, "How many people will be at dinner?"

"Tonight? Anywhere from fifteen to twenty. It all depends on if any of the kids has a friend over or not. Or, one of them may be having dinner at a friend's house."

"How many kids do you have?"

"Five, and fifteen grandchildren."

The men approached the front door and Owen's anxiety grew. "Do I have to go inside?"

The old man stopped and looked at him. "I know this is an intimidating situation to walk into, but I can assure you everyone in there is anxious to meet you. They will all be on their best behavior."

"Unlike Luca?"

The old man laughed. "Yes, unlike Luca."

They walked inside; elder first. The younger man followed after closing the door. The house was filled with the sounds of conversation coming from the dining room. He saw the backs of a few heads through a doorway at the other end of the living room. Everyone appeared to be seated at a long table.

Owen had the overwhelming urge to run away as they breached the doorway to the hall. It was filled with people speaking Italian, and doing so fast enough it was impossible for him to recognize any words. He stifled his initial impulse and stuck close to his uncle. When the men were noticed the conversation subsided and everyone turned and looked at them. Those with their backs to the door shifted in their seats. Owen's breaths grew quicker and his face became flush. A young man seated across the table broke the silence. "*E sicuro che lei non ha un attacco di cuore?*"

Uncle Owen laughed. "He said he's afraid you're going to have a heart attack. By the way, that's the joker of the family, Sylvio."

The nephew smiled nervously, held his hand up and gave a quick wave. Before the tension became too great an elderly woman who sat near the head of the table stood and walked to its end and took her nephew by the hand. "My name is Maria. I am your aunt," she said proudly. That proved to be just what he needed to calm his nerves.

248

"It's a pleasure to meet you," he responded. "Your English is very good."

"Your uncle made sure we all spoke the language he grew up with. Everyone here speaks English." She glared at Sylvio. "Some choose to be rude and speak Italian when English is called for." Without saying anything else she tugged on his arm and led him around the table to a spot where there were two empty chairs. To the right was a beautiful young girl, and on the left sat Sylvio. Owen chose to sit next to the girl; away from his belligerent cousin.

The old man moved toward his seat at the head of the table and sat down. "Owen, I am not trying to be rude, but I know if I introduce you to everyone there will be no way for you to remember all of their names. You can get to know everyone at your own pace."

The nephew nodded his agreement with the man's assessment. With that, everyone seemed to simultaneously re-engage themselves in the conversation they carried on before the two men entered the room. Owen examined the table and its contents. There were three large casserole dishes that contained Chicken Cacciatore and three large, dome-shaped loaves of bread. It all smelled divine.

"Owen," the uncle called from the end of the table.

The nephew leaned forward and made eye-contact with the man. "Yes, sir?"

"Can you please go out to the warehouse and bring in a box of olive oil?" He held up an empty bottle. "We seem to be all out."

He was glad his uncle asked him to complete the task. It would give him the opportunity to decompress emotionally. Without hesitation he stood and walked around the end of the table and out of the room.

By the time he made it across the living room he felt the calmness he desired. Thoughts of how he chose to relax while in Key West crept into his mind. *I wish I had a joint I could smoke while I was out here.*

After traversing the courtyard, he opened the door to the warehouse and felt along the wall for the light switch. When he found it he had trouble with its design and could not figure out how to manipulate it properly. Owen stood staring at the switch until his eyes adjusted enough to see it was a knob that required turning. When the light came on he turned and walked toward the wall. Purposefully he examined all of the boxes. There was an open one on the top shelf, but he had no desire to get trapped under a pile, so he reached out at chest level and removed a box from the shelf in front of him. He held it in both hands as he walked to the door. After turning off the switch Owen walked outside and past the fountain.

Once inside he gently pushed the door closed with his foot. It seemed as though the closer he got to the dining room the softer the volume of the conversation became. Silence fell and he slowed his pace wondering what was happening. *Luca must have some practical joke up his sleeve*, he thought. His uncle had already apologized once for his cousin's behavior, so there would be no way the man would allow Luca to harm him.

Cautiously, he walked into the dining room and exposed himself to whatever waited inside. He stopped and looked around. Everyone stared at him. A snicker exploded from a young girl at the end of the table op-

posite the elders. Owen looked at his uncle and Maria.
Wide grins shined on their faces. He looked down the
row of faces in front of him. Everyone had turned in
their chairs to watch him enter the room. After he
scanned one side of the table he stared at the snickering
child. She shook her head as the smile grew on her face.
Owen then scanned the faces on the far side of the
table. So many new faces heightened his confusion.
What finally dawned on him was that there was only
one empty seat at the table. His eyes were drawn to a
young lady seated to the right of Sylvio. Familiarity
cleared away his uncertainty. He continued to stare at
her in disbelief. *It's Julia.* Upon seeing the recognition
of her in his face she smiled at him. He returned the
gesture, but did not move. Then he realized, *Oh my
God! She's a relative.*

    Julia saw that he was frozen so she stood and
walked around the far end of the table where his uncle
and aunt sat, prolonging the anticipation. She gently
grazed the shoulders of the old man with her hand as
she walked past. When she made the turn Owen saw
every bit of the most beautiful woman he had ever
known. He was speechless and unable to move. She
continued toward him. Her shapely legs extended beau-
tifully from her dress that was cut to mid-thigh. They
were athletic, brown and smooth. Every inch of her was
a pleasure to behold and he became caught up in it, so-
much-so that he did not see it coming when she drew
back her hand as she took her final step toward him. Julia slapped him across the face, not nearly as hard as
she could, but hard enough to let him know that she was
angry. "Don't you ever leave me again," she said, just
before throwing her arms around him. He still held the

box in front of him and could not embrace her. Everyone at the table laughed at the sight and applauded the couple.

Once she released him, Owen turned to his uncle. "Where do you want me to put this?"

"On that table against the wall," he answered, while pointing.

He did as he was told and removed one bottle and walked to his uncle and handed it to him. Julia did not move. The nephew turned and walked toward her. Feeling the effects of her strike he rubbed his cheek gently with his left hand while opening and closing his mouth to stretch away the pain. The determination to do something equally dramatic came over him as he made his way toward her. He stopped in front of her and looked into her eyes with an emotionless expression. Slowly he reached up to her face and held his hand just behind her ear and gently stroked her cheek with his thumb. He could see in her eyes that her demeanor was softening and she was transforming into a dreamy trancelike state. When the time was right he slowly pulled her face toward his and softly kissed her most perfect lips. Passion for her had not waned. Her lips were as soft as he remembered. She tasted wonderful. Nothing about her had changed. It was he who had changed and Owen knew it.

After they embraced long enough for the cousins to start whooping, they both knew that it was time to end the show and return to their seats. Once they sat Owen reached over and lightly touched her leg. At a table where almost twenty people were having dinner, it felt like just the two of them. Their energy drew them together. Occasionally they leaned into each other and tenderly touched shoulders. Finally, Owen asked, "Who told you that I was here?"

She pointed at Luca who was seated across the table and two chairs down. "Luca."

"How did he know about us?"

"He heard that you met a girl while you were here. Florence is a small town. If you know the right people to ask, you can find just about anyone … except someone who doesn't want to be found."

"I want to know what your reaction was when he came to you and said that I would be here."

Julia thought about his question. "I was afraid that you would show up with a woman you had met and fallen in love with."

Owen nodded. "When did you find out that wasn't the case?"

"Tonight, while you and your uncle talked at the piazza, Luca called me and asked if I wanted to come to dinner."

Owen looked at Luca, who had been listening to the conversation. "All is forgiven … and I actually owe you now."

Luca smiled. "You owe me nothing, cousin."

He was struck by the reference to their relation. A lump formed in his throat. It was the first time in his life he felt like a member of a family. He was unable to talk for fear of crying, so he shoved a piece of bread that had been dragged through a plate of olive oil into his mouth.

"I had another fear about tonight," Julia confessed.

"What's that?" he asked, through a mouthful of food.

"That you would reject me."

Owen hesitated with the words that came to mind. "I'm not sure how you can think anyone would reject you. You're the most beautiful woman in the world."

"You're sweet," she said, as she leaned in and kissed him on the cheek.

"Besides that, with the reception you gave me, if I had rejected you, you may have beaten the shit out of me." Julia laughed. The thought of rejection conjured the one memory that he had for so long tried to forget. He was compelled to ask. "What happened between you and Gianni?"

Her laughter was not appreciated. "Two things: Gianni works for my father, and there has *never* been anything between us." She waited for his reaction. When he said nothing, she asked the question she had wanted to ask for years. "Why did you leave so abruptly?"

Owen became embarrassed. There was no answer other than his impetuous nature, but he knew that would not suffice. Julia expected more from him, and after a few moments in thought he did not let her down. "I've always run away from problems rather than facing them. Thank God I have a friend who instilled in me that some relationships are worth an occasional painful episode." He was compelled to ask. "You obviously think I am the man for you. Why is that?"

She smiled. "Do you remember the first night we met?"

"Yes. We literally ran into each other."

"But when you introduced yourself to me you extended your hand. You didn't try to saunter up to me and act all cool. Not once in the two weeks we were to-gether did you ever try to grope me, or make love to me. I could tell that you would allow it to happen when it was right. You were genuine then, and you are now."

"Wow! I never thought I'd hear those words used to describe me."

Other than the piece of bread that Owen stuffed in his mouth, neither of them ate. They talked as if no one else was in the room. The others went about their business without eavesdropping. Nonetheless, Owen wished to be alone with Julia so they could continue their conversation in private. "Would you like to come back to my hotel with me? We can have drinks in the same lobby bar we did before."

Uncle Owen heard the question and answered for her. "You won't be going back to the hotel tonight, or any night. We've checked you out and made up a room for you here. Luca can show it to you." He saw the look of astonishment on his nephew's face. "Hey, it pays to know people around here."

"Is it a private room?"

To that Maria interjected. "Yes, you can have your privacy, but not together. I won't have that in my house as long as there is a breath in my body," she drew upon an old cliché. "If you want to sit and talk there is a bench outside under the old Sycamore tree."

That was all the couple needed to hear. They stood and walked around the table and toward the door. Just before leaving, Owen turned and looked at his uncle. "Tonight when you said you hoped I would find the perfect woman like you had; is *this* what you meant?"

The wisdom the old man garnered over his lifetime dictated he not answer. Either an affirmation or denial could influence something he knew to be destiny, regardless of the circumstances. So he just gave a wry smile in response.

As Owen followed Julia outside, her words rang inside his mind. His genuine nature with her was a reflection of the purity of her soul. It was the same with Monica. Then it became clear. An attribute he never knew he possessed was obviously innate.

Chapter Thirty-One

The sun shined through the sheer curtains that did not completely cover the window. Owen had not slept all night and the light burned his eyes. He pulled the pillow over his head and tried desperately to block the unwanted intrusion. When the once cool pillow became warm and uncomfortable he became frustrated and tossed it onto the floor. While struggling to grasp onto the sleep he cherished, the sounds of someone working outside his window made his goal unattainable. The Italian language being spoken along with something obviously being loaded into the bed of a truck piqued his curiosity. Voices and the work being performed were both a mystery to him, but he was too damned tired to get up and look. One voice he could discern was Sylvio shouting something in Italian. His tone was angry and he uttered Owen's name.

Giving up on the notion of sleep, Owen interlocked the fingers of both hands and placed them behind his head and stared at the ceiling. Discomfort was still in his eyes, but he would not have traded the time he spent with Julia the evening before for anything. The mere thought of the arrogance he displayed when he stormed out of her life gave him pause to question the viability of any long term relationship with her. His instincts had never failed him. What he had yet to understand was that trust was best spent, and not horded.

The neigh of a horse came from below his window and interrupted his thoughts. He sat up and looked through the opening at the sky. Within seconds he heard the door open and soft footsteps as they made their way upstairs toward his room. The sound stopped just outside his door. Owen avoided rushing to open it, not wanting to appear anxious. Silence was interrupted with a soft knock. Slowly he got out of bed and moved across the floor. Just before opening it there came another gentle rap. Leisurely, he turned and pulled the doorknob. A smile grew wider on his face as he anticipated seeing Julia. His expression was quickly erased when he saw his frail uncle standing just outside.

"Did I wake you?" the old man asked.

"No."

"Good, because today is the last day you'll stay here without working." He turned and began walking down the stairs. "Get dressed and come outside. There's something I want to show you ... and hurry up. It'll be gone soon."

Hurriedly, Owen rummaged through his suitcase. He found a pair of jeans and a polo shirt, which he hastily draped over his body. Finally, he grabbed a pair of sandals and slid them onto his feet. He ran out of the room and down the stairs.

When he emerged onto the courtyard the morning sun blinded him temporarily. Looking down at the ground to shield his eyes Owen made his way toward an old buckboard where his uncle sat atop a bench mounted onto metal brackets. He stepped inside a stirrup that hung down from the frame of the wagon. Simultaneously, Owen thrust himself upward while grabbing the seat-back. He looked at his uncle who held the reigns. The old man shook his head and pointed toward the rear of the carriage. Not until he was fully mounted on top did he see Julia sitting on a stack of hay. They exchanged smiles. Once he had made his way next to her and sat down, he asked, "When did you get here?"

258

"I stayed here last night."

"You did?"

"Yes. There is a beautiful guest room in the main house. There is a huge four-poster bed made of mahogany. It's very sturdy, but soft and comfortable, with silk sheets. You really should come see it."

"You mean to tell me that we could have spent the night together last night and I had no idea?"

Julia assured him, "Even if you would have shown up in my room last night, there's no way I would have let you in my bed."

The two laughed as the wagon jerked forward. Uncle Owen guided it down a narrow path away from the family compound. They descended into a valley. Fog surrounded them and was so thick they felt the moisture on their skin. Owen scooted next to Julia and held her closely to shield her from the chill in the air.

"You didn't even kiss me goodnight last night," she whispered into his ear.

Owen looked at her. Julia's soft brown eyes embraced his soul with their warmth. "When you told me you knew I was the man for you because I shook your hand and did not try to make a move on you, you pretty much guaranteed any show of affection has to be initiated by you."

She shook her head. "No, you have my permission to show me how much you love me in any way you like."

He hesitated. "You'll have to be patient, I've never known how to love, so all of this is new to me."

Julia smiled. "I know this may sound odd, but in order for you to be able to give love, you have to love yourself. Be proud of the man you are and you will be able to give something you value, and it won't be lost on its recipient."

Owen smiled as he gently stroked her cheek with his thumb. She looked up at him longingly. He leaned in and kissed her. Holding her, he pressed his hand against her back and pulled her body into his. Their excitement grew into an intensity they knew couldn't be satiated at that moment.

Julia stroked her hand across his chest and his shirt fell open. She saw the St. Christopher medallion she had given him. "You still have that?"

Owen looked down and laughed. "You would be amazed at what I had to go through to keep this."

"I'm surprised I didn't notice it last night."

"Me too," he responded, and then added. "I haven't taken it off for several weeks."

"Weeks?"

"Yeah. When I realized that I would be coming back to Florence I put it on, and left it on."

"Were you hoping to see me again?"

His face turned melancholy. "I'm afraid I had lost all hope of that happening."

"So, why did you keep the necklace?"

"Even though I haven't worn it in a long time I always kept it near."

"Why?"

Owen drew in a deep breath and admitted, "You are the only person I have ever known that I wondered, '*what if?*'"

She laid her head on his chest, shifted as closely to him as she could possibly get, and said, "Now you know."

Uncle Owen guided the wagon through the rough, hilly terrain of the plantation. He derived a great sense of pleasure in bringing these two together. His smiling face exacerbated his wrinkles as he looked back and saw the lovers arm-in-arm. The carriage rocked back-and-forth as the wheels rolled into and out of holes that speckled the ruts in the road. Thirty minutes into their ride the path flattened and began a gradual ascent. Owen and Julia had to shift their weight to maintain the balance that kept them close. Neither had any idea where the old man was taking them, but they trusted him implicitly.

The carriage rocked forward and backward as the horses strained to pull its weight over the highest point on the property. It was their destination. Once the wagon was free of the gravity that pulled against it the ride became effortless. The old man pulled back on the reigns, stopped the equine power, and then turned to face the couple. "If you get out and go sit on that rock you'll get the most amazing view of Tuscany you will ever see."

Without a word Owen jumped to the ground below and then held Julia's hand as she crawled over the side, let go and fell into his arms. He gently set her on her feet.

"I'm going to turn the wagon around down there." The old man pointed down the road. Neither lover understood exactly what his plan was, but agreed without protest.

The boulder was well over ten feet high and they noticed there were natural notches that had been worn into it; which made for perfect steps to climb upon the makeshift perch. He helped her up and then followed. Before he made it to the top he looked up at her and saw a look on her face that spoke volumes. Amazement radiated from her eyes. Something inside told him to turn and enjoy the sight, but he refused the impulse. Instead, he wanted to be next to Julia so they could witness it together.

Once he had situated himself next to her and secured his arm around her body he directed his gaze over the landscape. What he saw was the most stunning sight he had ever beheld. The valley was filled with morning fog. A gentle morning breeze caused the surface of the mist to undulate like mild ocean waves. The lovers held each other tightly as they watched in awe. Two olive trees broke through the surface of the clouds only to disappear moments later as the ripples continued. Owen pointed at them. "Do you see that?"

"Isn't it amazing?" she responded. He sat captivated by the display, unsure of how to convey his awe. When he said nothing, she continued. "I feel like we are on top of the world, and that I am witnessing an awakening … how do you say, *Genesi?*"

"Genesis?"

"*Si, Grazie.*" She hesitated. "Does that make sense or am I crazy?"

"No, it makes perfect sense to me."

"What do you see?"

He thought of Monica and how she accused him of copping out for not having an original thought when she asked what he was looking for in a relationship. Julia had described the scene so perfectly that he had no idea how to improve upon it. Moving closer and holding her tightly was a means to buy time while he thought of an adequate answer. When he leaned his head against hers, it all made sense to him. Softly, he whispered, "I see two vibrant life forces that will never lose hope no matter what torrent swirls around them."

The beauty of Owen's words filled Julia with the desire to experience the love they felt without boundaries. She initiated an embrace and they kissed for several minutes. They thirsted for each other and their desire was voracious to the point of discomfort. Their souls ached to be one, but they knew they would have to wait.

When they heard Uncle Owen driving the wagon on the road in front of them they loosened their embrace. Each one coyly looked at the old man as if they were teenagers who had been caught by their parents. Everything was so fresh and new they felt juvenile. The morning Sun had begun to burn away the clouds, but the two trees still stood out among others that became visible.

Pointing toward the valley, the old man explained. "We call them *Nonna e Nonno*. They are over four hundred years old."

It gave Julia great pleasure to translate. "He said they are called Grandmother and Grandfather."

The uncle pointed to the rock where the couple sat. "I proposed to Maria on that rock on a morning not unlike this one."

The couple exchanged a giddy smile, but said nothing to one another. Reluctantly, Owen slid down the smooth rock face and landed feet first on the ground below. He turned and helped Julia down, bringing her feet softly to the earth. They walked hand-in-hand toward the wagon. After helping her inside he looked at his uncle. "Did you say anything special to Aunt Maria when you proposed?"

The old man smiled as he recalled the most pleasant of memories. "I told her that there would be times in our relationship that she would not understand me, but that if she accepted me for the man that I am the energy between us would sustain our relationship forever."

Chapter Thirty-Two

Uncle Owen was true to his word. For over a month his nephew toiled in the olive orchard and earned his keep. Every meal was served promptly during the breakfast, lunch and dinner hours and everyone was expected to attend. At first it was a shock to the younger man's system. For so long he had lived recklessly. Never once did he miss his life in Key West. He did however miss his friends. They occupied his thoughts constantly as he worked and sweated amongst his family, including Sylvio who always looked upon him with a jaundiced expression.

Owen took pride keeping his body in shape, but after a few days of labor almost every muscle he had ached. His cousins enjoyed giving him a hard time about it, but eventually he gained their respect by not letting the pain slow his work. They ultimately compared him to his uncle, who years earlier had gained the reputation as the hardest worker on the plantation. It was refreshing to accept the favorable comparison to a relative.

Julia returned to work with her family's bank in town. They owned several small depositories throughout Tuscany. After university she began working as a teller. Over the course of several years she had been employed in every job in the bank, including that of a runner who delivered paperwork from branch-to-branch. Her eagerness as well as her amicable disposition endeared her to everyone. Both of their hectic schedules left little time for them to be together, and when they were most of it was spent as Julia rubbed away the aches in Owen's back.

Tension between Sylvio and Owen escalated. It began with Sylvio's caustic sense of humor displayed from the outset of their relationship. The two never really hit it off and the longer they avoided each other the deeper their resentment became. During work days they refused to make eye contact whenever they passed one another. Luca tried to intervene once to no avail. The most awkward times were spent at the dinner table. By choosing the seat he had the first night Owen was fated to sit near his cousin at every meal. He was afraid to ask for help for fear he may alienate someone else. It had not occurred to him that this was the first time that he had not simply removed himself from an uncomfortable situation. There was too much at stake.

Weekends were the only time Owen and Julia had a chance to devote their full attention to each other. Her parents owned a villa in the small hillside town of Cortona that had been in the family for over two hundred years. It was kept as a reminder of their humble beginnings.

On their first trip to the house she offered to let him drive, but he was not comfortable with the task so he refused. When they arrived he was taken by the beauty of the countryside. The house sat atop a hill that was one of many that made up the landscape. Stones of varying sizes had been cobbled together to form its walls. He was astounded at the craftsmanship and dedication it took to build a structure that survived for centuries.

When he walked into the house all of the windows and shutters were closed and it was quite dark. Julia immediately went about opening them so fresh air could replace the stale. Owen hesitated not knowing what to do to help, so he stood in the middle of the living room and watched, waiting for instructions.

He noticed the interior walls were plastered with white stucco and several exposed beams supported the ceiling. A large fireplace made of the same stone as the house was obviously used to cook meals at one time in its history. It was large enough to hold a kettle and there were remnants of iron supports mounted into the firebrick.

Owen saw the only bed was in a loft above the living room. Stairs ran up to it along the back wall. The railing was made of hand-hewn wooden posts he surmised were from trees felled somewhere near the property. Julia worked busily as if he were not there.

Once she settled into the house Julia instructed him to take their bags upstairs. He hesitated wondering if he should offer to sleep on the sofa. She sensed his reticence and insisted that *their* luggage be placed in the loft. After he completed his appointed task he sat on the bed and was overcome by silence. There was not a single appliance to offer a distraction.

Julia brought a list of chores prepared by her father. Although he did not look forward to spending their valuable time working, there was no way he would let any task be left undone. He even searched for needed repairs that weren't on the list in order to make a lasting impression.

After dinner they moved outside and consumed a bottle of wine. Marriage was discussed, but the topic was kept at a distance recognizing its potential for rabidity. Julia offered to leave her family and move to Key West. Owen offered the sale of his house and a similar move to Italy. Both seemed willing to do whatever they knew would make the relationship work. No matter how right it felt for them to be together, both were skeptical of merely spoken words. Actions were what both yearned for, but neither knew how to give or receive love absolutely without feeling selfish. Physical desires were always present, but neither gave in to their cravings.

After completing their work on Saturday, they took a long walk into town and strolled through several quaint shops that lined the main thoroughfare. Cortona was not the busy tourist mecca Florence was, which allowed for a leisurely pace. Passing others occasionally on the sidewalk a pleasant '*Ciao*' would be exchanged along with a smile.

A small wine shop near the end of the avenue offered the perfect spot to stop and eventually begin their journey home. The bell mounted above the door frame rang obnoxiously disrupting an otherwise tranquil environment as they entered the store. From behind the counter the couple watched a little old lady make her way toward them, hobbling as she walked.

"*Ciao. Posso aiutarlo?*" the old woman asked, as she came to a stop in front of them. Hearing the language intimidated Owen so he walked away and looked at the various bottles on the shelves that covered the walls.

"*Stiamo cercando una bottiglia di vino per un'occasione speciale,*" Julia responded.

"*Appena siete stati sposati?*"

Julia smiled at the woman and shook her head. "*È definitivamente l'uomo che sono stata significato per sposarse, ma non siamo sposati ancora.*"

Curiosity drove him to ask, "What are you two talking about?"

"Aside from what kind of wine we are looking for, she wanted to know if we were married."

Owen smiled. "Your response was a lot longer than, 'no.'"

An impish grin grew on her beautiful face. She walked over to him, wrapped her arms around his waist, pulled him close and gave him a kiss. "I told her that we were not married, but that you were the man I was meant to marry and be with for eternity."

Owen looked deeply into her eyes. Their darkness and the way she looked at him longingly exuded emotional warmth and he found them comforting. "Thank you."

She was taken aback by his response. "For *what*?"

"I've never known anyone who spoke in terms beyond immediate indulgence," he admitted.

"*Non farei mai qualche cosa danneggiarti.*" Her native language instilled comfort and assurance. "I would never do anything to hurt you."

Never before had Owen uttered a response to romantic words he knew to be absolutely true. "I know," he replied as he held her tightly.

The little old woman shuffled behind the counter and disappeared into the back room. Owen and Julia eventually loosened their embrace and continued to look around the shop.

When the woman emerged she held a bottle of wine. It was dusty and appeared very old. Owen was the first to recognize a tear rolling down her cheek. He nudged Julia and instructed her with his eyes to look at the shopkeeper. When the two women saw each other the old woman handed the bottle to Julia. "*Ciò è stata significata affinchè la mia figlia Partiva con il suo marito sulla loro notte di nozze. È morta come infante. Posso vedere che il vostro amore sia speciale come era. Desidero darti questo.*"

Julia began to cry along with the shopkeeper. The women embraced. Owen felt isolated. He said nothing, allowing them to express themselves. Julia held the woman's arms as they released their hug. Tearful smiles were exchanged. She turned and grabbed his hand and led him out of the store.

On their trek home she explained the old woman had a daughter who died as an infant. The bottle of wine was from their family's vineyard and was meant for her wedding night. Although he shed no tears, the gravity of the gift was not lost on Owen.

That afternoon the first cold front of the winter moved through town with a vengeance. Owen spent most of the morning chopping wood in anticipation of the changing weather. Bitter cold eventually made it impossible for him to hold the ax firmly. He wanted desperately to chop an extra cord or two so the next visitors would not be left without fuel for a fire.

The evening was spent watching the orange glow emanating from the stone fireplace. He sat on the sofa with Julia's head in his lap. She was covered by an afghan her grandmother knitted. Neither said a word. The silence allowed them to examine their brief history together. Each desired the other more than anyone else, but neither knew how to ensure their future wouldn't be as tumultuous as their past. No one prepared them for the kind of love they found in each other, and they knew it was special. Julia knew the act of making love to Owen would stand apart based on the energy between them. He was not so sure of himself. The feelings he had for her were unadulterated by anyone or anything he experienced during his life. It had to be the same for their love-making and he had no idea how to make it happen that way.

They sat silently for so long that he questioned whether she had fallen asleep. His uncertainty was quelled when she asked about the proverbial elephant in the room. "Will you make love to me tonight?" Julia was sure the time and place were perfect; Owen was not.

"I can't," he admitted.

His answer was met with silence. She laid still wondering what the reason could be for him not wanting to make love to her. *Is he no longer attracted to me?* Each question she asked herself was totally contrary to how she felt and how she knew he felt. The ridiculousness of her thoughts finally caused her to ask for clarification. She sat up and scooted along the sofa until her back rested on its arm. She folded her legs in front of her, looked him directly in the eye and asked, "Why can't we make love tonight?"

"Because I am just not sure that tonight's right. I want it to be special for the both of us."

She shook her head. "How can it *not* be special?"

Owen was as captivated by her as he had ever been. The animal in him was ready to pounce, but he knew that was not the right thing to do. Everything about her physical being was dark and smoldered and needed to be experienced in the most basic manner. She needed to be touched and tasted, but not until he was sure he knew how to make love to her in a manner that transcended the physical. Monica's influence provided the impetus for him to strive for perfection. "I want to make sure that everything is right for us."

Exasperatedly, Julia responded, "What's not right?" she asked, as she threw her arms out; palms skyward.

"Everything *is* perfect between us. From the moment I met you I've felt something deep within my soul that you, and only you, brought out in me. It was the first time my character had been enhanced by another person. I simply want to make sure that when we make love it will be all about us."

Julia looked around the small house. "There's no one else here!"

Owen thought carefully. "I know that I love you more than a man has a right to love a woman. It consumes me. Making love is the ultimate expression of the feelings I have for you, and I don't want to settle for anything. I want it to be the best for the both of us."

"It will be," she implored.

"I need to make love to you somewhere without all the history that this house holds."

"But it's my family's house, and has been for generations."

Directness was something he hoped to avoid, but he had shunned it his entire life and that had gotten him nowhere. The only thing left to do was blurt out his concern. "I don't want to make love to you in a house where you may have come with some other lover, or a

272

high school boyfriend who you snuck away with in order to simply explore each other's bodies." Julia's silence acted to confirm his fear. Thoughts of her with other men did not bother him, it validated his desire for purity in their relationship. "Don't worry. It's not a deal-breaker. This is what I need in order to have a clear vision of our future together."

Julia smiled. She understood what he wanted and appreciated it. "Should we go to Key West?"

Owen laughed. "No. I'm afraid there is too much of me spread all over that island." He paused. "Is there some place in Italy you've never been that we could call our own?"

"I've never been to the Italian Alps."

"*Really?*"

She shook her head. "We always spent our vacations traveling across Europe."

"But it's so close."

She nodded. "I promise, I've never been there."

Owen threw up his hands in frustration. "No, that's not what I meant. I believe you. It's only a couple hours drive from here, isn't it?"

"More like four."

"Do you trust me to make the arrangements?"

She smiled as they leaned into one another. Just before kissing him, she said, "Of course."

After a long, soft, slow kiss Owen leaned back, breaking the bond between them. "There is one thing I'd like to do tonight, with you, that I have never done before."

"What's that?"

"I'd like to sleep with you naked."

"You're not afraid that will lead to something?"

Owen shook his head. "I know it won't because I have made up my mind to do whatever it takes to make this relationship the best one in the history of humanity."

"It's going to be very cold tonight. Are you going to get up in the middle of the night to tend to the fire?"

"Of course, but I hope that we will generate enough heat between us to suffice."

When it came time to retire for the evening Julia made the bed with a large down comforter she removed from a foot-locker at its end. Owen stoked the fire and stacked several logs on top, but not too many that one may roll onto the floor. When he was done he ascended the stairs to find her standing beside the bed in a nightgown that was sheer and left very little to the imagination. Every inch of her body was perky and erect in the cold night air. The bed was turned down.

"Is there something wrong?" he asked.

"Other than me standing half naked in the bitter cold … no."

"Crawl in bed." He pointed to it.

She shook her head and shivered, simultaneously. "No. You are going to have to look at what you will be missing."

Owen smiled wryly. "Then you'll have to do the same." He removed the sweater and shirt that he wore in one motion by grabbing the tail of both and pulling them over his head. Once he began to remove his pants Julia reached up with both hands and pulled the straps of her nightgown down off her shoulders, allowing it to drop to the floor. Owen could never have imagined a woman could be so beautiful. To his amazement he re-

mained flaccid. Sex was no longer a mission with a cul-
mination. It had become an expression that would last
forever. There was no need to rush eternity. Owen felt it
every time he thought of her.

The two lay in the same position throughout the
night. Skin-to-skin contact was continual and gentle. In
those hours there was more communicated between
them than ever had been.

During the night, as they slept, Julia received
confirmation of the purity Owen desired. Not once did
he intrude into her physical realm. Yet a single act displayed by her unconscious lover spoke volumes about
his intent. At a time when his mind was free of influ-
ences from outside forces he reached toward her hand,
interlocked his fingers in hers, and gently squeezed.

Chapter Thirty-Three

Owen drove down the long, winding dirt road that lead to the house. When it came into sight he noticed his uncle sitting on an iron bench in front of the fountain. He smiled at the old man as he drove past. The gesture was returned with an added wave that called the young man to join him. After parking he did just that.

For so long he thought the man he had come to live with was dead. It was difficult to divorce himself from the mythical notions about him that were concocted in his adolescent mind to fill the void as he daydreamed about the man with whom he shared a name.

A lot of effort was required by the orchard and the warehouse; so-much-so that work was plentiful seven days a week. Owen did his fair share, but his uncle had shown a great deal of leeway by allowing him to have his weekends free to spend with Julia. Guilt overcame him as he worried the man would tell him he could no longer spend time with his love.

Owen quickly made his way to his uncle's side. The old man patted him on the top of his thigh and smiled.

"Was there something you needed?" the young man asked.

"Just your company," the old man said. Owen worried weighty topics were being readied to inject in an otherwise benign conversation. He continued, "You really love Julia, don't you?"

"I sure do." Owen hesitated. "It scares me to know how into her I am."

The old man laughed quickly and briefly. "I was the same with Maria."

"What's your secret?"

"Persistence. I have applied that concept in every aspect of my life and it has served me well." He looked at his nephew. "When I became an adult I realized I faced the challenges of a man, but my father had never taken the time to communicate to me what to expect from life. I felt like I had been set up for failure, and promised to never do that to any of my children. There are going to be times when you will question whether or not you and Julia were meant to be together. That's when you'll need to remind yourself how much you love this woman. There is nothing wrong with questioning yourself. *Knowing* the answer before the question is asked prevents you from making the mistake of a lifetime."

The nephew swung his leg over the bench, enabling him to turn and face the old man. "Did you ever question whether you had done the right thing by staying here and not returning to the United States after the war?"

The old man shook his head. "I knew once I began to dream in Italian this was my home."

Every experience the young man had with women flooded his mind simultaneously. "There had to be times when you wondered whether Maria was more interested in another man … or some other man may have been more suitable for her."

The old man chuckled. "I can tell you're a relative. Most men are instilled with arrogant confidence, but you and I seem to have been raised to feel unworthy of someone as wonderful as Maria and Julia." Owen said nothing as the old man considered his question further. Circumstances that were woven into the fabric of his fifty year marriage had become part of a completed quilt. Not everything was pleasant. Some threads were weak, but never to the point of an emotional tear. "Yes … there were times when I wondered if I could be the man Maria wanted, or desired."

"What did she do to allay your fears?"

"It isn't what she did. It's what I did." He paused to collect his thoughts. "Women will remember every single detail of each encounter they have had with a man throughout their lives. It's your job to make sure Julia understands how special she is to you, and you have to do that daily. There is no memory strong enough to undermine the sense that she is desired by the man she loves." When there was no response by his nephew, the old man asked, "Is there something wrong?"

"No. There's something right." Owen paused. "And I guess there *is* something wrong. Not until now did I realize that not having a father meant that I had no one to turn to for advice."

The smile that grew on the old man's face was genuine and emanated from his soul. "If I ever had any doubt about never going back to the U.S. I think you just eased those concerns."

"You have given more of yourself to me than I ever expected anyone would. Thank you."

"Surely you've had special relationships?" the old man inquired.

Owen shook his head. "I never knew what to look for in the people I associated with. Most of them have been insignificant."

The old man shook his head as he gazed into the distance. "I've never had a relationship that was insignificant, no matter how brief the encounter. Everyone I've met I've tried to take something positive away from our time together. Now, I'll admit some of what I have gleaned from people contains brushstrokes that I have chosen to paint. As long as they are bright and colorful it would serve you well to take on a positive disposition." When he saw that his nephew did not fully comprehend his words, he tried another approach. "Owen, there are people who will tell you the sun drains you of energy; that it's detrimental. I choose to believe that it releases the power inside all living things in order for them to thrive. Don't hoard your essence. Make sure it's released positively and allows for growth of not only yourself, but everyone around you!" He paused briefly, gathering thoughts he formed for nearly eighty years. "I believe that within all humans resides the energy that created the universe. Not until we learn to shake away the prejudices caused by life's defeats can we selflessly share that energy and live eternally with our loved ones." He focused on his nephew. "Have you ever had any pals you grew up with that you could have a completely honest exchange of hopes and fears?"

Owen shook his head. "It seems every person I've chosen to confide in has used the information against me. Is sleeping with the girlfriend of a friend such an accomplishment?"

The old man shook his head. "I assume your question is rhetorical?"

"It was, but if you have anything to offer I'm all ears."

"The best advice I can give you is that when that happens, just remove yourself from the lives of people who treat you poorly."

"But that's how I lost Julia the first time."

The old man laughed heartily. "You and I really are a lot alike." He gathered his composure. "I think people are programmed to either try to take advantage of others or they choose to see the good in everyone. We are from the former. When we encounter the latter their kindness has a tendency to hit us like a club, and we don't know how to handle it. That's what happened with Maria and me before we got married. She stopped me at the railway station before I had a chance to board the train. I came very close to making it back to the U.S. Knowing when to walk away and when to stay and fight for what is right is what separates those who ultimately find happiness with those who don't."

Owen thought about Monica and the Bahamians. He was still unsure he had done the right thing. "How do you define that line, and when it's okay to cross it?"

The old man thought carefully about his answer. "In order to fight for something truly worthy, you must be willing to die. When death becomes an alternative you will know it."

"How?"

"When the life you fight for is not your own, and you envision it thriving because of the sacrifice you've made."

"So, I have to surrender to death in order to prove my love for Julia?"

"No, but you must be willing to die for her, and the beauty of true love is that you won't even have to tell her. She'll know."

The wisdom of the old man was evident in its subtlety. He was finally able to forgive himself for causing the death of the two Bahamians on his boat. Monica was alive because of his actions, and his willingness to accept the ultimate sacrifice in exchange for her life. Freedom from guilt lifted his spirit to a level he had never before experienced. His uncle liberated him from a lifetime of self-destructive behavior, and his future became sanguine.

Trepidation overcame him as he realized Monica was the only person he ever had a completely selfless exchange of hopes and fears. Confusion permeated his soul. Would Owen have to take his relationship with Julia to death's door in order for it to be as special as his with Monica? At that moment he realized the only time he romanticized his uncle's existence was when he was a mere memory.

Chapter Thirty-Four

The olive harvest had reached a critical time. Fruit weighed down tree limbs and was rife with the oil that needed to be processed into its finished product. A narrow window of time existed to bring it in and everyone worked hard in the orchard. Uncle Owen resisted with every ounce of his soul the mechanization of his operation. He did not trust machines to handle his trees with the amount of care he knew his family would. Some embraced automation to reduce the amount of time spent in the fields. The old man knew this. Secretly, he feared the break-up of his clan more so than the changes in how his business operated. Maria was the only person in whom he confided his concern.

For his American nephew the week was crucial. Each day he was the first into the fields in the morning and the last to leave at night. All of his work had to be completed by Friday afternoon so he could take off the first two days of the following week. A room at the Hotel Ancora in the city of Cortina D'ampezzo awaited he and Julia. Their hideaway was nestled amongst the Italian Alps and several fine shops where he fantasized spending their days roaming about hand-in-hand. It was not peak season for the resort town and Owen counted on few visitors to disrupt the feeling they had the city to themselves. Of paramount importance was a place they could call their own. That need was not lost on either of them.

On his final day working the harvest Owen was perched atop a ladder that leaned against an olive tree. In his hand he held a wand-like pair of tongs he used to rake ripe olives from its branches. They fell onto a waiting canvas stretched out on the ground below. From his vantage point he saw the two-rut road that encircled the field. He had only taken enough time at lunch to quickly eat a sandwich. His Italian relatives jeered at him while lying on the ground, laughing and joking at Owen's expense. It did not bother him. He refused to listen, choosing to focus on the task at hand.

Suddenly, his attention was diverted by movement at the top of the hill, near the house. A large car moved down the road toward the orchard. He shook away the desire to stop and stare, and continued busily raking olives onto the ground. Regardless, it was difficult to not look. Even at such a great distance, Owen could tell it was an ostentatious vehicle and moved with urgency. It was a convertible and someone was seated in the back seat, but he could not tell who it was. Once again, he forced his attention away from the distraction and back onto his chore.

Vigilantly working, he refused to look away as the car got closer. That proved difficult because he noticed as it came closer how quiet the engine was. All he heard was the hum of the tires as they approached. Finally, he stopped and began to stare. It looked to be a 1940's sedan of some sort that appeared to have emerged from a Newsreel story. Owen watched as every member of the family stood and walked to the road, lining each side of it. He tossed his implement to the ground and made his way down the ladder to join the others.

Once on the ground he walked between the mature trees and made his way to where the others stood. The car stopped and everyone began clapping and cheering. It was the end to another successful harvest and Uncle Owen brought out his 1940 Packard 180

Darrin Convertible Sedan, as had been the tradition for nearly forty years. The car was purchased so he and Maria could take drives and enjoy the beautiful Tuscan countryside together. Driving into the fields at the end of the harvest had become a tradition, but no one was sure exactly what year it started.

The old man's nephew stood clapping and smiling with the others. Not since his days on the boat had he felt part of something of great importance. A sense of accomplishment engulfed his psyche. He became lost in his thoughts and did not see his uncle motion for him to approach the car. Anthony nudged his American cousin, shaking him out of his malaise, and pointed toward the old man. Owen exchanged a warm smile with the man as the two made eye contact. Uncle Owen's boney hand shook as he waved his nephew toward him. The young man hastily made his way toward the senior member of the family.

"You have worked very hard, Owen," the old man said.

"Thank you."

The old man patted his nephew's hand as it rested on top of the car door. "I must say that I have great hopes that you and Julia will get married and take your place here on the estate."

Living such a life had never been a part of his dreams and Owen was unsure he could live up to those ideals. The only thing he could think to say was in support of his uncle. "To be able to live out my life the way you have would give me a great sense of accomplishment."

The old man was wise and understood his nephew's comment was meant to deflect additional inquiries about his intentions. "I've said what I have to say. Now you go have fun in the mountains, but when you come back be good and ready. Just because we've finished the harvest doesn't mean the work is over."

His visit to the estate had cleansed Owen of the toxins that kept him from moving forward with his life. However, repeating the same routine year-after-year was not appealing to a man who embraced variety. He could not confess that fact to his uncle. The connection between the two men grew stronger as they gazed into each other's eyes.

Suddenly, he understood what his uncle had been trying to convey in their short time together. Everything around them was meant to one day pass. Physical elements contained and stabilized energy that would otherwise radiate unchecked. A wry smile was exchanged between the men. The younger man finally understood that in order to get the most from life he must embrace the eternity contained within each moment.

Chapter Thirty-Five

Cortina was only accessible by taking a series of trains and a bus. During the trip Owen skimmed through several brochures about skiing the Italian Alps. The only time he had donned snow skis was a trip to North Carolina when he was twenty years old. Photographs of professionals intimidated the inexperienced skier. It didn't help that Julia told him about her family's annual trips to the Swiss Alps. The normally brash and careless man worried there would be no way he could satisfy the person he knew was the woman of his dreams.

When they emerged from the bus depot and onto the street chilly air brought their progress to a halt as they stopped to put on the coats they held in their hands. Owen's duffle bag was slung by its strap over his shoulder and he pulled Julia's wheeled suitcase behind him. It wobbled as it rolled over the cobblestone street.

Looking through the window of a small cafe the couple saw one party of a few patrons having a late dinner. Several bottles of wine were scattered about their empty dishes. Muffled, yet uproarious laughter could be heard through the glass.

The streets were empty and void of warmth. Owen imagined what it must be like during the season and how the excitement in the town must be magical. It was inconceivable that it could be any more enchanted than spending time with Julia.

Gas lamps lined the street and flickered in the cool breeze. Shadows caused by the moving flames danced across the street as they walked toward their hotel. Owen stopped in front of a building he thought was their destination. He removed a brochure from his pocket and looked at the picture. It was the right place. He shoved the pamphlet back where it came from and the couple hurried inside to escape the cold.

Standing in front of the desk they waited patiently to register. It was late and they had to ring a bell in order to roust someone from a room behind the counter. Owen preferred Julia do all of the talking, and she did. He looked around the lobby at the ornate decorations. To his untrained eye there seemed to be an eclectic mix of Italian and Austrian antiquities adorning the lodge's interior. Nervously he looked about the place, attempting to displace the tension he felt that weakened his legs. Owen was about to spend an extended weekend with the most beautiful woman he had ever known and the prospect made him unsure of himself.

Julia filled out the registration card and Owen watched every move she made no matter how slight. She was truly stunning. There was not a flaw to be found in her body. Her face was smooth and without a blemish. Any man would eagerly forgo the majority of his time on Earth for the opportunity to be seen with this woman. She was Owen's to lose and he had no intention of allowing that to happen. The realization he never had a relationship last more than a year was a pall that hovered over him. He could not shake the feeling and it made him uneasy.

After registering, Owen carried their luggage to the room. When the couple came to the door adorned with the number six they stopped. Julia inserted the key, turned the lock and entered their hideaway. A short hallway led into the room. She made her way to the end of the vestibule and stopped to look around. The fact that this would be their sanctuary forever provided warmth in an otherwise wintry room. Owen placed his hand on her shoulder gently, not wishing to interrupt the thoughts that occupied her mind.

The room was beautiful. A fireplace at the foot of the bed was prepared with wood and kindling. There was enough stacked neatly on the hearth to last through the night. Everything about the room conveyed warmth. Owen waited patiently for his love to move into the room. Without saying a word she turned to him, leaned in, and gave him the softest, sexiest kiss she knew how to give. He let go of the luggage to embrace her. Her bulky winter coat would not allow for a pleasurable tactile experience. She backed away from the kiss and looked deeply into his eyes. The only thing that could break the mood was an unwanted chill, and it did.

The better part of an hour was spent readying the room for a comfortable night. Julia sat huddled in a leather chair in the corner waiting patiently as her man fastidiously tended the fire. He lit several slivers of kindling and backed away, coming to rest on the floor at her feet. She gently rubbed his shoulders while they watched anxiously, hoping it would take on a life of its own. Never had a rendezvous meant so much to either of them. It must be perfect.

When the warmth of the fire began to fill the room the couple removed their coats. Once they settled Owen realized they had not had anything to eat since leaving the train station in Florence.

"Are you hungry?" he asked, dropping his head backward into her lap and looking up at her.

"I could eat something, but I really don't feel like going out."

"If I can find a place that will deliver would you like me to order something?"

Julia shook her head. "The front desk clerk has gone to bed. The town is deserted. Let's just go to bed." She leaned over and kissed him.

Suddenly, he pulled away. Owen crawled over to the fire on his hands and knees, grabbed the poker and stirred the flames. Orange sparks flew up and disappeared into the chimney. Julia stood and walked into the bathroom, closing the door behind her.

As he changed into his pajamas, the remaining chill caused him to choose, and quickly remove, the long johns from his bag.

When Julia opened the door they saw that the other had chosen to don thermal underwear. Each chuckled at the frumpy manner they had chosen to spend their first carnal night together.

The couple made their way to bed. Owen paused. "Will these be our sides of the bed for the rest of our lives?"

"They are the same sides we have slept on for the past four weekends."

He nodded. "I guess they are."

She felt the need for confession. A quirky pleasure she engaged in on their trips to the family's country cottage in Cortona created a silly guilt for her. "Whenever you got out of bed I would slide over to your side and lay my head on your pillow."

"Why?"

"I like the scent you leave behind. It brings me comfort."

Owen pulled back the quilt and slid into bed. "Comfortable won't lead to complacency in our relationship, will it?"

Julia followed him. She pulled the comforter over her shoulder, laid her head on the pillow and faced him. Looking into his eyes she shook her head. "I almost lost you once. I won't allow that to happen again. I will do whatever it takes to make sure we are together until the day I die."

Owen had never known such conviction. It felt good. The two lay next to each other silently. He traced his fingers along her flank while she sketched the outline of his lips with hers. Occasionally they looked into each other's eyes. Whenever Julia's hair fell over her face, he gently brushed it back and they exchanged smiles. She appreciated that he ensured every move was done with care.

"Have you ever heard of nihilism?" Owen asked.

"Nietzsche?"

"Among others," he nodded. "I've lived most of my life in a self destructive manner. I've never been a big proponent of the social-change aspect of nihilism, but I've turned those principals on myself. I cannot remember a time when I liked the person I was and I came very close to destroying myself because of my self-loathing." Owen tried desperately to choose the right words. "You make me feel like I am worth something. You're the most beautiful, intelligent woman I have ever known and you accept me."

Julia smiled as she moved her hand from Owen's face to his shoulder. "I am not sure what has happened in your past, but it's obvious to me that all of your experiences have made you quite a man … a man that I have thought of every day since we met, and I smile at every memory. We've had our problems and we will continue to have some, but there is no doubt in my mind we were meant to spend the rest of our lives together."

Owen closed his hand and stroked her cheek with the back of his fingers. The deep, intense stare was broken by the desire to kiss. He leaned back. "I don't ever want to lose the ability to look into your eyes." A puzzled look crossed her face, and he continued to explain. "There have been times when I have gotten so frustrated with a friend … "

" … or lover?"

" … or lover." Her addition made him uncomfortable. It was never his intention to bring old relationships into theirs. "I've allowed it to reach the point that I could no longer look them in the eye. When I look into your eyes I feel like you are inviting me into your soul, and I thrive there."

She smiled. "You've been a part of my soul since the day you knocked me down in the piazza. You were totally taken off guard by what happened and I knew what a genuine person you were by the way you were more worried about me than your own well-being."

Owen laughed. "You saw something in me before I did."

"Sometimes it's difficult to see ourselves as others see us."

Monica entered his thoughts. She was the first person he knew that saw some intangible in him that needed to be freed from the constraints he allowed others to place on him. He sat up, stood and walked toward the fireplace. A base of orange coals lay beneath the grate. He removed the two largest logs from the hearth and positioned them on the fire for maximum burn. Quickly he hopped back into bed to escape the still present chill in the room.

"What was the first thing you thought when you saw me for the first time?" Julia asked.

"Before or after knocking you to the ground?"

Laughing, she responded, "After, when you helped me up."

"That I had never seen someone so beautiful in all of my life."

"Since that day have you met someone more beautiful?"

Owen smiled. "The more I get to know you the more beautiful you become. There is no way *any* woman could come close to matching your splendor, Julia."

His compliments warmed her more than the fire. She leaned over and kissed him. They scooted closer to each other and removed the bulky comforter that sagged between them. Beneath it they embraced, still donning their thick pajamas. He slid his hand underneath her shirt and caressed her bare back before pulling her closer.

Even though they had waited years to make love the time still did not feel right. More needed to be said, and they talked all night. Owen appreciated how the flickering glow of the flames lit Julia's face. The dark features of her visage smoldered steamily, piquing every sense in his body. Whenever there was a break in the conversation the two kissed and petted softly. They were in no hurry. The knowledge that they would spend eternity together made coupling more about the soul and less about the physical.

Before they knew it, dawn broke and sunlight illuminated the once dark room.

The time for talking had passed. By the end of their extended day they knew more about each other than they had ever known. Emotional wounds were reopened for the sake of understanding each other. They realized when they met years earlier neither was the same person who was ready to commit to an eternity together.

Julia rolled over, straddled Owen, and sat up on him. Her nubile portrait was titillating. The manner in which her dark features came together; her hair, her eyes and her skin, smoldered sexuality. Fear that he would succumb to her feminine wilds before she surrendered to his masculinity gripped him.

At the moment when both were the most vulnerable Owen confessed something to her that he had kept to himself. "You have occupied my thoughts every day since we first met. You are like a song that got stuck in my mind. I was never able to get over you," he admitted.

Julia collapsed softly on top of him and held his naked body closely to hers. She whispered in his ear. "I stopped living the day you left."

Every undulation of their bodies and each heartbeat pulsed in unison. Morning gave way to afternoon and then evening without their passion yielding to the degradation of time. No longer was sex about simple pleasures. It became the vehicle with which to transcend the physical and bring together individual forces and deny the polarizing affect of their flawed psyches. Their combined energy produced the sustenance required to move forward into eternity.

Chapter Thirty-Six

The estate and its never ending work require-
ment awaited Owen upon his return. When he dropped
Julia off at her house a piece of him was left with her. It
was a welcome ache because he knew she provided the
comfort he needed when they came together again.

His eagerness to get into the orchard was fueled
by completing his work so he could see her free of consternation. Jogging down the two-rut road that led into
the field he heard the explosion of a rifle coming from
behind the house. Instinctively Owen ran off the path
and into the trees, stopping behind the stoutest trunk he
could find. Peering through the branches he saw Luca
sitting in a chair atop the hill, firing into the grove.
Each shot ended with the explosion of an olive without
disturbing any limbs. It amazed Owen someone could
possess such incredible marksmanship. Then it occurred to him that the size of a mature olive was about
the same as the Puma logo on the back of his running
shoes. Anger raged within him as he realized it was
Luca who had taken a shot at him that morning after his
run. Aware that a challenge to his cousin would be one
against many he chose to move into the open and wave
his arms in the air until Luca noticed he was in the
fields. When the shooter saw him he promptly removed
the remaining cartridges from the gun and placed it in
its case, which lay on the ground next to his chair.

Soon the other family members joined Owen
and everyone worked without discussion except Sylvio.
Almost as if his movement had been choreographed he
sauntered from one worker to another; each just a little
closer to where Owen toiled. Whenever he stopped he
feigned work while talking loudly in Italian. Owen

could not help but feel his cousin's words were obnoxious in nature and directed at him. Mostly, those feelings were supported by the astonished looks on the faces of the others who understood what the man said. Finally, he made his way to the tree where Owen worked and circled it while speaking loudly at his American cousin who was perched atop a ladder. There was not a single word of English and it irritated him. Calmly, he descended and stood face-to-face with his nemesis.

"If you have something to say to me, say it in English, if you have the guts." Neither man noticed that everyone had stopped what they were doing and congregated around them.

His thick accent caused Sylvio to speak slowly and deliberately so that his message was properly conveyed. "I said … that your girl … friend makes me itch," he grabbed his crotch, "down here. Justa by looking at her … I want to sticka this in something … any … thing." Remarkably, Owen controlled his anger, allowing Sylvio to say everything he wanted, and then the rift between them would be settled physically. The Italian continued. "For the opportunity to make love to her … I woulda sticka dis in the olive crusher. There is no way an American can satisfy a woman with such fire. You will neva maka her happy."

That was all he needed to hear. His first punch had little impact. He tried to surprise his cousin and brought it up from his hip and was unable to generate any thrust. Nevertheless, the Italian staggered backward slightly before lunging toward Owen. Sylvio buried his head in his opponent's chest and tackled him by wrapping his arms around his legs and pulling his feet out from under him. Both men hit the ground hard and dust billowed into the air. For a brief moment Owen worried his opponent's countrymen would join in, making the fight un-winnable. The best he could manage were several punches to the side of Sylvio's rock-hard head that seemed to do little damage. The Italian had the advantageous position on top, and used it as he raised up several times and thrust punches with all of his weight behind them into Owen's face. Blood poured from his nose and a cut below his eye. He felt defeated until he heard one of the bystanders yell, "Come on, Owen!"

Having at least one member of his family behind him gave Owen the strength to send his adversary reeling as he pushed him mightily from his perch. Both men stood and Owen lunged into Sylvio and landed a punch that opened a gash that ran along his cheek-bone and under his eye. Blood squirted profusely from the wound and sprayed Owen's shirt.

Just as both men recoiled to muster as much energy as they could into the punches that would follow, the action was interrupted by a gunshot. Onlookers stopped cheering and the two men stopped fighting. Everyone looked in the direction of the explosion. On top of the hill behind the house stood Luca. He waved the rifle in one hand and the other over his head to get their attention. When he was sure everyone saw him he yelled down to them. "*Fretta*! *Lo zio Owen sta morendo*!"

Sylvio looked at his American cousin and said, "Hurry! We hava to get-a to da house." The man's compassion surprised Owen, but also communicated the gravity of the situation they faced.

Everyone ran to the house, led by the two combatants. As they ascended the hill Luca shouted his dire news in English. Only then did Owen realize that the man he had fantasized about all of his life was dying. His legs became weak, and the only thing that kept him moving was the realization that he may not have the opportunity to tell the only man who had ever meant something to him how much he loved him. Of all his sins that omission was one for which he would be unable to forgive himself.

When they reached the house Luca let them both pass and kept the others from entering. He understood the importance of allowing his American cousin time with his uncle.

Maria openly wept at his bedside. The old man's eyes were closed and Owen feared they were too late. When she saw them standing in the doorway she squeezed her husband's hand, and motioned for the two to come inside and stand next to the bed. The old man opened his eyes and slowly rolled his head on the pillow to look at them. He did not acknowledge the cuts and bruises on both men's faces. With all the might he could muster he held his hand up for Owen to hold. The young man took the boney, frail hand in his, knelt at the bedside and listened intently.

In a voice that was nothing more than a strained whisper, the old man said, "Nephew, I'm afraid that I've not been completely honest with you."

Owen shook his head nervously in short repeating strokes. "It doesn't matter. We're together now."

The uncle inhaled deeply in order to get the next sentence out. "We have been together once before." A questioned look flashed across the young man's face.

He searched his memory for a time when they may have met, but memories from decades earlier had been repressed too deeply. The old man drew in another breath and spoke. "Do you remember playing catch with a middle aged man when you were about five years old? It was in a park near your home." Owen acknowledged the memory with a nod. He let the man speak. "That man was me. Do you remember that when it got dark the only light was in a gazebo and we stood inside it tossing the ball?" He strained to smile. "I did not want that night to end." Tears streamed down the cheeks of both men. Another breath was drawn into his lungs. "When I found out I had a nephew who had been named after me, I had to see you … at least once." He inhaled. "Twenty years later you came here looking for my final resting place." Breathing became laborious for the old man. "Maria taught me how to love. You've shown me how love can transcend time and space. That knowledge brings with it peace. I know we will all be reunited one day, and I look forward to seeing you again." Breaths became shallow and he struggled to fill his lungs with oxygen.

"My love for you is eternal too, uncle."

There was not another word spoken that night. The greatest accomplishment of the man who meant so much to so many in Tuscany was perhaps that he saved the life of someone who had been discarded at a young age. That salvation did not happen in the few short weeks they spent together. The ability to care deeply had been bestowed upon the young man many years earlier by the man for whom he was named.

Chapter Thirty-Seven

Death knells rang throughout Tuscany the day after Owen's death. The estate hosted almost the entire population of Florence during that time. Some visitors came by car, but many walked from nearby farms; carrying on a centuries-old tradition. Owen spent the day hovering around the periphery of the mourners, not really knowing his role. Occasionally, Sylvio came over to check on the emotional state of his American cousin. For all of the bitterness he displayed at the outset of their relationship, the man had become extremely compassionate. Suspicion over his true intentions could not be avoided.

Several people approached and greeted Owen, most of whom spoke no English. He surmised they were conveying their condolences. Not until the expressions of sorrow took on the feeling of consistency did he realize there were a lot of people aware of his presence in their community. It became clear the ease with which his uncle was able to locate him the second time was because he had a lot of help from his neighbors. For someone who never felt like he could rely on the kindness of others, it opened a pathway unto which he hesitantly moved toward trust.

The day grew old and the ache in his heart was matched by pains in his legs from standing all day. Julia had been by his side most of that time until he convinced her it was okay for her to go home. She had to work the next day, and he felt the proceedings had become a burden on her. Hesitantly, she left after assuring him she would do whatever he needed. He was grateful that he could count on her emotional presence when she was not by his side. That fact provided great comfort.

Darkness blanketed the estate and he knew there would be no way he could sleep, and as he had done so many times before, the desire to swallow his pain along with copious amounts of bourbon became an all too familiar alternative. He mentioned that fact to Sylvio, who told him of an out-of-the-way restaurant in town that had been around since the Renaissance where they could go and experience some local flavor. It sounded like the remedy he needed.

When they arrived the men sat at the bar. The owner looked at the two and made a laughter filled reference in his native language to the cuts and bruises on both of their faces. Sylvio spoke to the man, and not once did Owen feel anything said was of a derogatory nature. He viewed his Italian cousin as a passionate man, and wondered if his willingness to defend Julia at all costs had won him over. Maybe his uncle had instilled the same philosophy of a fervent death over uninspiring life. Regardless, it felt good to have yet another person he could trust.

"Cousin, I needa to apologize for being an ass to you," Sylvio said, as he drank from his Lemoncello.

"Don't worry about it." Owen sipped from his drink. "But, I have to ask you, why did hate me so much. You've never known me."

"I was a jealous. Uncle made such a production of-a bringing you here, and then he sent-a Luca to retrieve you. I was-a angry." He paused. "And, uncle spoka of you often after meeting a-you that day in da park."

Owen thought about everything Luca had done to him in Key West; all in the name of good humor. He worried what Sylvio would have done if he had been sent instead. Maybe that shot into his running shoe would have found its way into his back. "Speaking of Luca, I owe that guy a date in the boxing ring."

Sylvio laughed. "So, you think-a you will-a stay at da house for a while?"

He nodded. "It's the only place on earth where I feel like I belong."

His Italian cousin smiled and raised his glass into the air. "*Salute!*"

Owen mimicked his cousin and they drank to their good fortune.

The Italian placed his glass on the bar and wiped the excess from the corners of his mouth as he looked over his shoulder at the diners in the restaurant. A look of astonishment grew on his face when he saw Julia walk in with a man. Before he had the chance to gain his composure his cousin saw the expression and turned to see what was causing it. In the instant it took him to recognize her, the numbness associated with experiencing a passing emanated throughout his body. The lovers made eye contact. Anger could be seen in his face; astonishment in hers.

He finished his drink, placed the empty glass on the bar, stood and walked out of the restaurant without a word to her or Sylvio. It was best he continue drinking elsewhere.

The cracks in the cobblestone path caused his ankles to roll-over as he made his way through the piazza. His legs had been weakened more by betrayal than alcohol. Before he could get halfway across the square he heard Julia call his name.

"Owen!" He refused to turn around. "Owen! Stop!"

Reluctantly, he stopped and turned to see her running toward him. When she made it to where he stood, he asked sarcastically, "What do you want?"

"It's not what it looks like."

"It never is … and don't tell me he's your cousin."

"Antonio is an old lover of mine … yes. But he brought me here tonight because he is asking his girlfriend to marry him."

"Oh! Let me guess. That girlfriend is you, right?"

"No. I have not been his girlfriend since before you and I met the first time. We were mere teenagers, and had no idea what having a relationship meant."

"So, why does he need you now?"

"He asked a favor of me … a very personal favor."

"Stop playing games with me. If you can't tell me what it is there's obviously nothing between us. Whatever happened to the complete honesty we professed to bestow upon each other? I guess we were both wrong about our feelings for each other."

Julia inhaled deeply, and then exhaled. "I will never breach Antonio's trust, except for you. But you have to promise that you will *never* say anything to anyone about what I tell you."

"Sure." His tone was tinged with sarcasm.

"When I got home tonight, there was a message from Antonio. I hesitated to call him back, because we had talked about a week ago and he asked a favor of me."

"Favor? What kind of *favor*?"

"I'm getting to it." She paused. "I was worried that after having fulfilled his first favor it may have opened the door to another. I called anyway. He wanted to take me to dinner to thank me and show me the ring he is giving to his girlfriend." Owen opened his mouth to say something, but Julia held her hand up in front of him. She wanted to finish. "Antonio is very much in love with Claudia. He is a man of little means, but a gigantic heart. My cousin is a jeweler, and he asked if I could get my cousin to work with him on the price or payment of the ring. I did. If that got out it would be mean great embarrassment for him, and I have no desire to cause him such pain. That's all."

Owen had no idea how to react. Twice she had given him the opportunity to display complete trust in her and both times he failed miserably. A mere apology seemed inadequate. He knew every word she said was true, but yet again, the man he was could not help but react in the manner he always had. The only thing he had to cling to was the lesson his uncle passed along before his death. "There's only one question I have and you must answer honestly."

"Okay."

"Would you be willing to die for Antonio?"

A crooked; unconvincing smile appeared on her face. "As a silly teenage girl I would have answered, 'yes.' As I stand before you tonight I tell you the answer is no; now and then. I had no idea what love was until we met. I have lost Antonio before. I have lost you before. I could not stand losing you again. There is energy between you and I that would live on if I had to sacrifice myself, and I would without hesitation."

Owen held her by the arms and pulled Julia toward him. He gently kissed her. "I have more love for you than I know what to do with." She smiled. "Now go back inside and enjoy your dinner. You're a good person and you deserve a nice evening."

"Please come with me."

He shook his head. "That would make Antonio uncomfortable, and I believe he is not deserving of the awkwardness. Besides, my gift to Antonio is an evening filled with people seeing him accompany the most beautiful woman who ever lived. It feels good to share my fortune." He paused briefly. "Enjoy your friend." Reticence filled his next request. "Just please stay away from Sylvio."

"Neither are half the man you are, even if you combined them."

He watched her walk away, comfortable that she was more true to him than he had ever been to himself. Before disappearing into the restaurant she turned and they exchanged waves. Monica helped him to understand forgiving himself of his past was the only way he could have a future. For Owen, overcoming both his and Julia's former lives presented a challenge that could prove insurmountable if allowed.

Chapter Thirty-Eight

Owen sat at a table staring at the station's twenty railway platforms; some filled with trains and some empty. He nervously tapped the edge of his ticket on its surface. Schedules quickly rolled across the message board and he feared he may miss his train to Rome. His glance moved nervously from the trains to the board and back. The clicking and clacking of the ever changing times echoed through his head. Everything that happened over the last few months was replayed in his memory at a frantic pace. His uncle came into and out of his life too quickly for his liking. Family members he had only begun to know became an indelible part of his life. Above all else, the woman who occupied his mind every day since they met cared for him as much as he did her.

The ear-piercing screech of metal wheels grinding caused him to shudder and lose concentration. He looked down the tracks toward a train that was leaving the station and saw a beautiful woman pushing a luggage cart and walking toward him. On top of the bags lay a young girl wearing dark sunglasses. Her hands were behind her head and she casually enjoyed the ride provided by her mother. The woman brought the cart to a stop at the table next to Owen. She sat down and the little girl climbed to the ground and began to inquisitively wander about the station.

Owen looked at the woman, "*Qual e suo nome?*" He hoped that he got the words right. She had dark features and a metropolitan flair about her.

"Carina," the woman responded without a smile.

Owen sensed a great deal of sadness from her. He wanted to say something that would brighten her mood. "*È bella!*" The compliment about her daughter's beauty only lifted one corner of her mouth in a half-hearted attempt to acknowledge it. She was such a beautiful woman that her sadness seemed paradoxical.

Realizing he could say or do nothing to brighten her mood, he turned his attention to the young girl. He smiled at her and waved gently. The girl's eyes darted toward her mother for approval to approach this strange man. She gave it with a nod. When she walked toward Owen he held his hands out, palms skyward, inviting her to play a game of *Patty-Cake.* At first, the amusement progressed slowly. Carina giggled as she sped up the pace, seeing that Owen was having difficulty keeping up with her. The giggling turned to laughter as his hands got tangled in hers. Owen turned to look at Carina's mother as he laughed. She sat sternly with her arms folded across her chest; without a smile. He looked back toward the child but she had lost interest and walked toward an older couple two tables away.

Once again, his uncle entered his mind. The man's words were repeated, *I've never had an insignificant relationship. No matter how short the time that I knew someone I've always tried to take something away from the experience.* Slowly, he turned his head toward the woman. She had not changed her posture. The dynamic between mother and daughter perplexed him, but at the same time he recognized that his perception of their reality was influenced by his own experiences.

The young girl skipped through the terminal without a care in the world. It was obvious by everyone's reaction she brightened their day. The caution she displayed earlier had been summarily disposed of and

replaced by a playful temperament and an apparent
openness to every experience the noisy railway depot
offered.

The woman sat, un-phased by the joy being experienced by those coming in contact with her daughter.
Owen felt the pain of her experiences. She wore it like
armor. A chill came over him as he worried this woman
may miss out on so much of her daughter's life. He
laughed to himself realizing that his own anxiety was
being projected onto her.

Before he had a chance to think any further
about how the little girl's situation paralleled his own
childhood, he saw Julia walking sternly toward him.
She did not reach him before the inquiries burst forth in
a rapid fire manner. "Where are you going? What was
all that talk last night about dying for each other? I
guess you never said you'd die for me? Did I take
something for granted that wasn't true?"

Owen tried to convey a calm demeanor. "Didn't
I trust you implicitly last night?"

"Yes," she answered, sheepishly.

"Can you trust me as well?"

"Yes."

Sincerely, he asked, "How was your dinner last
night?"

"It was very nice, thank you."

"Did Sylvio make a move on you?"

"No. He was quite the gentleman. But … he did
say something I found strange."

"What was that?"

"He told me to tell you that he was never really
that fond of the olive crusher." Owen laughed. He un-

derstood that was his cousin's way of communicating his apology. "What does that mean?"

"I'll tell you some other time."

Calmly, Julia readdressed her main inquiry. "So, where exactly are you going?"

"There is something I need to accomplish before our relationship can progress any further."

She nodded slowly, unsure if she was going to get a straight answer to any question she asked. "Is this the end of us?"

"It's just the beginning."

"Then where are you going?"

"There is someone I need to see before we can move forward. That's all."

Julia looked skeptically at Owen, but knew she must show him the same faith he had shown her.

Chapter Thirty-Nine

Her apartment in the heart of Florence was as empty as her soul. Julia knew Owen would come back, but at what cost to their relationship? She held a glass of wine on her thigh as she sat on her sofa and stared through an open window. The view across the Arno dissolved up a cypress dotted hillside into a blue Tuscan sky. *I should never have gone to dinner with Antonio*, she thought. *Maybe it's not me. He did lose his uncle, and that's tough on anyone. It has to be hard on someone who's never had a family, then gotten one, and just as suddenly loses the only father he's ever known.*

For years Owen occupied her thoughts, and nothing had changed. He was the only man for whom she was ever concerned. It was his sensitivity that hooked her. Never had he been afraid to show his true feelings. There was no bravado; no facades. She knew when he said something to her he meant it. The only times he refused to communicate was when he left years earlier, and after her dinner with Antonio. Only then did she understand he did not know how to confront matters of the heart. Her realization made him all too typical in relation to other men.

Time had been of little consequence for the years they spent apart. Feelings had not changed nor their intensity. At some point she must consider herself over all others. It would be hard to let go of him, but if she had to do so for her own good, that was a decision with which she was coming to terms. She knew he would always occupy a space in her heart, but maybe he truly wasn't the man for her. Emotional fantasy created wonderful memories, but stability always won the battle for life-long love.

Her malaise was interrupted by a knock on her door. *Owen?* she hoped. Quickly she stood and made her way to the front of her apartment and answered the query. Disappointment was overcome by surprise when she saw the old woman from the wine shop in Cortona standing in her doorway. "*Ciao.*"

The old woman nodded graciously. "*Ciao.*"

"*Cosa ti porta a Firenza?*"

"*Posso entrare?*"

"*Sono spiacente. Entra per favore.*" Julia was so stunned to see the woman she neglected to ask her inside. She stepped aside to allow her to pass, and they made their way to the sofa. The old woman wrung her hands nervously, and was unsure of herself.

"*Vino?*" Julia asked as the two women sat down.

"*Si, grazie. Did you enjoy the bottle of wine I gave you?*"

"*We haven't yet. It's being saved for a special occasion.*"

"*That's nice.*"

Julia hesitated, avoiding the appearance of abruptness. "*What brings you here?*"

"*After my daughter died my husband was never able to truly find the joy in life ... and neither did I. We did our best to make the most of our time together, but her absence left a hole where some of our happiness drained away. We never had anything to fill it.*"

"*I have the feeling there is something I can do to help you.*"

The old woman nodded sheepishly. It embarrassed her to make such a bold request. "*I have the opportunity to experience the joy that has been missing in my life.*"

"*How?*"

"*I am an old woman who has no one left ... except a sister who lives in Ethiopia. She moved there after World War II when the country gained its sovereignty to open a school for the children. My family was angered by her desire to leave and we cut off all communication with her. I have not seen her since I was a teenage girl. Please, Julia, go with me there. I cannot travel alone.*" The old woman saw hesitation in her expression. She knew Julia must come with her. "*Please! You are the only person who I can count on. I recognized your sincere compassion the day we met in my shop.*"

Her answer was filled with reticence, although her words evoked complete sympathy. "*Yes, of course I will go with you.*"

Wherever it was Owen felt he had to travel before continuing his life with Julia was okay. He would have to understand she was equally compelled to help her friend make contact with her sister before either of their deaths.

Dread overcame her as a chill shuddered throughout her body. The last question Owen asked her was if she were willing to die for him. Did he consider death to be a romantic alternative for their love? He had spoken of the challenge of taking their love beyond the physical, to an eternal state. Certainly he had no desire to give up on their next fifty years together. She had no desire to return from Africa and find that he was dead. Her parents had given her the name of the tragically romantic Juliette because they hoped that one day she would find love so pure that matters of the flesh would be inconsequential to her existence.

She looked at the old woman who sat next to her. Creases in her face conveyed wisdom. Living beyond experiences, no matter how painful, was the only way she knew to extract every bit of life from the time she had been given. Her love for Owen would never fade, regardless of the ideals he held dearly.

Chapter Forty

A week after agreeing to the trip Julia found herself in Dire Dawa; the women's final destination. Their journey took them by train from Addis Ababa toward the Gulf of Aden and the port town of Djibouti. They strolled through the market-place accompanied by the smell of roasting coffee beans.

Julia basked in the immense history that permeated the faces of the town's citizens. The school Francesca founded was on the outskirts of the city. Agriculture was the chief occupation and the ex-patriot felt that as the farmers made their way into the market they could drop their children off at school. Local resistance was overcome by determination and will. The elder sister had become a revered member of the community, known and respected by all.

More than once the ladies were forced to move aside to allow cattle to pass along the path everyone traveled. Heat radiated from the scorched earth beneath their feet. Mud-hut buildings dissipated into open fields as they made their way along the road to the school house. Julia pulled her scarf over her head to protect it from the dust being blown by a wind that was no longer blocked by buildings. She interlocked her arm inside the old woman's to help her move into the stiff breeze. Their destination was in sight, but the distance was exacerbated by the elements.

The schoolhouse was constructed of mud-brick and its tin roof was suspended by wooden pedestals on top of its walls. Once inside the structure Julia chuckled at the notion she expected some relief from the heat.

A group of children played soccer behind the school, completely oblivious to the adverse conditions.

Screams of joy followed each strike of the ball by a child's foot.

When the women walked through the door and uncovered themselves they noticed someone seated at a desk in front of the class. A chalkboard covered the wall behind it. The words *A single seed provides perpetual life* had been scrawled in chalk. Julia noticed the teacher was older, but not nearly old enough to be the sister they sought. She feared facing Francesca's death when they had come so far. Once the woman noticed them she stood and walked to the back of the room.

Smiling, she asked, "*May I help you?*"

"*We were looking for Francesca DiMario,*" Julia said. "*Can you tell us where we can find her?*"

Sadness came over the teacher's face. "*Francesca died over a decade ago.*" She reached out and grabbed Julia's hands. "*I'm sorry.*"

Julia looked at Sophia. "*We're too late.*"

Her travel companion smiled, and then looked at the teacher. All three shared a smile; only Julia wasn't sure why. "*Did you get my letter, Victoria?*"

"*Yes. It came just yesterday.*"

Julia became confused. "*You two know each other?*"

Sheepishly, Sophia admitted, "*Victoria and I met ten years ago when I came to visit my sister for the last time.*"

She acknowledged her understanding with a nod. "*I should have known there was something going on when you spoke to us in Italian.*" The two older women laughed. "*So, why did you bring me here?*"

Victoria pointed toward the windows at the rear of the building. They were dusty and it was difficult to

see through them, but Julia saw children chasing a soccer ball around an open field. Slowly, she walked
between the rows of desks, her mind filled with possibilities. Not until she reached them did she see a familiar
figure. Slowly, she traced his miniature outline with her
finger along the pane. He held a soccer ball high above
his head, then threw it into the mix of children; all of
whom screamed joyously.

Julia turned and looked at the two women, who
grinned widely. Without a word she quickly made her
way back through the maze of tables and chairs and
through the front door. She pulled her scarf over her
head as she ran around the building and into the field.
Children stopped and watched her run across their play-
ground, and the manner in which the two adults focused
intently on each other.

"What are you doing here?" Julia asked after
pulling away from their embrace.

"It's a long story."

"I've got my whole life to listen."

Owen looked over her shoulder and saw the two
women watching through the rear windows. "I saw
Sophia at my uncle's funeral and we began to talk."

"You two talked?" Julia asked, incredulously.

"Yes ... it was one hell of a conversation, let me
tell you. But, with Sylvio's help we were able to
muddle through our language barrier. Anyway, she told
me about how her sister left after the war to build this
school. Her story was so similar to my uncle's that I
could not help but feel a great kinship toward her. There
has been a great deal of tragedy in both of our lives. I
will be forever grateful that I was able to be with my
uncle for the few short weeks I had him in my life. But,

those kinds of short-sighted sentiments have defined my life and family for far too long. Our perspective has been narrowly focused on small victories. My uncle told me the way I would know that my love for you was true would be when I realized that I would gladly die for your prosperity, and I would. I'm convinced that no matter how gladly I would trade my life for yours, the most to be gained from our relationship is to embrace all that it has to offer. Sometimes we need to break away from our families in order to grow beyond their boundaries. From the moment we bumped into each other in the piazza you gave me something without even realizing it. Every day since then I have had hope. My biggest fault is that I am a student of history. It has always proven prescient for me to learn from my own past, but the problem with that is, by doing so I allowed others to control my destiny. Living in the past became nothing more than a self-fulfilling prophecy, and I could not recognize that fact. Erasing it is the only option for me to move forward into a life that will grow infinitely." He saw consternation on Julia's face. "Don't worry, you're the reason I've reached this epiphany. My uncle gave me several bits of advice in the short time I knew him. Whenever he did it seemed cryptic and vague. Now I realize that he had to speak specifically about his own experiences, yet in a manner that I could apply them to my own life in order to learn." He paused to collect his thoughts, but the words came as naturally as his love for Julia. "What I felt for you the moment we met I've only just begun to understand. It's a bond so tight that if I were to betray you I would also be giving away my own value. You've struck a chord within me that I did not know was there. It's the most basic of senses; an awareness that together we can accomplish anything. If I had not bumped into you in that piazza I could very well be a dead man today. You have consumed my thoughts daily since that meeting. I considered my attraction to you as an addiction because of your beauty, and all I knew was that of the flesh. Just as my uncle will always live within me, so will you. You were the first to ever instill that sense in me. There is a worldliness about you, and I am sure that together we will grow spiritually every day until we die."

"Why did you have to bring me all the way to Ethiopia to tell me this?"

"You found the spark within me, but there was a woman I met in Key West who breathed life into it until its flames raged with the desire to live life to its fullest. She was so special that I was willing to die to protect her. It was the first time I ever felt like I had a true friend."

"Do you love her?"

"More than my own life, but not for the reasons you may think. She taught me how to love based on a bond less physical. Because of her I *know* that I can love you without question for the rest of our lives. If it weren't for Monica I would have no idea how to bridge the gap between our physical beings and our souls. There is a part of me that wants to strip away my flesh and combine our individual energies into one that is completely balanced."

"How do we accomplish that?"

"Whenever we are cheek-to-cheek I make sure the opportunity to bridge the gap between the two is not wasted." He smiled at her before divulging his most fundamental secret. "Every breath you inhale contains

318

the essence of your soul. That airy manifestation per-
meates your body. When we come together I seek to in-
dulge myself in your spirit." He paused. "I do that by
tasting it in your aroma and the gentle flavor of your
flesh."

Julia wavered at the compliment. It was something she never considered and it took her completely
off guard. Humor was meant to mask her inability to respond in an equally poignant manner. "I feel like I need
to bathe."

Owen saw through her attempt. "You showed
me what to search for when you confessed that you lay
on my pillow for the same reason."

She launched herself into his arms. As they
hugged she asked, "So, why Ethiopia?"

"Because I've experienced the two extremes life
has to offer. Death was a viable alternative with Monica. Eternal life is what I desire with you. I can only
imagine when the first men and women stood shoulder
to shoulder at the edge of the Gulf of Aden and looked
across the water, the hope that burned inside must have
been so strong that it did not matter what awaited them
over the horizon. Their hope was so resilient that it
blossomed into an undeniable faith in one another. I
have that strong belief in you, and it will never wane."
Her smile conveyed the gravity of his words. "The purity of your essence sweeps away all obstacles, just like
the first humans saw nothing that would stop them from
experiencing all life had to offer. You unlocked that
same passion in me from the moment we came together.
We will always stand shoulder-to-shoulder and peer
over a horizon all our own. Just beyond it is an immeas-
urable treasure that is not there for us to hold, but to

embrace. Every moment of the rest of my life will be spent carrying you in my soul. Wherever you find yourself in this world I will be there with you and for you."

"So what about that special someone you needed to see?"

"You're that someone! Your kindness is so unlimited that you'd accompany a near stranger half way across the globe to a place that most consider the end of the Earth. In actuality it's the beginning of human existence. Before meeting you my perspective was just as skewed, but you've shown me what eternity looks like, and I want to spend it with you. I'll no longer view every relationship as having an end. Now I can envision an existence that not only reaches so deeply into my soul it touches the beginning of time, but I know that it will never cease. You are the truest love I've ever known."

11144136R00184

Made in the USA
Charleston, SC
02 February 2012